Islam Today

Continuum *Religion Today*

These useful guides aim to introduce religions through the lens of contemporary issues, illustrated throughout with examples and case studies taken from lived religion. The perfect companion for the student of religion, each guide interprets the teachings of the religion in question in a modern context and applies them to modern-day scenarios.

Available now:
Christianity Today, George D. Chryssides
Hinduism Today, Stephen Jacobs
Judaism Today, Dan Cohn-Sherbok

Forthcoming:
Sikhism Today, Jagbir Jhutti-Johal

Islam Today

Ron Geaves

continuum

Continuum International Publishing Group

The Tower Building
11 York Road
London SE1 7NX

80 Maiden Lane
Suite 704
New York NY 10038

www.continuumbooks.com

British Library Cataloguing-in-Publication Data
A catalogue record for this book is available from the British Library.

ISBN: HB: 978-1-8470-6477-6
     PB: 978-1-8470-6478-3

Library of Congress Cataloging-in-Publication Data
Geaves, Ron.
  Islam today / Ron Geaves.
     p. cm.
  Includes bibliographical references and index.
  ISBN-13: 978-1-84706-477-6 (HB)
  ISBN-10: 1-84706-477-9 (HB)
  ISBN-13: 978-1-84706-478-3 (PB)
  ISBN-10: 1-84706-478-7 (PB)
  1. Islam--21st century. 2. Islamic renewal. 3. Islam--Essence, genius, nature. I. Title.

  BP161.3.G4354 2010
  297--dc22

                2009053427

Typeset by Free Range Book Design & Production
Printed and bound in Great Britain by CPI Antony Rowe Ltd, Chippenham, Wiltshire

Contents

Acknowledgements

Above all I wish to thank my wife Catherine, whose forbearance is magnificent when I am researching and writing. Thanks also to my son, Dominic, who only wants daddy to play. He reminds me that there is more to life than work, even when work is cherished. I want to mention Liverpool Hope University, which has given me an environment where my research is supported, and finally all the hundreds of Muslims worldwide who continue to open their hearts and their homes to me and make my work possible.

Chapter 1

Introduction

To begin the story of Islam a decision has to be made whether to approach the subject from an insiders' or outsiders' point of view. If we were to begin with the latter, the birth of Islam would begin in the Arabian Peninsula in the sixth century, focused predominantly on events in the two cities of Makkah and Madinah and concentrated on the life and activities of Muhammad (570–632) and the first Muslims. But no devout Muslim would acknowledge the historical events in Arabia as the birth of Islam. To do so, would place Islam in the realm of sects and cults that are created by human beings for their own devices rather than the eternal verities of divine nature and the primal relationship between the divine being and humankind. Yasin Dutton makes a distinction between 'original Islam' and 'primal Islam'.[1] The first, he suggests, describes the Islam that was revealed to Muhammad and taught to his companions based upon the Qur'anic revelation and was then 'inherited and transmitted' to following generations. In other words the religion that was practised by those who lived where Muhammad lived, accepted him as the final Prophet of God, and believed the sacred text revealed to him to be the eternal and perfect word of God. There are those amongst Muslims who believe that this 'original' Islam was passed on to three generations in its purest form[2] and, after that, it was maintained and kept alive to the present by a succession of *mujaddids* (renewers of the faith). Historically, this version of Islam spread outwards from the Arabian Peninsula after Muhammad's death and was introduced to conquered lands by the Arab tribes who had embraced it wholeheartedly as their religion. This historical narrative of the birth of 'original Islam' will be recounted later in the chapter.

Primal Islam, on the other hand, refers to the eternal and only true religion of God that was originally taught to Adam and Eve and passed on to a succession of prophets who preached it to the people of their time and place. This primal religion shown by God to chosen messengers has needed from time to time to be renewed as various generations of people have always corrupted it or failed to understand it. What then is primal Islam? To Muslims the story begins with the creation of the first man and women.

Myths of Origin

The primordial religion of God begins with an act of cosmic disobedience which results in the human race becoming a battleground for a titanic struggle between Allah and Shaitan (Satan). The Qur'an speaks of three kinds of being, each created from different elements: the angels from light, the *djinn* from smokeless fire and human beings from clay. All were created to worship God but both *djinn* and human beings possess the gift of free will and can *choose* to do so. When Allah created the first man and woman (Adam and Eve) out of clay he requested the angels to bow before them. Iblis, a powerful *djinn*, who the Qur'an informs us kept the company of the angels because of his piety and love of God, baulked at the idea of humbling himself before the newly created human pair. Addressing his Lord, he complained: 'You created me from fire and you created him [Adam] from clay.'[3]

Muslims believe that Iblis was the first being to look at his self and make a comparison with another, in which he judged himself to be superior. In his pride he refused to prostrate himself. The Qur'an states, 'When We said to the angels, "Prostrate to Adam," they prostrated except for Iblis. He refused and was arrogant and was one of the unbelievers.'[4] Of interest here is that the Qur'an does not define unbelief as a lack of faith in God, but rather as an act of disobedience. The Muslim struggle is to obey God. In Islamic belief, it is Iblis who scores the first victory in a titanic struggle for the allegiance of the human being. His motivation is twofold: first, he desired revenge for humanity's part in his own downfall and second, he wished to justify his act of defiance by demonstrating to Allah that human beings were not worthy of divine trust. Iblis determined that the best course of action is to guide all future human beings into disbelief and disobedience to God and thus deny them re-entry to Paradise and condemn them to the punishment of hellfire. Most significantly, Iblis decides to subvert human beings by leading them to neglect God's worship and remembrance.

But Allah remained secure in his trust for his new creation and permitted them to continue to choose between the right path and the temptations laid in front of them by Iblis. Medieval Muslim accounts indicate that Adam and Eve were initially separated from each other after their expulsion from Paradise. Eve, the mother of the human race, wandered in the desert, coming to a halt in the vicinity of Makkah. Adam was allowed a glimpse of the true worship of God when he was permitted to see the host of angels circumambulating the divine throne. After successfully pleading for forgiveness they were reconciled with each other in Makkah. Adam was asked to establish a place of worship that would imitate the actions of the angels that he had been permitted to witness. It is this myth that explains the origins of the act of circumambulation at the Ka'aba. However, it was Iblis, now known as Shaitan, who again and again distracted the Arabs from the worship of God and the Ka'aba became a place of idol worship. It was restored again by Ibrahim and finally by Muhammad. To the present time, when Muslims gather in prayer throughout the world, facing towards the Ka'aba and circumambulating it on the great pilgrimage of the Hajj, they believe themselves to be performing the eternal rite of prostration and worship performed by the heavenly hosts. Final victory over Shaitan will come when all human beings join in true obeisance to the Creator by circumambulation of the Ka'aba in the final days.

Thus a cosmic struggle ensued: a fight for the heart of the human being. On one side, there is the 'respited' Iblis, freed from the confines of death, allowed to retain his great power and ability until the battle is ended. On the other side, there is Allah, who in his mercy sends assistance to human beings through revelation; a clear reminder of the 'straight path' that leads back to him. The messengers and the book used to convey revelation are also powerful allies against Shaitan's machinations. Also, all around there are clear signs in creation for the discerning, which will warn them of the right and the wrong way, bringing inspiration and wisdom. The Qur'an speaks of a succession of prophets (*nabi*), righteous and God-fearing men, who are chosen to remind human beings of Allah's worship and to act as exemplars of surrender to the divine will. Some of the Prophets (differentiated as *rasul*) are chosen to bring a book of revelation to guide human beings. Foremost among them are Moses (Torah), David (Psalms), Jesus (the Gospels) and finally Muhammad (the Qur'an).

But the succession of prophets from Adam to Jesus was met by derision and disbelief by the majority. 'Then We sent Our messengers in succession; every time there came to a people (*umma*) their messenger, they accused him of falsehood.'[5] Although not a bringer of a Book, it is Ibrahim (Abraham) who exemplifies for Muslims the ideal of Islam. Before the advent of Muhammad and the Arabian revelation, Ibrahim's model was most fully exemplified in the Jewish and Christian communities marked out as special by the Qur'an's designation of *Ahl-i Kitab* (People of the Book). However, these two religious communities fell into error. Their sacred texts of revelation were adulterated by human additions and they introduced doctrines and practices that endangered the primordial monotheism of Ibrahim. A final revelation was needed to bring victory to the faithful and restore humankind to the path of surrender. The final struggle is entrusted to the Arab nation, the successors of Ishmael who have not been blessed with prophets as have the Jews, the successors of Isaac. In Muslim mythology it was Ishmael who was taken to be sacrificed in an ultimate act of surrender to the Will of God performed by his father.

It is Ishmael and his mother, Hagar, who became the key figures in the possibility for God's religion to be upheld by a small number of Arabs. Leaving Ibrahim with Sara and Isaac, the two exiles wandered in the desert until saved by divine intervention and the miraculous appearance of a divine spring known as Zamzam. The place where the two settled became the city of Makkah, in an otherwise hostile valley where previously life would have been impossible. It was Ibrahim, visiting his second family, who built the shrine known as the ka'aba for the worship of the One God, but according to Muslim belief on the site of a previous location created by Adam. Thus it is believed by Muslims that Makkah became a place of pilgrimage to the one God, with its rites established by Ibrahim and Ishmael. However, it is believed that over the course of time, the shrine fell into disuse and became a centre of idol worship. The well of Zamzam was filled in by the Jurhamites, invaders from South Arabia, who had been driven out but decided that no other people should benefit from possessing the oasis. It is said that a powerful tribe of Abrahamic descent, known as the Quraysh, settled in the area, and it was one of them named Qusayy who ordered his people to build houses around the shrine rather than inhabit tents. Thus the settlement of Makkah came into existence.

At this point myth blurs into history. The story tells us that Qusayy gave the right to be the keeper of the keys of the shrine to his son Abd al-Dar and his descendants, whereas Hashim, his first-born son, and his descendants were granted the privilege of providing food and shelter for the pilgrims. Hashim had a son from a woman of Madinah who was brought to Makkah by Hashim's brother. He did not consider his own sons fit to succeed him at the task of taking care of the pilgrims adequately. The young boy inherited the right to feed the pilgrims and loved to sleep in the sacred confines of the Ka'aba. One night in a vision, he heard the voice of a supernatural being commanding him to dig. After some days of disbelief, he finally rediscovered the spring of Zamzam and his clan was given charge over it to assist in the feeding of the pilgrims. Like Muhammad, Muttalib, the son of Hashim, is reputed to have never prayed before idols but only to have offered worship to Allah. It is believed that there were a number of significant individuals among the Quraysh who remembered the old religion of Ibrahim and remained true to its monotheism.

Muttalib had nine sons of whom the best loved and youngest was named Abd Allah. In a parallel story to the famous sacrifice attributed to Ibrahim, Muttalib had made a vow to sacrifice one son if God blessed him with many. The drawing of lots selected Abd Allah but the women of his clan prevented the sacrifice and camels were slaughtered in his stead. Abd Allah died whilst trading in modern-day Syria or Palestine, leaving behind a pregnant wife named Aminah. According to tradition, on the day of the birth of her son a voice spoke saying: 'Thou carriest in thy womb, the lord of this people, and when he is born say: I place him beneath the protection of the One, from the evil of every envier; then name him Muhammad.'[6]

Historical Origins

To tell the historical version of events, to some degree known by all Muslims from childhood, requires a little background knowledge of the Arabian Peninsula at the time of the birth of Muhammad. The Qur'an accuses the Arabs of idol worship and certainly the prevalence of tribal or household gods appears to have been the norm. Even in Madinah, where Jewish tribes were in the ascendancy, tribal deities appear to have flourished. Amongst Orientalist scholars of the pre-Muslim period there has been a prevalent view that such worship was already in decline when Muhammad began to preach the monotheism of Islam, thus explaining the relative ease with which the Arabs embraced the new religion. Muslim accounts of the early converts frequently contain stories of idol worship prior to contact with Islam but there are also tales of individuals who had rejected the tribal norms and clung to a primal form of monotheism unconnected with either Christianity or Judaism. These prototype monotheists were treated with great respect by the first Muslims and were known as *hanifs*. Monotheism would also have been present in the region through the aforementioned Jewish tribes in Madinah and various forms of Christianity existing in Syria and its surrounds. Arab merchants could not have travelled far without coming into contact with the Byzantine Empire. But it is unlikely that the largely illiterate Arabs would have known much of either Christian or Jewish practices and teachings except what came to them as traveller's tales or campfire stories.

There are also scholars who argue that the Arabs of the desert were indifferent to religion and were more concerned with fighting, drinking, gambling and sexual activity.[7] In this view the tribal gods were only significant at times of distress or in battle against other tribes. In the city of Makkah the gods were more important, as they were part of the merchant's livelihood. The historic pilgrimage that took place annually allowed the tribes to visit and trade under protection of a religious armistice and as such it would have benefited the trading families who were residents.[8] Generally, the Islamic view of pre-Muslim Arabian society is that it was *jahiliya*, a godless and immoral system where the laws and ethics of God given through revelation did not apply. Otherwise, Makkah, the birthplace of Muhammad, was not a particularly significant place. It existed outside the influence of the two powerful but declining empires of Christian Byzantium and the Zoroastrian Sassanids of Persia. Economically, life was difficult: the land was arid and agriculture sparse. The Makkans relied upon camel caravans for their livelihood, either as a trading post or for movement of their goods to either Byzantine or Sassanid territory.

It was into this harsh environment that Muhammad was born around 570 CE. The world of the desert nomads was little changed and continued in its traditional tribal forms, where protection against feuds was essential and patronage of the strong defended the weaker. The main cities were Makkah and Madinah, and the former was the most important city in the Arabian desert. The city was ruled over by the dominant tribe, the Quraysh, and it was their task to control the city's political and economic systems and ensure the defences were sound enough to keep out enemies and maintain their own dominance against Arab rivals. It is not known to what degree Muhammad's teachings of absolute monotheism, final judgement, and the existence of paradise and hell would have been familiar to the citizens of Makkah, but even if they had some prior knowledge through contact with earlier monotheistic religions, the socio-political impact would have been revolutionary and threatening to the religious, economic and political structures of this early seventh-century urban social system.

Muhammad was a member of the dominant Quraysh tribe but not from one of the powerful ruling clans. At an early age he lost his parents and was brought up by his paternal uncle, Abu Talib, who sent him to the desert to learn the traditional ways of the nomadic tribes, customary for small boys of good families born in the city. Muhammad's biographers state that he was involved in trade as an adult and took part in many caravans, thus coming into contact with Byzantine Christians, Jews and Persian Zoroastrians.[9] At the age of 25 he married Khadijah, an older woman, widow and a successful caravan trader. He had previously worked for her and tradition states that she asked for his hand in marriage. They were married for 15 years, his only wife until her death. Their marriage produced two sons and four daughters but only their daughter Fatima outlasted her father and played an important role in Muslim history.

Muhammad had a reputation amongst the citizens of Makkah for honesty, integrity and fair play. It is stated that he was often called upon to resolve arguments and was known for his wisdom. It is also said that he had a contemplative nature and, between trading, would often leave the city and spend time in the desert. At these times he would ponder upon the nature of existence but also the social injustices of Makkan society. Tradition states that he had a religious disposition but had never worshipped any of the city's idols. The story so familiar to all Muslims is that, from the age of 35, he retreated during the Arab month of Ramadan to the cave of Hira, near the summit of Jabal al-Nur, above Makkah.

It was on one such occasion, when Muhammad was 40 years old, that an experience took place in the cave that not only changed Muhammad's life and the society around him but was about to have dramatic and long-lasting consequences for the whole of human society. It is said that a divine being, later identified as Jibreel or Gabriel, and functioning as a divine intermediary or messenger, appeared before Muhammad and commanded him to 'Read'. The command was made three times, as Muhammad was not clear what he was supposed to recite. The order would have been more confusing if Muslim tradition is correct in saying that the Prophet was illiterate. Finally, the first verses of the Qur'an, the latest and last of the great revelations of God to humankind, was heard and recited back by Muhammad. 'Read, In the Name of your Lord who created; created man from a clinging clot. Read: your Lord is the Most Bountiful, Who taught by the pen. Taught man what he did not know.'[10] Muhammad was uncertain as to what had befallen him and rushed home to Khadijah afraid. She assured him that he was a virtuous and honest man and that nothing evil could befall him. With his wife's reassurance, Muhammad began to be convinced that the message was from God and thus began the last great prophetic encounter between the divine and the human race.

The newly called Prophet of God began to teach secretly amongst his intimate acquaintances and family members, testing out the message before he publicly preached in the city. The first followers were Khadijah, Muhammad's cousin Ali ibn Abi Talib and the Prophet's old friend Abu Bakr. Also amongst the early followers of Islam were Umar ibn al-Khattab and Uthman ibn Affan. Each of the four men was destined to become a leader (Caliph) of the Muslim community after the Prophet's death.

For 10 years, Muhammad preached in Makkah, gathering around him a loyal group of predominantly young believers in the message of total submission to an almighty Creator-God of the Universe, who invites humankind to worship, charity and social justice. However, paganism was also condemned and the majority of the Makkan merchants were strongly opposed to the new creed. It was not only their gods that were denounced but also their way of life. Slowly the opposition hardened as the powerful and the prosperous in the city began to organize resistance, and persecution of the Muslims began. In the meantime, the Islamic revelation was more fully enunciated by further revelations of the Qur'an to the Prophet. These were collected and memorized by those who sat before Muhammad when he preached. When the persecution reached a pitch that the Prophet considered unbearable he advised the first Muslims to seek refuge with the Christian ruler of Abyssinia. After a large number were accepted by the king there, the Makkans decided upon a boycott of the community of Muslims who remained in the city. It lasted for three years, during which time no trade, marriage or even conversation was permitted with them. At the end of this period of hostility, Muhammad suffered the dual blow of losing his two great allies, Khadijah and Abu Talib. The loss of his beloved wife, who had been the first to support him, was emotionally a great privation. But the death of his uncle meant that Muhammad no longer had a powerful protector in the city. His life was now in danger from his enemies.

As plots to kill him were being organized, he was invited to leave Makkah and come to the oasis city of Madinah to arbitrate and resolve certain tensions in the city resulting from tribal conflicts and the inability of the leaders of Madinah to forge a community from its disparate factions. As the situation with the Makkan leaders grew tenser, Muhammad sent his followers ahead of him and then, barely escaping an attempt on his own life, departed in the middle of the night.

The move to Madinah in 622 transformed the situation. From a despised religious leader in Makkah, Muhammad came to be a political figure with both temporal and spiritual leadership that provided him with the authority to establish a community which found its unity in God and his revelation and which agreed to guidance under the authority of God's Prophet. Although there were factions that undermined and resisted this development, especially amongst the Jewish tribes around and within the city parameters, Muhammad appears to have welded the people together through the worship of one God. As described in a unique and historic document called the *Constitution of Madinah*, the Muslims of Makkah, the new converts in Madinah and other tribal allegiances were forged into a community that overruled the primacy of blood ties in favour of a supra-tribal alliance that acknowledged belief in Allah and the leadership of his Prophet. The flight to Madinah is known as the *Hijra* (migration) and is so significant in Islamic history that it marks year one in the Muslim calendar.

From hereon in, faith would become the criteria for community membership and an examination of the Qur'an's revelations after the *Hijra* provides insight into a community that is incorporating God's new law, especially in the realm of personal family law, to create an organized political and social life, where the laws and customs of tribal loyalty were carefully negotiated to create a religiously bonded community governed by Allah's ordinances. In Madinah, Muhammad finally broke his ties with the older revelations of Judaism and Christianity, and as a part of this process of separation and distinction, the unique religious rituals and observances of Islam were formulated.

Muhammad's trials were far from over. Even if his fledgling community appeared successful in Madinah, the Makkan merchants remained deeply cynical and antagonistic. The skills of warfare taught by his uncle and his youthful stays with the desert Arabs were both now to be called upon in a series of armed conflicts with the forces of the Makkans. The Battle of Badr in 627 would transform Muhammad's reputation amongst the tribes of Arabia in a way that was as significant as his new role in Madinah. The inferior force of the Muslims and their Madinan allies were to engage in battle with a much stronger enemy gathered together by the Makkan confederacy and pull off a victory that was to surprise even the Muslims and bring Muhammad increased respect amongst the tribes of Arabia who, above all, admired strength.

The consequences of the victory had a considerable impact on the religious sensibilities of the Muslims. Their prophet had led them to a significant victory over powerful forces, deemed to be the strongest in the land. The Qur'an was to speak of it as 'Manifest Success', and most Muslims would thereafter link success in the world with proof of God's favour. But there are also negative effects of such a theology for the victorious. Worldly success may indicate to religious believers that they are the chosen of God, but failure results in religious crisis. We will see that this has had an impact on Muslim patterns of behaviour to the present time. More immediately, the Muslims in Madinah would face the problem of how to integrate into their faith community the tribes who would come to offer Muhammad their allegiance and seek his protection and patronage but whose motives would be very different from the original followers.

From now on Muhammad's life would revolve around the quarrel with the Makkans, but so powerful would he become as a result of new allies drawn to him from the Arab tribes that the Quraysh decided to pragmatically negotiate with the Muslims. When Muhammad requested to come on pilgrimage to the Ka'aba, they initially agreed. But when they resisted his terms and reneged on the agreement he brought the weight of his forces to camp outside the city. The city decided to surrender, and in 628 Muhammad entered the precincts of the Ka'aba, destroyed all the idols that were contained within it and announced that forthwith the shrine would only exist for the worship of Allah. Both parties were satisfied and there was no bloodshed. The Muslims of Makkah could return to their family homes and all could take part in the rites and practise their religion, but the merchants of the Quraysh would not lose their traditional income from the shrine as the city was now even more successful as a focus for pilgrims rapidly embracing the religion of the victors.

Four years later, Muhammad died. His submission to Allah had established the new faith on the Arabian Peninsula, and his own reputation amongst the Arabs was assured. At his last sermon delivered in Makkah on the occasion of Muhammad's final pilgrimage, we see some of his concerns for his community. Although he mentions some of the ethical codes bequeathed to his community concerning the rights of women and the treatment of others, it is the overwhelming simplicity and power of the lines speaking of equality before God that generate something of Muhammad's religious conviction.[11]

After the death of Muhammad, the Arab tribes, invigorated by their new-found allegiance to Islam, came out from the Arabian Peninsula and quickly conquered Persia and parts of the Byzantine Empire. Within sixty years of the Prophet's death, Muslims had reached China and Africa. Not all were interested in religion. Arab traders and warriors took Muslim culture far and wide and, along with them, went the religious preachers and the pious keen to bring the final revelation of God to the far corners of the earth. Nothing seemed to be able to stand in the way of Muslim success and within centuries of the advent of Islam two great dynasties had become empires and centres of civilization. Ruling from Damascus and then Baghdad, the Umayyads and Abbasids transformed the power structures of the world. The old Christian Empire built upon the decline of the Roman Empire could no longer dominate and slowly retreated before the forces of the Arabs. Only Roman Catholic Europe stood firm.

Core Belief

The primary Islamic doctrine concerning God is *tawhid*, the unity and uniqueness of the Creator, and the two aspects of the Oneness of God. All the core beliefs and practices of Islam stem from this powerful and uncompromising monotheism. The doctrine of *tawhid* is embodied in the first clause of the *shahada*, the great witnessing of Islam's monotheism, which proclaims *la illaha illa'Llah* – there is no god but God. However, it would be a mistake to consider *tawhid* as merely a rejection of idols. If there is a negation contained in the notion of *tawhid*, it refers to anything that is given primary significance in human affairs and therefore denies God the sole sovereignty and loyalty of his human subjects.[12] The negative in the first clause of the *shahada* goes far beyond the worship of plural gods, but rather asserts that there is nothing that should be put in the way of divine rule. This can be interpreted politically and leads to revolutionary ideas concerning governance, or spiritually as an inner realm of surrender defined as reintegration with the divine will through self-purification.

But above all else, *la illaha illa'Llah* is the primal statement of the divine describing its own reality; and then manifested in nature, human relationships, social organizations, worship and ritual and even the material dimension of the religion. Kenneth Cragg once described Muslims as the 'people of the point'.[13] He was referring to the geographical locus of the Ka'aba in Makkah as the point in which the emotional focus of all Muslims is directed in prayer. Five times a day millions of Muslims around the globe face towards Makkah, whilst those in Makkah itself face towards the Ka'aba, thus creating geometric patterns of human beings all directed towards one point, a feature which is unique in the world's religious history.

But the idea of the 'people of the point' can be taken to explore the way in which Allah's oneness and uniqueness is manifested in human affairs to create unity. As Allah is one, so has he created one religion (*din*) for human beings to worship and submit to his sovereignty. This unity of religion is manifested in revelation, continuously renewed through messengers, and sometimes when required a divine book, both acting as agents to draw human beings and their Creator even closer to each other by providing the details of how human beings should live on the earth in harmony with the divine will. All of this is premised in the unity of human nature, the idea of *fitra*, the original instinctive nature of the human creature that is inclined towards the good and the worship of God. Islam does not posit the idea of a corrupted being fallen from grace through original sin but rather of a person, although prone to forgetfulness and weakness, whose innermost being is altruistic and drawn towards godliness, exemplified by the possibility of complete submission and obedience as seen in the lives of the prophets. The Qur'an describes Islam as '*Din al-fitra*', the religion most closely associated with the primordial nature of human beings.

The unity of God is also replicated in human community. The Qur'an promotes the concept of community not in a Western sociological sense, but rather as a group of people, a tribe or a nation, that are united not by blood ties, language, culture, food or customs, but by their relationship to God. All other outer markers of community identity would ideally be established through the process of obedience to God's revelation; thus eating habits, dress codes, family structures, governance and ritual would be determined primarily by religion, although cultural diversity would be recognized as long as it did not contradict the primary loyalty to God. The ultimate manifestation of such a community would be the whole of humankind living in accordance to God's will.

In concrete terms, unity is demonstrated through the ritual life of the Muslim. Although individual prayer is not discouraged, it is in communal unity that Muslim religious life is fully implemented. Although the *du'a* prayers, individual prayers or group prayers of supplication, take place daily in the mosque, before and after the *salat*, it is in the ritual of the latter that the spirit of *tawhid* is discovered. Muslims gather in rows, shoulder to shoulder, facing towards Makkah, repeating with each other a series of movements and words of praise and supplication, culminating in prostration, an act of submission before the overwhelming awesomeness of Allah's unity and uniqueness. In the month of Ramadan, the sacred time when the Qur'an was first revealed, when the barriers that divide the divine world from the creation are thin and easily bridged, all adult Muslims should fast and millions do; abstaining from drink, food and sex from the hours of sunrise to sunset. In *zakat*, the divine imperative to provide for the needy, the thrust towards community is strengthened.

But, arguably, the most marked series of ritual actions to demonstrate and to encourage the sense of unity takes place on the annual Hajj, the pilgrimage to Makkah. In a series of activities, beginning in and culminating in the circumambulation of the Ka'aba, millions of Muslims, male and female, of all nations and cultures, rich and poor, try to surrender their individual identity into the religious *gemeinschaft* by wearing the same garb, a single white cotton sheet, and shaving their heads whilst performing identical ritual acts. Each performance re-enacts a special mythopoeic moment in the relation between God and humankind, uniting each Muslim into a sense of oneness that bridges a sacred past and the present time, overwhelming the usual human divisions of culture, language, status and wealth.

Although the term *tawhid* is not found in the Qur'an, the principle of God's oneness is embedded in the central message of the revelation and is proclaimed on numerous occasions. The Qur'an states on 13 occasions that Allah is the 'sole divinity', and in a further 29 instances proclaims '*la illaha illa huwa*' (there is no divinity other than He), a variation on the first clause of the *shahada*. Islam has even been called *ahl al-tawhid* (the way of unity) by some Muslim authors and jurists.

Islam Today

The creation of the Arab and other Muslim empires had a significant impact on Islam and its relations with Christian Europe which are still felt to this day. The first was theological, the second political, and the third is to do with perceptions of each other. In many ways, Europe's relations with the Muslim world and events taking place in that world are the inheritance of Europe's colonial enterprise and the decline of Muslim power.

1. Theology

The victory at the Battle of Badr had already created in the Arab religious psyche a sense that victory was divinely ordained as part of God's plan and proof that the divine will worked with the new people of revelation. However, as indicated earlier, there is a problem with such 'Manifest Success' theologies. As long as worldly success keeps on coming, the faith of the believers remains unchallenged. Defeat brings with it a spiritual crisis. The believers either have to lose faith or alternatively seek religious reasons for the military or cultural decline. Defeat is explained as God's warning to an aberrant people and brings with it a wake-up call to restore the pristine faith. A pattern is established that whenever a serious disaster befalls the Muslim world, there is a corresponding religious revival. Muslims were not seriously affected until the Mongol invasion in the thirteenth century – which resulted in the sacking of the centres of Arab culture and civilization, political administration and religion – led to considerable self-questioning; in fact, this is a perfect example of the conditions that lead to Muslims seeking to reform and renew their covenant with Allah. Ibn Taymiyya (1268–1328 CE) lived through the traumatic period after the Mongol sacking of Baghdad in 1258 and the fall of the Abbasid Empire and he sought to discover reasons for the inconceivable; the defeat of the Islamic world by apparently barbaric and polytheistic infidels. As a learned scholar of the Hanbali school of law, the most conservative of the four schools of law, he called for a literalist interpretation of the Qur'an and *Sunna* and the observation of Islam based on the period of the Prophet in Madinah and continuing through to the end of the first four Caliphs, who had been Companions of the Prophet.

2. Religio-political Causes

The Muslim world recovered from the Mongol invasion as a result of the invaders embracing Islam and creating their own Muslim dynasties in Central Asia and India. But far worse was to come. From the eighteenth century onwards the Muslim world retreated under the military, economic and cultural onslaught of the emerging European powers. This time it appeared that divine providence had rewarded the older people of God – the Christians – with 'Manifest Success', resulting in a number of European victories over Muslim forces and the subjugation of Muslim territories.

From Southeast Asia, Arabia to Africa, significant Muslim figures created movements to reform Islam. Out of these simultaneous revolutionary responses, perhaps influencing each other through significant meetings at the Hajj, the most important has to be the radical attempt to reform the original heartlands of Islam – Arabia – by Muhammad ibn al-Wahhab (1703–92). Joining with the temporal power of Muhammad ibn Saud, a local tribal chieftain, the combination created the first Islamic state, to be henceforth known as Saudi Arabia, but more significantly a global religious movement that to this day remains influential as it promotes the ideals of its founder throughout the Muslim world as the 'authentic' and 'pure' version of Islam. This movement was to become known as Wahhabism, but is more often invoked by their enemies and rivals in the Muslim world, extending it beyond the actual heirs of Muhammad ibn al-Wahhab to include any movement or ideologue that espouses similar ideas or promotes renewal and reform.

Although the jihad (in this case literally meaning armed struggle) movements that appeared in the various parts of the Muslim world during the eighteenth and nineteenth centuries generally disappeared as a viable response to colonization because of the superior firepower of the various European forces, the goal of reform and renewal based on the ideal of a return to Islam's pristine past did not. Invariably, the eighteenth-century movements turned to education of their own local Muslim populations, attempting to safeguard them from contamination from Western culture and ideas. Even the Wahhabi regime of Saudi

Arabia saw more mileage in spending its new-found oil wealth on education of Muslims worldwide than in promoting revolution through armed struggle. Consequently, the Wahhabis lost their radical edge and became neo-conservative forces within the world of Islam by the time of the creation of newly independent Muslim states in the twentieth century. It was left to others to create new movements that responded to the post-colonial situation. However, the twentieth-century ideologues such as Maulana Mawdudi (1903–79) or Sayyid Qutb did not stray far from the historical roots of reform and renewal that arose out of the theology of Manifest Success.

The growing new middle-class elites had benefited from Western education and appropriated the values of the European colonizers. They began to emphasis loyalty to the nation (*watan*) state rather than the Islamic *umma* (the universal Muslim community) promoted by those with a religious worldview. A new pan-Arabism replaced the older pan-Islamism and the religion was only perceived as a source of ethics to be drawn upon for the service of the nation and the new needs of the era. In such examples, Islam remained as a national state religion that would primarily function to supplement national culture and identity. Borrowing upon nineteenth-century European nationalism, the nation-state became the key unit which, drawing upon a common Arabic language and a distinctive cultural identity, should be able to unite diverse ethnic and religious identities, creating a distinctive unit where the first loyalty is to the *watan*.

Shortly after the end of the Second World War, these Western-educated elites were able to secure control of the newly emerging independent Muslim nation-states by dint of their leadership in struggles to overthrow the colonial powers. Britain and other European empires had been weakened by several years of total warfare and were unable to resist such struggles for independence. Thus the new Muslim governments embraced sovereignty with the borrowed ideals of secularism, socialism and nationalism that they had imbibed from their former rulers. Introducing European legal systems and the secular ideal that separated religion and politics was never going to be fully compatible with the worldview of devout Muslims. The West remained politically and economically dominant and those who professed loyalty to the *umma* began to enunciate ideas of statehood that were deemed Islamic. The idea of removing foreign cultural accretions to revive Islam by restoring it to its pristine purity was adapted to become part of an urgent call for an Islamic state governed by the law of God.

Thus a heated debate on the nature of the state and the question of loyalty took place throughout the Muslim world. Each Muslim nation arrived at its own individual solution but there is no doubt that the twentieth century was to witness a fundamental shift of territorial loyalty to the nation-state. In this respect the concept of *umma* was to take on a new symbolic meaning, more amongst the Muslim minority communities than in the Arab heartlands. For the Arabic-speaking nations '*umma*' was a term used in everyday language to denote various types of community. Where Arabic was not spoken as everyday language and Muslims lived alongside other communities, the ideal of the *umma* came to be a very powerful cultural and religious symbol which could be drawn upon to promote Muslim identity against the majority population of the respective nations.[14] In addition, throughout the latter half of the twentieth century, it also took on an ideological significance as a new kind of Muslim revivalist struggled to impose the values of Islam over the ideal of nationalism and patriotism to the fatherland.

Throughout the nineteenth and twentieth centuries in most Muslim nations the *shari'a* (Islamic legal code) was modernized by the replacement of traditional Islamic legal codes with those from the legal systems of the former European colonial powers. In some places, even Muslim family law – the heart of the *shari'a* consisting of the laws of inheritance, divorce and marriage expressly addressed by the Qur'an and the major force for governing the social lives of Muslims everywhere in the Islamic world – began to be tampered with by the new Muslim rulers, even though usually left intact by the former colonial rulers. An Islamic rationale was provided by Muslim governments wishing to reform their legal codes, who proclaimed the right to practise *ijtihad* in order to revitalize the Muslim world in line with modern Western nation-states. The *ulema* either cooperated with the governments by working as state-sponsored imams in government-built mosques and *madrasas* or alternatively felt powerless to halt the process even while they viewed it as profoundly contrary to the revelation of God enshrined in the Qur'an and Muslim tradition.

The new Muslim nation-states have inherited all of the above problems of governance since their independence and have not been able to challenge the dominance of Western political, economic or military power. So far, they have not been able to create a society that claims the allegiance of all their people, nor have they established themselves as the primary locus of Muslim identity, although, since the revolution, Iran could claim to be the first of the Muslim nations to approach this ideal. Generally, the state has sought to appropriate to itself those loyalties that Muslims ideally would have given to the universal religious community established by Muhammad, yet this has not been fully successful. This is further complicated by the artificial borders of a number of Muslim nations carved out in the twentieth century, where different ethnic groups with a distinct identity exist within the frontiers of individual nations. Such groups are not always successfully assimilated within the ideal of the nation-state. For example, the Kurdish populations of Iraq and Turkey or the populations of Indian Muslims that migrated to Pakistan during Partition in 1947 have not been fully integrated into their respective nations. In other countries there are tensions between rival religious groups such as Shi'a and Sunni Muslims, as is the case in Iraq.

Besides the conflicts between the Western-influenced ruling classes and the traditional *ulema*, there exists a third major division. The massive injection of European ideas gave impetus to the Islamic revivalist groups, whose central tenets had always included the idea of removing foreign cultural accretions to revive Islam by restoring its pristine purity. Although similar movements had existed in the past, they tended to criticize Sufi adherents of Islam as the innovators who introduced alien religious practices into the religion, but, in the twentieth century, revivalist movements appeared with an agenda to remove Western influences from Muslim nations. The leaders of these tightly knit, well-organized movements did not belong to the *ulema* and, unlike the earlier revivalists and reformers, they were not formed around the teachings of *madrasa*-trained members of the *ulema*. Prominent examples of such movements are *Jamaat-i Islami* founded by Maulana Mawdudi (1903–79) in the subcontinent and the *Jamaat al-Ikhwan al-Muslimin* founded in Egypt by Hassan al-Banna (1906–49). Such organizations rejected both nationalism and the hidebound, ineffective traditionalism of the *ulema*. They fought against the idea of loyalty to the nation-state, or at least those that were founded upon principles derived from the West. Instead they asserted that the primary loyalty of Muslims should be to the global community of Islam, even if initially it meant the overturning of Muslim governments and their replacement by an Islamic state. Reinterpreting the old label of *jahiliya* (ignorance) used for the decadent condition of the pre-Islamic Arab society, they asserted that such a state of godlessness now pervaded the whole of humankind, including those societies that would normally be called Muslim but that do not implement the *shari'a*. Thus a simple choice was advocated between loyalty towards Islam and participation in *jahiliya*. The common demand of the revivalists was addressed towards Muslim nations to implement the *shari'a* in its entirety and revolutionize their governments and society to become Islamic states freed from Western influence.

Thus in the twenty-first century, the global community finds itself facing a crisis as Muslims try to resolve these differences between themselves. Although originally caused by the loss of Muslim power and the tensions created by European colonial supremacy, they have now been further complicated by the supremacy of global capitalism after the fall of the Soviet Union and the accompanying globalization of secularism and an aggressive Western insistence that liberal democracies are the superior form of political, economic and social organization for nation-states. A number of Muslim organizations have developed a radical and violent form of revivalism that has gone beyond the strategies of the older movements and created an Islamism that is prepared to inflict damage on Western institutions and civilian populations through armed struggle. The activities of such movements culminated in the iconic events of 11 September 2001 (commonly known as 9/11) and subsequent acts of violence in various parts of the world. The USA responded by its call for a 'War on Terror' under the Bush government.

The situation was further complicated by mass population movements that brought significant Muslim populations into the West and confused the traditional ideas of boundaries between the Muslim and non-Muslim worlds. Both migration and terrorism caused a renewal and re-emergence of historic attitudes towards Islam that had been originally forged during the collision between Islam and Christianity in the medieval period and were further reinforced during the colonial period.

3. Perceptions

Heeren suggests that historic rivalry has led to an 'ignorance of the ordinary Westerner towards Islam'.[15] However, it is equally true that misconceptions of Western culture and the teachings of Christianity are held by Muslims. This needs to be understood in the context of a historic relationship and the appropriation of the East in the colonial era that has become known as 'Orientalism' since the publication of Edward Said's seminal text by the same name.[16] For those writing after 9/11 the temptation is even greater to demonize, marginalize and distort; to set Western freedom and civilization against Muslim superstition and ignorance. In such an environment, the old myths and fabrications reappear in new forms and then the temptation for those on the liberal left who resist colonialism and corporate capitalism is to enlist Muslims to their cause, and to paint too rosy a picture that conveniently forgets gender issues, homophobia, and social injustices in the Muslim world. In short, Orientalism, in both its negative and positive aspects, still rules the roost when it comes down to media depictions of Muslims.

In the next chapters we will be picking up many of the issues touched upon in this introductory chapter and exploring them in more detail. In examining Muslim diversity, fundamentalism, gender, ethics, and relations with the West in the following chapters it will become clear that all these issues have been affected by the situation described in this chapter. In Chapter 2 we will detail some of the major divisions in the Muslim religious and political spectrum, including Shi'as, Sufis, Wahhabis and some of the twentieth-century revivalist movements.

Chapter 2

Muslim Diversity

Abdullah bin Amar (RA) relates that the Holy Prophet (peace be upon him) said "Surely things will happen to my people as happened earlier to Israelites, they will resemble each other like one shoe in a pair resembles the other to the extent that if anyone among the Israelites has openly committed adultery to his mother there will be some who will do this in my Umma as well, verily the Israelites were divided into 72 sections but my people will be divided into 73 sections, all of them will be in the fire except one." The companions asked, "Who are they? O Messenger of Allah." The Holy Prophet (peace be upon him) said, "They are those who will be like me and my companions."[1]

The above Hadith is regularly cited in Muslim meetings throughout the world to demonstrate that sectarianism was prophesied by Muhammad and therefore Muslims should not be surprised to discover that it exists. Of course each movement in the spectrum of Islam considers itself to be the one that is saved and regards all the others as belonging to the symbolic 72. In the main the divisions within the Muslim community have learned to live alongside each other relatively harmoniously accepting the Asharite position that only Allah can know the secrets of the heart and therefore who is faithful or not. However, from time to time political, economic or social tensions lead to violence in the name of religious authenticity. Before looking at contemporary situations where such differences are problematic, this chapter will outline some of the main schisms in Islam and the causes of division.

Any attempt to explore the causes of schism within Islam has first to acknowledge the powerful rhetoric of unity that is constructed upon the ideal of *umma*. The *umma* is held together not by any formal organization but by a collective act of will, inspired by personal conviction and embodied in the ritual duty of daily prayer, the month-long fast of Ramadan and the annual pilgrimage to Makkah. Five times a day, millions of Muslims face Makkah all at the same time to observe the same ritual prayers. This core of shared ritual practices combined with observances of the *shari'a* is integral to Muslim life and creates the bonds that tie the *umma* together.

Despite the ideal held by many Muslims of a single, divinely revealed and united Islam, there have been and continue to be diverse interpretations of Islam. So successful is the rhetoric that a general perception of Islam is one of a monolithic religious entity that overrides the diversity of nationalities and ethnicities that form the whole. This ideal is maintained by Muslims themselves, who though aware of the diversity of religious positions across the Islamic spectrum still persist in presenting the ideal of a single community of believers in the one God to outsiders.[2] So successful is this strategy arising from a powerful sense of an imagined community that few outside the knowledgeable are likely to know more than the fact that Islam has two main branches, the dominant Sunnis and the minority Shi'as.

The initial division occurred over the issue of the leadership of the *umma*. Other divisions were created concerning the nature and shape of the community itself. Major stress was also placed on the *umma* by the spread of the Arab empire and its attendant rapid incorporation of older, more sophisticated cultures brought into the fold of Islam. Any attempt to formulate an overriding theory of schisms in Islam would need to take account of these factors and also acknowledge both religious and political tensions. It is also important to note that the original schism that produced Sunni and Shi'a Islam set up divergent patterns for future divisions in the *umma*. Sunni sectarianism will take place within a different context to Shi'a. The various Shi'a movements, some of which have developed into separate religions outside the fold of Islam, would appear to have been formed over disagreements around leadership, often at a juncture occurring upon the death of the charismatic founder. It would be tempting to analyse this category of schism within the framework of the relationship between institution and charisma classically provided by Max Weber. Sunnis, on the other hand have tended to disagree on matters of interpretation of law or over changes in a group's doctrines and/or degrees of strictness arising out of such processes of legal/religious interpretation. Yet caution needs to be taken in either of these analyses as splits can also be driven by ethnic, tribal, racial, or national fault lines.

The Original Schism

The death of Muhammad was to be the catalyst for the first main schism in Islam. Wallis argues that new religious movements are marked by unstable authority and can be destabilized by the death of a charismatic leader, although he admits that where processes are put into place to prepare for the transfer of authority at death, the impact of such destabilization can be negated and legitimacy can be smoothly passed on from one kind of leadership to another with little disruption from competing claims.[3] The Prophet left no son to be his heir or to take his place, and it is uncertain whether primogeniture was observed in Arabian culture. The election of the aged Abu Bakr as the first Caliph (632–4) would appear to have marked a return to the traditional tribal method of choosing a leader and could be said to represent a move away from the type of charisma represented by the Prophet to a more institutional form of leadership based on political authority.

If this is an accurate estimation of the change of leadership brought about by the demise of the Prophet, then the first schism of Islam can be explained – using a straightforward Weberian analysis of charisma and institutionalization – as an attempt to restore charismatic leadership. According to Shi'a narratives the origins of the division go back to an incident that took place not long before Muhammad's death, when he was returning to Madinah from his farewell pilgrimage to Makkah. The Prophet and his Companions stopped near a pool called Ghadir Khumm. It is said that after asking them if it was true that he was closer to them than they were to themselves, he said something of major significance for the succession. The Shi'a believe that Muhammad took his son-in-law and cousin, Ali, and said, 'He, of whom I am the patron, of Him Ali is also the patron.' To many this signified that Ali was Muhammad's chosen successor.[4]

Ali was married to the Prophet's daughter, Fatima, and was the father of Muhammad's grandchildren. Even the Qur'an appears to endorse the specialness of Muhammad's family and direct bloodline. 'And Allah only wishes to remove all abomination from you, Ye Members of the Family, and to make you pure and spotless.'[5] In Shi'a conviction, Ali was blessed with a charisma similar to Muhammad's own: one who shone with Allah's light on his countenance. Shi'a tradition states that Muhammad came to know that Ali was his successor when it was revealed to him on the Night Journey, the mystical ascension to the divine presence.[6]

However, the Shi'a religious sensibility was to be based on a cult of suffering, which began with this first moment of error and deprivation. Shi'as came to believe that on the Prophet's deathbed, when his family was gathered around him and performing the rites of death, the elders of the tribes met and chose Abu Bakr. Yet there were those who never accepted the decision, believing it to be in opposition to the Prophet's wishes, and these people became known as the Party of Ali – Shi'at Ali or Shi'a.

Whatever the historical events may have been surrounding Ali, there is no doubt that for the Shi'a he and the surviving direct descendants of Muhammad, the *ahl al-Bait* (the 'People of the Household'), all became significant figures of their religious imagination, doomed to suffer on behalf of their community and deprived of true recognition by the majority of Muslims who had cast their lot with the Sunni Caliphate. The Shi'a developed the theological and political position that Ali should by right have been the first Caliph, handing the Caliphate on to the 'People of the Household', the Prophet's direct family descendants, thus giving the leadership of the Muslims over to a rule of the bloodline that mysteriously contained some of Muhammad's spiritual power and authority. In many ways, what took place was a classic sociological dilemma that occurs at the death of a founder and the loss of charismatic leadership. The Umayyad rulers who came into power after the period of the four Caliphs were content to accept the more institutional leadership of the community, begun with the choice of Abu Bakr. The shift from charismatic leadership to a fully institutional leadership took place gradually for most Sunnis with the first four Caliphs providing a bridge between the two types of authority. As we shall see later, not all Sunnis felt this way and some were able to resurrect charismatic leadership through the institution of sainthood. The Shi'a, on the other hand, utilized the doctrines of the pure and unsullied 'People of the Household' to retain charismatic leadership and resist the dominant institutional power established by the Umayyads.

After Ali's death, the Shi'a may have been inclined to accept pragmatically the reality of Umayyad power but only with the retention of a sense of grievance. It is a central belief that Ali and

Mu'awiyya, the first Umayyad ruler, made a sacred pact after the battle between their forces, in which Ali agreed to Mu'awiyya's succession to the Caliphate but only if he renounced the right of his son Yazid to follow him. On Mu'awiyya's death, the leadership of the Muslims was to revert to the grandsons of Muhammad, Hassan and Hussain.

Whatever the facts, it is a religious truth believed by the Shi'a that Hassan, the elder of the two grandsons, was persuaded to relinquish his claim to the Caliphate, and retired into exile in Madinah where he died in strange circumstances. According to the Shi'ite version of the tale, he was poisoned by the Umayyad leadership. Thus the tale of the woes of the family continued: destined to be martyred and deprived of their birthright as the Sunnis grew from strength to strength. But the real fateful story that grips the Shi'ite religious imagination, in effect marking out their differences from the Sunnis and providing the myth for a theology of patient suffering, is discovered in the tragic circumstances of the death of Hussain, the Prophet's sole surviving grandson.

After the death of Mu'awiyya in 680 CE, his son Yazid inherited the Caliphate, thus beginning a hereditary dynasty. The details vary according to which side is telling it. One version states that Yazid placed a repressive general to subdue Ali's stronghold in Kufa. It is said that the Kufans called for Hussain to liberate them, promising to support his right to the Caliphate. Hussain was intercepted on his way to the rescue by forces loyal to Yazid and persuaded to move in another direction. He then departed for Karbala where he set up camp on 2 October 680 CE (the second day of Muharram). Other accounts claim that Hussain marched on Damascus from his father's old stronghold in Kufa with a force of 72 loyal followers, believing implicitly in Allah's promise to bring victory to the righteous even by miraculous means as described in the Qur'an after the defeat at Uhud. After arrival in Karbala, he was trapped by the Umayyad armies of Yazid under the command of Umar ibn Sa'ad, who insisted Hussain could not leave unless he submitted to the authority of Yazid.

Hussain's small force was attacked in Karbala on the tenth day of the Muslim month of Muharram by an overwhelmingly superior army comprising five thousand armed troops. In Shi'a accounts, the fighting raged all day on the tenth day of Muharram, a day to be known henceforth by the Shi'a as Ashura. By the afternoon, Hussain remained defiant, cradling his own dead son in his arms, only to be cut down with his last surviving companions. Those who survived were beheaded. Hussain's widow, Zaynab and his surviving son, Ali, were brought in chains to Yazid, who gloated on his victory for days over the decapitated head of Hussain. Eventually the widow and her son were released.

Thus it is believed that a wicked and ruthless tyrant came to usurp the Caliphate that rightfully belonged to the family of the Prophet. This motif would run throughout Shi'a interpretations of history. Henceforth the Shi'a would view the mainstream of Sunni Islam, although ostensibly successful and representing the majority of Muslims, as representative of an illegitimate and degenerate empire that could never be the true people of God. The escape of Hussain's son, Ali, from the slaughter ensured the survival of the true inheritors of Islam, the direct line of the Prophet, replete with their special powers inherited through his bloodline that permitted them to know the inner secrets of the Qur'an, and thus qualified them to lead the faithful. For the Shi'a these were the true leaders of the community, known as the Imams and differentiated from the Sunni imams, who are merely leaders of prayer.

Amongst the Ithna'ashariyya – the Twelver Shi'as as they are known, still the dominant group in Iran and Iraq – there are believed to be 12 Imams, beginning with Ali. But all Shi'a groups are united in acceptance of the first six Imams: Ali Ibn Talib, the cousin and son-in-law of Muhammad; Hasan ibn Ali (d. 669), the son of Ali and brother of Hussain; al-Hussain ibn Ali (d. 680), the son of Ali, the *Sayyid ash-Shuhada*, the 'Prince of Martyrs'; Ali Zayn al-Abidin (d. 713), the son of Hussain, and supposedly quiescent in the struggles between Shi'a and Sunni; Muhammad al-Baqir (d. 731), the son of Ali Zayn al-Abidin, a significant scholar, attributed with the development of Shi'a laws and doctrines; and finally, Ja'far al-Sadiq (d. 765), the son of al-Baqir, also quietist and scholarly in his approach to the Caliphate. It was during his period that the Shi'a doctrine of the infallibility of the Imams was developed. Fuad Khuri makes the observation that the choice of the title 'Imam', used in opposition to 'Caliph' by all Shi'a groups, is intentional and indicates how such sectarian movements utilize moral authority as a means of legitimacy.[7] The Qur'an is regarded as the ultimate exoteric authority but it is the Imam who governs the esoteric realm, which holds sway over the exoteric realm. The Imam is exemplar, the perfect religious model to be followed and a visible salvationary symbol of the hidden realms, the completion or embodiment of religion. According to Khuri, the Sunnis perceive the sects as a natural product of historical processes whereas the Shi'a sects see themselves as expressions of divine will.[8]

Schisms amongst the Shi'a

Momen reminds us that when the Arabs expanded into territories that lay within the Fertile Crescent they were to meet with ancient civilizations that had already developed complex religious systems. Zoroastrianism, Mazdakism, Manichaeism, Judaism and various sects of Christianity all rivalled each other and added practices and doctrines to the worldview of the area. When they crossed into Islam, these prevalent ideas, such as transmigration of souls, occultation, the descent of the spirit of God into man, divinely inspired guidance, and delegation of God's powers, became jointly known as *ghulat* or extremist by the orthodox amongst Muslims.[9] Momen suggests that the converts to Islam from this region adopted Ali and his successors as an embodiment of the above religious speculation, providing them with a hero-martyr and a priestly succession.[10] When Ali moved his headquarters to Iraq it was natural that he would gain loyalty from the local populace. The death of Hussain and the second-class status attributed to the non-Arab Muslims of this area provided political aspirations to overcome the Syrian Umayyad hegemony.

Thus it is difficult to assess the historical accuracy of the various Shi'a accounts of the Imams. The prototypical Shi'a certainly took time to develop the full salvationary narrative around the Imams and, in particular, the role of the final Imam or Mahdi. Shi'a writers tend to depict the Imams as quasi-legendary figures rather than historical. These hagiographical accounts come complete with wondrous birth stories, performance of miracles, possession of supernatural knowledge and authentication tales to legitimize their succession. Consequently it is difficult to ascertain whether they had the qualities of charismatic leadership. Even Shi'a texts describe Ali as corpulent, short-sighted and balding, hardly the epitome of charismatic appearance. The focus is on his heroic traits and popular depictions show him wielding a two-pronged sword fighting against the opponents of Islam or wild animals.[11] He is also considered to be eloquent. Thus it would seem that the Imams can be defined as possessing a constructed charisma rather than actual personality or character traits. This constructed charisma needs to be explored within the context of its role in the theoretical 'invented tradition' first developed by Eric Hobsbawm.[12]

Invented traditions form a set of practices and organizational structures that are heavily dependent on continuity with a historic past, a reference to old situations which consist not only of tacitly accepted rules and rituals and norms of behaviour heavily reinforced by repetition, but also of historic relationships with rival Muslim movements.

A mention has to be made of the final Imam or the doctrine of the Mahdi that has become central to Shi'a movements. The classic model is found amongst the Twelver Shi'a. The Shi'a's embracing of a cult of suffering based upon their sense of being Allah's righteous minority struggling against the sins of the world would be reinforced by their conviction that all their infallible Imams, the true servants of Allah from Ali to the eleventh Imam, were victims of violence by their enemies. The sense of being under continuous threat led to the practice of *taqiyya* (dissimulation), whereby Shi'a leaders and their followers could conceal their true beliefs to avoid persecution by their enemies. However, this pragmatic decision was deemed insufficient to avoid martyrdom, and when the twelfth Imam provided no direct progeny, the significant doctrine of *ghayba* (occultation) appeared, in which Allah protected his last Imam by taking him to a special place of concealment. This event was supposed to have occurred in 874 CE and after this date a succession of official representatives known as *babs* intermediated mystically between the Imam and the faithful. In 941 CE, the period of the greater *ghayba* began, where the Imam was and is incommunicado until his return as the Mahdi at the end of time to bring final vindication.

It is the belief concerning the occultation of the Imam and when this occurred that generally marks out different Shi'a sects. The Zaydiyya or Zaidis believe that the son of the fourth Imam was the true successor based on his argument that the Imamate can be claimed by any descendant of Ali and Fatima who is pious, learned and who comes out openly to make his bid. Zaid and his half-brother, the fifth Imam Muhammad al-Baqir, disagreed over several points of doctrine. After his death in battle several Zaidi imams rose in rebellion. On several occasions various groups of supporters claimed they were the final Imam and in occultation. Subgroups of the Zaidis are the Jarudiyya, the Jaririyya and the Butriyya.

The death of Ja'far al-Sadiq, the sixth Imam, resulted in one of the most notable fragmentations of the Shi'a community. Ja'far appointed his son Isma'il to succeed him but he died. The community experienced another major division. The Twelvers believed that his death annulled his Imamate and moved on to another branch of the family but another group came to believe that the Imamate ended with Isma'il. The Isma'ilis are therefore known as the 'Seveners'. The pure Isma'ilis believe that he did not die but was taken into occultation. Other groups were to follow the descendants of Isma'il.

In Shi'a circles, the many subgroups – some of which are no longer in existence – are divided into three categories:

1. *Ghulat* (the extremists) are those groups who hold to beliefs that assert there are prophets after Muhammad or who believe that God can incarnate as a person. They may also believe in the transmigration of souls.
2. *Waqifa* (those who hesitate or stop) applies to any group that denies or hesitates over the death of a particular Imam and refuses to acknowledge any further Imams.
3. *Qat'iyya* (those who are certain) applies to any group who are sure about the death of an Imam and go on to the next Imam.[13]

However, it is not only differences over the Imam that can create divisions amongst the Shi'a. There are also eschatological groups that appear from time to time announcing an imminent end to the world and following a leader who is proclaimed to be the Mahdi. Even *babs*, the mystical intermediaries between the Imam and the faithful once he has entered occultation, can cause new sects to arise. The most notable example would be the Baha'i, who went on to become a separate religion. The Baha'i's origins lie in the life and teachings of Sayyid Ali Muhammad Shirazi (1819–50) who first claimed to be the Bab or Gate to the Imam but who went on to assert that he was the returned twelfth Imam and that the Islamic dispensation or revelation was abrogated in favour of a new prophetic cycle.

Another independent religion to emerge from the Shi'a accused of *ghulat* doctrines was the Druze. Located today in Israel, Syria, Lebanon and Jordan, the Druze originally emerged as a breakaway from the Isma'ilis. According to Robert Betts, Druzism appeared as a reaction to the failure of the Isma'ilis to create a messianic kingdom out of their Fatimid dynasty with its capital in Cairo.[14] In reality the state was little different to that of the Abbasids or their Byzantine enemies. Saviour figures began to emerge and one such was the Fatimid Caliph al-Hakim. Around 1009 CE several leaders in Cairo began to proclaim al-Hakim as the fulfilment of scriptural promises and to acknowledge his divinity. Al-Hakim is a contested figure, judged by Western historical scholarship to be a megalomaniac. Certainly some of his actions are not what is normally expected of a religious founder, albeit that one of his foremost followers, Hamza ibn Ali ibn Ahmad al-Zuzani, a Persian Isma'ili theologian, was able to successfully spread the religion throughout the Fatimid Empire. After al-Hakim's probable assassination in 1021 CE, the usual myth of the hidden Imam in occultation emerged. However, Betts argues that even in its early stages, Druzism saw itself as a new religion aiming to establish a new world order.[15]

Sunni Schisms

Although there are clearly sectarian divisions that have even led to new religions manifesting out of the Shi'a schism, the Sunni majority has always considered itself normative and undivided. It would be difficult to get Sunnis to admit that there are schisms in Islam's dominant grouping. It is here that the myth of the *umma*'s unity is found in its strongest expression. The Sunnis have been the dominant group and historically the political rulers of the Muslim world with the few exceptions of Iran and the Fatimid dynasty, for example. As rulers they were able to utilize the state as the main means of organizing religious life. Indeed, Fuad Khuri goes so far as to state that Sunnis feel 'lost' when deprived of centralized power.[16] If this is true it has implications with regard to Sunni reactions to the loss of power and whether this impacts on the development of diverse Sunni religio-political movements whose *raison d'être* is the revival of religion as a means to regain power.

The Caliph or Sultan has ideally embodied both governance and piety, but ruling through the implementation and execution of *shari'a*, the divine law. Ideally he is not there to create laws, as these have already been given in entirety by Allah in the Qur'anic revelation. Any difficulties of interpretation are resolved by bodies of *ulema* or religious scholars, who are experts in jurisprudence. The situation in contemporary Muslim states is diverse depending upon the form of government, but most religious Muslims would still consider that it is not the role of the state to create law but rather to implement God's law. Whereas the Shi'a are more likely to speak of justice, oppression and expected salvation, the Sunnis are more likely to speak of consensus and unity. Khuri goes so far as to argue that the Shi'a sects have historically been the refuge of the oppressed and underprivileged and that such sects are a means to reject the centralized authority of the Muslim state.[17]

A number of elements can contrive to form separatist or rebellious movements against the unity of state and religion within Sunni Islam. The degree to which Islam is actually practised by Muslims can be controversial and even a cause of political rebellion. The question of whether nominal Muslims were within the fold of Islam arose early in Islam's development and was a continuation of the 'hypocrite' concerns that arose in Madinah where the motivations of the Arab tribes seeking allegiance with the Muslims were questioned. The first movements to declare war against the Umayyad state were the Kharijites, who were unequivocal that the defining feature of Muslim identity was piety and who controversially claimed the right to declare jihad against nominal Muslims, stating that they were *kufr* or unbelievers. The state was quick to recognize that such a position led to unrest, civil wars and anarchy, and adopted the Asharite position that only God could judge the condition of *iman* (faith). Nevertheless the Kharijite position has never disappeared and has re-emerged dramatically in the twentieth century amongst various jihad movements.

Similar to the Kharijite position on individual allegiance to Islam is the issue of state loyalty to the religion. In practice the union of revelation and governance has not always been watertight. Many rulers have been at odds with the *ulema* with regard to authority and not all have implemented the *shari'a* fully. Most of today's Muslim states have either discarded *shari'a* law or mix it in varying degrees with legal systems adapted from various European codes. Even in Shi'a Iran, the Islamic revolution has not fully removed French law, despite its attempts to introduce an Islamic state. Generally, it is only family law that has remained sacrosanct. This compromise made by the political union of *din* (religion) and *dunya* (world) has led to some movements and organizations that condemn the state and seek to implement an Islamic revolution, sometimes through violent overthrow.

The justification for such movements in Sunni Islam is to reform or revitalize Islam, and they base their actions, as did the Kharijites before them, on a verse in the Qur'an: 'Let there arise out of you a band of people inviting to all that is good, enjoining what is right, and forbidding what is wrong. They are the ones to attain felicity.'[18] Originally revealed in Madinah, probably as a reaction to the recruiting of various tribes whose religious motives were suspect, the political and religious significance of this verse can be highly subversive for Muslim states that are seen by the devout to have compromised God's revelation. In the twentieth century, a number of revivalist movements have set themselves up as a righteous vanguard to renew Islam and purge the community of anything that is perceived to be a threat to the religion.

The third factor to impact on the appearance of Sunni radical or revolutionary reform movements is the complete or partial loss of state power, especially to a non-Muslim invader. The doctrine of Manifest Success provides an underlying pattern that repeats itself throughout Sunni Muslim history. Malise Ruthwen refers to Islam being 'programmed for victory' and argues that it is a 'triumphalist faith'.[19] Yet the fall from power that resulted from European colonialism was to be the biggest shock of all – for the new imperial powers brought before Sunni Muslims the vision of a revival of Christian authority – a religion that God was supposed to have supplanted by Islam as his new community of salvation. From the eighteenth century to the present the response was a succession of regional religious revivals, for defeat could only be interpreted as a sign of God's disfavour. To restore favour to His last community it was necessary to be self-critical, and seek revival and the reform of Islam.

The process of renewal of the faith to keep it to the pristine purity of the original revelation is contained in the two concepts of *islah* and *tajdid*. *Islah* is mentioned in the Qur'an in the context of the warnings of the prophets to their respective communities to return to the ways of God. *Tajdid* refers to the process of renewal. Thus throughout the centuries there have been those who have called for renewal and worked to restore Islam to their own understanding of the contents of the original message and its implementation. Implicit in such renewals is the understanding that the community is divided and requires purging of un-Islamic behaviour or accretions that are foreign to the faith in order to restore unity. The various revivals created a number of movements whose revolutionary zeal gradually died down, to be replaced by newer more radical groups, which in turn became 'tamed'. Often such movements can develop around the charismatic leadership of a *mujaddid*, a pious individual believed to be a rejuvenator of the *umma*. Sunni tradition insists that such individuals arise at the beginning of each new century of Islam's history. Any movement with a new charismatic leader endowed with personal piety and the energy to impact on the world around him can claim that their leader is the *mujaddid*. A special *mujaddid* is also believed to appear every thousand years. The followers of both such personalities are likely to become a subdivision of the Sunni community.

In the twentieth century, these religious revivalist movements have largely taken place in the context of nationalism and the confrontation between conflicting loyalties to state and religion. This is amplified when the state has moved towards a Western secular model of statehood. As we have seen in Chapter 1, the overwhelming factor in determining Muslim political and religious thought and activism has been relations with the West. Economic control in the eighteenth century gradually became political and military domination in the nineteenth and returned full circle to economic and political domination in the post-colonial era of the latter half of the twentieth century. The *ulema* were found to be inadequate to deal with the new situation, preferring to cling on to their old traditional ways, retreating to the mosques and the Muslim seminaries (*madrasa*), a domain where they could retain control. Essentially schooled in the *madrasa* system, with a curriculum unchanged since the medieval period, they were increasingly challenged by a superior European technology and military might that was founded upon economic power and the new discoveries of science. In addition, they had to deal with a new worldview rooted in philosophical and political history that had given rise to democracy, nationalism and secularism. The Muslim crisis arose primarily from the fact that they were powerless to stop the European powers from taking control of or dominating Muslim territory. This provoked a crisis within the faith which the rigidly traditional religious leadership were ill-equipped to resolve. With an educational methodology based on *taqlid* (blind imitation), innovation and adaptation to the new situation was difficult and foreign domination by non-Muslims raised questions concerning the health of Islam and the reasons for the apparent loss of divine favour, which appeared to no longer provide success to the *umma* as it had in the past.

There was disagreement concerning the means of achieving this return to success. Such disagreements, although initially intellectual responses, were to polarize into positions that politically and religiously divided the Muslim world to the present time. In brief these positions can be described as modernist, secularist and Islamist. Each is united by their desire to revive the Muslim world but divided by the means in which they feel this can be achieved. Modernists hope that Muslims can rediscover their power by rejuvenating the morality and ethics of Islam but meanwhile learning from European developments that have been made in science and technology. The crucial element is to restore the glory of Islam by reviving the essentials of the faith but to reform Islamic legal, administrative and educational institutions along the lines of the West. The objective is to compete favourably with the power of Europe. Nations such as Tunisia, Malaysia and the Gulf States would fall into this category. The liberal and modernist reformers of the nineteenth and twentieth centuries believed that creative interpretation of the Qur'an and *Sunna* was open to all Muslims in order to discover the way to adapt Islam to the changing conditions of modern society, thus permitting legal and social reform. These reformers accused the *ulema* of holding back progress by being out of touch with the modern world. Key modernists call for a thorough reinterpretation of the Qur'an that acknowledges its metaphorical and cultural content as opposed to more literalist interpretations.

The problem of inner decay had already been prominent in the minds of a number of Muslim thinkers and reformers, but now they had to consider the possibility of Muslim civilization being unable to survive this new external threat from the West. Most of the responses to the crisis agreed upon the necessity of Islamic revival in order to restore the past glories of the Muslim *umma*, but there was disagreement concerning the means of achieving this. These disagreements, although initially intellectual responses, had polarized into positions that have politically and religiously divided the Muslim world to the present time. Jamal al-Din al-Afghani (1838–97) and Muhammad Abduh (1849–1905) were to become the leading proponents of a position that proclaimed that Muslims could rediscover their power by rejuvenating the morality and ethics of Islam but meanwhile learn from Europe the developments that had been made in science and technology. The crucial element was to restore the glory of Islam by reviving the essentials of the faith. Then Muslims could go on to reform their legal, administrative and educational institutions and once again compete favourably with the new power of Europe.

A new intellectual class of Muslims, educated to Western standards, taking on the values of the colonial powers and lacking the religious outlook of the reformers, gradually developed to challenge the authority of the *ulema*. Influenced by nationalism, they stressed loyalty to the nation rather than the *umma*. Rifa'a Badawi Rafi al-Tahtawi (1801–73), an Egyptian writer resident in France for five years as the imam to a student mission, and influenced by French ideals of republicanism, appears to be the first to have introduced the idea of the fatherland (*watan*) and patriotism (*wataniyyah*) into the Arabic medium.[20] More significantly, in the milieu of the rapidly collapsing Ottoman Empire, the Muslim sociologist Ziya Gokalp (1876–1924) propounded the theory of Turkism. He saw Islam as a source of ethics which could be adapted to the needs of the time and the service of the nation, but religion and nation had to be separated for the common good of both. He argued that it was possible to retain Islam's fundamental values and principles but to develop a modern Turkish national culture in which religious law would be replaced by secular law. Islam would remain in place as a national state religion that would primarily function to supplement Turkish culture and national identity. It could be used to develop connections with the wider Muslim world but the interests of the Turkish nation must always be paramount. For such thinkers, the nation was a natural integrated unit which, through the medium of a common language and a distinctive cultural identity, brought together diverse ethnic and religious identities and welded them into a distinctive unit where the primary loyalty was to the *watan*. Although not all Muslim nations were to go to the lengths of Turkey, the ideal of primary loyalty to the *watan* was to become pre-eminent.

In the twentieth century, revivalist movements appeared with an agenda to remove such Western influences from Muslim nations. Prominent examples of such movements are *Jamaat-i Islami*, founded by Maulana Mawdudi in the subcontinent, and the *Jamaat al-Ikhwan al-Muslimin*, founded in Egypt by Hassan al-Banna. Such organizations rejected both nationalism and the hidebound, ineffective traditionalism of the *ulema*. They fought against the idea of loyalty to the nation-state, or at least ideas of state organization that were founded upon principles derived from the West. Instead they asserted that the primary loyalty of Muslims should be to the global community of Islam, even if initially it meant the overturning of Muslim governments and their replacement by an Islamic state. Reinterpreting the old label of *jahiliya* (ignorance) used for the decadent condition of pre-Islamic Arab society, they asserted that such a state of godlessness now pervaded the whole of humankind, including those societies that would normally be called Muslim but that did not implement the *shari'a*. Thus a simple choice was advocated between loyalty towards Islam and participation in *jahiliya*. The common demand of the revivalists was addressed towards Muslim nations to implement the *shari'a* in its entirety and revolutionize their governments and society to become Islamic states freed from Western influence.

The foremost ideologue of the Islamic state was Maulana Mawdudi (1903–79). Ishtiaq Ahmed describes him as 'the ablest theoretician of the Islamic state in the Muslim world'.[21] The new state of Pakistan needed to establish an industrial base and this required the expansion and dissemination of modern skills through an education system that was secular and not dependent upon a received religious wisdom. On the other hand, the ideological underpinning required to successfully establish a common national identity and sense of patriotism had to be imparted to various ethnic groupings with distinct local cultures and languages. Both these transformations of Pakistani society were a challenge to traditional views. Whereas the ideal of the *umma* could be utilized to unite various ethnic groupings under one identity, it did not necessarily sit easily with the ideology of the nation-state. In addition, Islam itself was divided between Sunnis and Shi'as. Amongst the Sunni majority, traditional shrine-based Sufism was dominant but its leadership was intensely locality based and other-worldly in orientation. The Sufi *pirs*, with their strong devotional followings, had been challenged since the eighteenth and increasingly in the nineteenth century by reform movements in India, with their agendas to reawaken Muslim society based on a more literal interpretation of the Qur'an. These historic divisions continued to cause tensions in the new Muslim state of Pakistan.

The *ulema*, both those loyal to the *pirs* and those loyal to the older Indian reform movements, had failed to come to terms with the modernization process; increasingly the urban educated sectors of the population saw them as superstitious and clinging on to outmoded traditional ideas that were irrelevant in the world of new technology and discoveries. However, the secularization of culture that accompanied the processes of urbanization, and the development of modern science and technology, were seen by many as the heritage of the West and as a legacy of the colonial world that had been thrown off at independence. Yet freedom had not liberated the new Muslim nation from the colonial influence of the Western powers; for many, it had only changed the form of the oppression. The modernists were suspected of having compromised with the post-colonial exploiters, and the old Islamic reform movements, with their message that Islam needed to be cleansed of outside cultural influences, were now part of the established *ulema*, and perceived as backward.

Stepping into the vacuum, Mawdudi recreated the reform message in a new form, arguing that a purified Islam needed to be practised within the confines of an Islamic state which would provide the correct ideological framework for the nation to address modernization. He argued that Islam was the better alternative to Western imports of either capitalism or socialism. Thus, in one stroke, through his theology of sovereignty, Mawdudi politicized the message of Islam within the context of contemporary struggles for power. He persuasively argued that the need for an Islamic state arose from the nature of the universal order, where God's laws govern all creation. It is only human beings that suffer from the delusion of independence. Nature is under the sway of Islam because it obeys God's natural law, but human beings have the capacity to obey or disobey. In order that they make the correct choice there is revelation. Human behaviour is therefore governed by revealed law just as the universe is ruled by natural law. The law that governs human behaviour is fully revealed in the Qur'an and the *Sunna* of the Prophet.

The key to understanding Mawdudi's ideas on the necessity of an Islamic state is his interpretation of the *shahada*, the witnessing to Islam required in order to be a Muslim. He saw the problem of history not as humanity's denial of the oneness of God but rather as an unwillingness to recognize the sovereignty of God. Mawdudi interpreted the *shahada* as a statement that not only proclaims the uniqueness of God as the Creator or sole object of worship, but also expresses the uniqueness of God as the master, sovereign, Lord and law-giver. Thus God alone has the right to legislate and command human affairs.

It is this revolutionary interpretation of the *shahada* that provided Mawdudi with his main critique of the intrusion of Western ideas and philosophies into Muslim society. Secularism, nationalism and Western models of democracy are all based on the Enlightenment ideal of the sovereignty of the people. Mawdudi revolutionized Muslim politics by arguing that the acceptance of any other authority as sovereign is a form of *shirk* (idolatry), and as such raises that authority to the status of being a partner with Allah. The great moral evil of the age, he declared, consists of accepting other sovereigns such as 'the will of the people' or the laws created by worldly rulers and setting them up in competition to the rule of God.

Thus true Muslims should band together to resist such 'idolatry' and strive for the creation of an Islamic society, as well as maintaining individual righteousness. For Mawdudi, the imperative of Islam directs individuals to develop a community of faith that promotes social change by creating a society fully obedient to God's law. Mawdudi called this state the 'Caliphate based on the Prophetic

Pattern' or *Khilafah 'ala Minhaj al-Nabuwah*.[21] It has no power to make new laws, but will work within the limits prescribed by Allah through fully implementing Islamic law without any compromise with Western legal codes or the ideologies implicit in nationalism, secularism and Western-based democracies. For Mawdudi, a Muslim society that either creates its own constitution or borrows legal or constitutional frameworks from outside Islam breaks its covenant with God and therefore loses its right to be considered Islamic. Mawdudi's political understanding of the sovereignty of Allah provided a blueprint for Muslim radicals to challenge the modernists and secular Muslim governments and work tirelessly to create Islamic states where the *shari'a* was reintroduced as the sole means of governance.

The new Muslim nation-states have inherited all of the above problems of governance since their independence and have been unable to challenge the dominance of Western political, economic or military power. So far, they have not been able to create a society that claims the allegiance of all their people, nor have they established themselves as the primary locus of Muslim identity, although Iran, since the revolution there, could claim to be the first of the Muslim nations to approach this ideal. Generally, the state has sought to appropriate to itself those loyalties that religious Muslims ideally would have given to the universal religious community established by Muhammad, yet this has not been fully successful. This is further complicated by the artificial borders of a number of Muslim nations carved out in the twentieth century, where different ethnic groups with a distinct identity exist within the frontiers of individual nations. Such groups are not always successfully assimilated within the ideal of the nation-state. For example, the Kurdish populations of Iraq and Turkey or the populations of Indian Muslims that migrated to Pakistan during Partition in 1947 have not been fully integrated into their respective nations. In other countries there are tensions between rival religious groups such as Shi'a and Sunni Muslims, as is the case in Iraq. Such divisions and tensions have been opened up by Western intervention and military conquest as part of the 'War on Terror'. The undermining of nation-states forged with difficulty out of the post-colonial situation has led to crises between ethnic groupings and religious groupings. Such crises exist in Iraq, Afghanistan, Sudan, and Pakistan, where loyalties to the nation are undermined by older commitments to religion and tribe.

One more division within Sunni Islam demands our attention. In some senses this division could be described as part of the crises described above; that is, the response to the loss of Muslim power. It has it roots in theological and theosophical differences with regard to Islam's central doctrine of *tawhid* and therefore goes back much further into the early centuries of Islam. Some Muslim writers have mainly focused on the oneness of God in the context of opposition to polytheism. Mawdudi and the proponents of an Islamic state were more complex and theorized polytheism as anything, created either by God or human agency, whether an object or an ideal, which is placed alongside God, usurping his supremacy as the sole object of human worship. Others have gone further and promoted the idea of 'all-inclusiveness' as their understanding of God's unity and oneness. Although there are dangers in this approach to *tawhid*, in that monotheism can easily become pantheism or monism, the Qur'an itself speaks of Allah as both immanent and transcendent. Certainly the primary emphasis of the Qur'an is on transcendence, a remote Supreme Being who exists beyond his creation but brings all creation into existence, yet the Qur'an also declares that Allah is closer to human beings than their jugular veins.

For many Muslims, especially those belonging to revivalist religio-political movements, the fear of diluting *tawhid* results in an emphasis on transcendence to the exclusion of considering Allah's immanence. In such forms of uncompromising monotheism the emphasis is on the uniqueness of God and His absolute 'otherness' or incomparability to anything in creation. On the other hand, as stated by Said and Funk, the emphasis on transcendence can lead to forms of orthodoxy where love and intimacy in the relationship between Creator and created are almost completely ignored. They both argue that this can lead to forms of Islam where *tawhid* is understood as remoteness, downplaying ideas of the unity of existence or the reflection of divine attributes in the human. In such paradigms, peace is perceived as merely the absence of war or the lack of civil order and there is likely to be a political element to the interpretation of *tawhid*, developed from a theology of sovereignty that spills over into Islamic political theory.[22]

Yet immanence is there in Islam. Although Islam is a religion of divine majesty, Allah is also manifested to his subjects through beauty and love. Love, by definition, requires a personal God who is able to be intimate with his people and the Qur'an states: 'And He is with you wheresoever you may be' (57:4). In spite of the overwhelming emphasis on the incomparability and omnipotence of God, the Qur'an indicates that he is both *tanzil* (far) and *tashbih* (near). For many

Muslims, the spirituality of Islam is discovered in the presence of Allah within his creation. The Qur'an describes Allah as *al-Muhit*, the all-encompassing (4:126) and *al-Mawjud*, the ever-present (10:32). Thus it is possible for the Muslim to find the divine presence throughout creation, and at the deepest level Allah is ultimately the universe itself, for he creates out of his own being rather than *ex nihilo*. Allah is the ultimate reality, the truth (*al-Haqq*) of existence (*al-Wujud*). For the Sufis, the mystics of Islam, the preoccupation is on the unity or oneness of the divine being, rather than his uniqueness, and is best understood by the idea of *wahdat al-wujud* (the unity of existence). The emphasis on divine unity and the belief in Allah's intimacy with the created has led to a different understanding of God, humanity and nature. In this paradigm, love predominates and peace is understood as a state of being where the human being lives in accordance with *fitra*, experiencing the divine presence both within the purified heart and without, in harmony with nature. In such a paradigm the whole universe has been created for worship rooted in experience of the divine presence. At its ultimate expression, *tawhid* is a human experience of oneness with the divine being rather than a statement about the nature of God. For such Muslims the experience of *tawhid* is the culmination of a life spent in remembrance of Allah, possibly resulting in ecstatic intimacy. The transformation of the simple statement of the oneness of God into an experience associated with a spiritual elite, able to attain a state where they are transformed to such a degree that they cease to exist before the overwhelming presence of God, offers a radical reinterpretation of *tawhid*. The danger is that it leaves the ordinary believer's understanding and practice of Islam, although sufficient, in a lower category of experience and comprehension. This effectively provides a two-level understanding of the Prophetic revelation in which the mass of Muslims operate only on an exoteric level of understanding and practice with just an elite able to achieve an esoteric possibility of oneness.

This deeply spiritual version of Islam has come to be known as Sufism. Sometimes defined as Islamic mysticism, it probably began as an ascetic reaction to Umayyad worldliness. From these early examples of asceticism and withdrawal appeared a variety of movements composed of disciples to various spiritual guides who taught paths to self-purification based on the remembrance of Allah's names. As Sufism formalized itself under the guidance of a number of skilled exponents of its disciplines, these variations on a theme based on the teachings of these masters became the distinct orders of Sufism with a lineage of masters that succeeded the founding teacher. These orders are known as *tariqa* and are considered by most Sufis to complement the outer practices of Islam (*shari'a*). Discipleship is therefore central to Sufism, to provide guidance to the *murid* (student) along the way of transformation from a self-centred existence to one which is God-centred.[23]

Over time these mystical doctrines and practices developed into a cult of sainthood in which a hierarchy of deceased saints, who are believed to maintain the spiritual well-being of the world from outside time, combined with popular belief and dependence upon living *shaikhs* to create the doctrine of *karamat* or special favour that was bestowed upon the saint to perform miracles and even intercede on behalf of those requiring Allah's mercy and assistance. This belief in miracles caught the imagination of the populace and led to extravagant and fantastic stories of the deeds of Sufis. When the *shaikhs* died the religious piety of their followers turned to the graves, which subsequently developed as important shrine centres and the focus of the continuing development of the *tariqa*. It was believed that the power to intercede and perform miracles was contained within the remains of the saint, who was in some way still alive awaiting Judgement Day in the tomb. The proliferation of shrines of deceased saints brought a new dynamic into Muslim belief and practices as millions of rural adherents of the faith concentrated their devotional practices and petitions around the tombs.[24]

The development of a fully-fledged theosophy of sainthood, both living and in the tomb, troubled many orthodox Muslims, especially amongst the ranks of the *ulema*. There was considerable criticism of the need to submit to the authority of charismatic men who claimed a special relationship to Allah through ecstasy. Some believed that Islam was being subverted through vicarious holiness arising out of dependence on holy men, pilgrimage to their shrines, adoration of their relics and total commitment of physical and mental resources to their service.[25] Arberry suggests that the cult of miracles led to the incredulous masses allowing themselves to be duped by impostors.[26]

Sufism came to be regarded as the traditional enemy of the neo-orthodox movements and Islamic revivalists long before they perceived the West as a threat. Before the domination of Muslim territory by European powers, any sign of decline in the Muslim community was blamed on inner lapses within the *umma* and often laid at the door of Sufism. For the neo-orthodox reformers, Sufism was the cause of Islam's decline and to be eliminated.

Conclusion

Throughout Muslim history, devout Muslims have been concerned with the question of what constitutes the true *umma* and how it should be maintained. Exactly who constitutes this category of true Muslim has been a source of contention ever since the Prophet's death. This debate has been exacerbated by the conflict between the respective values of Islam and the West. The result has been the division of the *umma* into many factions, each justifying their position by various interpretations of the message of Islam. Gibb stated that 'the first lesson learned by them was that the community must not be identified with or confused with political regimes. Thus political division in no way impaired the unity of the *umma*.'[27] He argued that the central doctrine of *tawhid* justifies Islamic totality and universalism. The aim has always been to establish a highly integrated and united *umma*. In reality, Muslim sectarianism has its roots in the political divisions of the *umma* and the various attempts to restore unity that in themselves create new factions. These factional differences in the community are in direct opposition to the ideal of universalism, which is preached to Muslims everywhere.

It can be convincingly argued that the integrated community of believers submissive to the will of Allah as proclaimed by the Qur'an has not existed since the death of the Prophet, but this has not prevented Muslims through the ages from chasing the ideal and attempting to renew the original vision. However, sectarian divisions over the question of authority split the community, and the various aspects of the Prophet's charismatic authority were passed onto several different institutions. Closer scrutiny of Islam reveals a number of divisions, not just the first major schism between Sunnis and Shi'a but also within both these major groupings. The intensity of the divisions reveals itself in a number of struggles and conflicts going on throughout the Muslim world. Some of these have ancient histories but are revitalized under the crises of modernity and other pressures unique to the contemporary period.

Chapter 3

Ethics and Morality: The Challenge of Textual Interpretation

The purpose of ethics, however, is to make human beings good. Human beings are good when their actions are good and as such governed by what is upright and just.[1]

What is the Good for man? It must be the ultimate end or object of human life: something that is in itself completely satisfying.[2]

Islamic ethics (*akhlaq*) is linked primarily to the ideal of 'good character', and is closely associated with *adab* (manners). Although the repository of such character is the individual who maintains it, there is implicit understanding that ethics has a very powerful social dimension. The body of law that contained the constituent parts of Islamic ethical life took shape gradually from the seventh century and was finally established by the eleventh century. It was not solely taken from the Qur'an but was a creative amalgamation of the teachings of the *Sunna* of Muhammad as recorded in the Hadith; the precedents of Islamic jurists; the aspects of pre-Islamic Arabian tradition that it was deemed appropriate to maintain, and some non-Arabic elements – adopted from conquered territory – which were perceived not to conflict with the Islamic revelation. Underpinning this coming together of various factors was the Islamic revelation as contained in the Qur'an and the first principle of such jurisprudence was that nothing should contradict the contents of the Book. The Qur'an and Hadith are therefore foundational to how Muslims deal with ethical issues such as gender, abortion, human rights, just war, animal rights and ecological issues. This chapter will not only explore a number of issues that are proving difficult for Muslims today but also assess the underlying challenge of interpreting a seventh-century Arabic text deemed to be the eternal and complete revelation of God to all humankind. One of the challenges facing the Abrahamic monotheistic religions with their central conviction that God shows Himself to humanity through historical revelation is how to resolve the difficulties created by a belief in a single act of God in which he intervened in human history through final or complete revelation of a divine law to which the chosen recipients are beholden until the end of time. A revelation which is judged to be comprehensive but revealed in a localized cultural milieu and geographical space in a particular event taking place in a moment of time contains tensions with its universal applicability as it moves through time and across territories. There are also challenges between divine immutability and the constant mutability of human society. These challenges have been sharpened by the rapid changes that have taken place in the twentieth and twenty-first centuries and the Muslim world's encounter with such transformations emanating from the progressive Western world.

The monotheistic God of Abraham, Moses, Jesus and Muhammad is marked by his knowledge of past, present and future events. Therefore a single revelation that is not going to be repeated by future updates must contain within it all the knowledge required by human beings until the end of time. The security of human beings is dependent on a merciful, just and forgiving deity endowed with omniscience. Yet both the Torah and the Qur'an were revealed to a particular people (the nomadic Jews and the tribes of Arabia) at a particular point in the development of human beings where human knowledge was limited to both a particular culture and the mores of the time. Yet for those who believe in the revelation it must be comprehensive, going beyond its apparent particularity and answering the questions of the faithful in all aspects of life even when the religion moves forward in time and across geographical space subsuming cultures and civilizations remarkably different from the original recipients.

The apparent solution, short of admitting cultural relativity to God's word, is the need for specialist interpreters, who are able to search within the hallowed sacred text that contains the revelation, applying it to new situations but not interpreting it. In other words, skilled practitioners, special sacred people, seek to discover the content that God would have already placed in the revelation. The revelation must at all costs be preserved in its entirety and in the pristine original form, because only there can God's knowledge of the human future be ascertained, understood and acted upon. In the case of Islam and Judaism, where it is believed that God provided a comprehensive way of life revealed as a binding covenant between human and Creator and as a legal contract with a Lord who is both Judge and Sovereign, such specialists are more jurists than priest. Their area of expertise is religious jurisprudence and they are not intermediaries between humankind and God in the way that priests are.

However, jurisprudence in modern Western societies is usually regarded as the science or philosophy of human law rather than skill in understanding God. Yet Islam went on to become the foundation of nations, empires and a civilization where the law of God was developed to become the law of the land. Those who had the training to interpret the original revelation contained in the Qur'an and the Hadith, as well as the corpus of law developed by their predecessors, were not merely philosophers and theologians but functionaries of the legal system, making decisions and passing sentences in law courts.

For the system to work, devout Muslims had to be assured that their judges and scholars were not diluting the word of Allah and creating a legal system based on their own judgements, however skilful and learned they may have been deemed to be. In addition, the scholars themselves needed to be secure in the knowledge that time-honoured practices existed for the application of God's law to new situations that could be trusted to protect them from human interpretation or error. The choices facing Muslims have always been simple: either the original revelation was not complete and needs to be supplemented by human law making; an unthinkable conclusion to the devout; or the original revelation and its subsequent development into a corpus of Islamic law were both somehow equally the activity of God. Another possibility that has been considered by some over the centuries is that the original revelation remains unchallenged as of divine origin but the subsequent creation of a body of law was a human construction as prone to error as all other human activity.

The difficulty is that the Qur'an itself does not appear to contain a prescription for every human activity and actually has very little to say even on statecraft and most matters of jurisprudence. It is detailed only on personal family law. Even though the Qur'an is supplemented by the four volumes of Hadith that contain the Prophet's actions and deeds, authoritative because he was considered to be an exemplar of obedience to the divine imperative, the genius of the first generations of Muslims was to codify all this into a system of jurisprudence. It would regulate not only the lives of Arab tribes but the far more sophisticated conquered territories of the Byzantine and Persian Empires, and succeed for most Muslims in maintaining the trust that the revelation had been placed in safe hands.

The process of developing this system of jurisprudence went far beyond a legal system. The *shari'a*, as it came to be known, provided comprehensive categorizations of God's commands and recommendations that were able to regulate every aspect of human existence from 'worship and ritual equal with legal rules, political, toilet, greetings and table manners'.[3] Joseph Schacht later claimed that 'Islamic law was the core and kernel of Islam itself'.[4] Fazlur Rahman states, 'It is the Way, ordained by God, wherein man is to conduct his life, in order to realize the Divine Will.'[5] Islamic law achieves this by prescribing all human activity, including how and what to eat; when to wash; what clothing to wear; how and when to perform religious rites, including fasting and prayer; commercial transactions; relations with non-Muslims; and rules of warfare and crime. However, as we shall see, although the law in its entirety must remain anchored in the transcendent from which its moral imperatives derived, there is a tension between the eternal law of God, revealed by a sending down (*tanzil*) in the Qur'an, and the systematic creation of a fully worked corpus of law in Muslim history. It has been up to human beings to utilize their moral and intellectual faculties to construct and reconstruct God's law through the process of *fiqh* (jurisprudence). There are dangers in this process, as recognized by S. Nomanul Haqq when he states: 'human knowledge could never claim, nor is it capable of acquiring, epistemological certainty or finality'.[6]

However, most Muslims today have made a crucial distinction between a moral system that is based upon the revelation of God and that which is considered to be independent of God and based upon humanistic understandings of what constitutes the best means to human well-being. There is also a powerful argument that without the guidance of a sovereign and all-knowing deity any classification of moral behaviour will lack clarity and sink in a mire of relativity. Religious morality, however, is based upon two fundamental tenets; the belief in God as the Creator of the universe, and the belief in the rewards and punishments of the Hereafter. Consequently it is not possible to separate correct Muslim ethical behaviour from the Islamic Concept of God. Morality arises out of Allah's absolute perfection, sovereignty and lordship. Perfection endows God with complete knowledge of what is best for human beings and his Lordship makes him the sole purveyor of power, mercy, and justice. A just God knowing the future afterlife of his chosen creatures would have an imperative of mercy to make absolutely clear a 'straight path' that would lead human beings to the rewards of paradise and away from the dire punishments of hellfire. In the process of choosing the good and following the wisdom of God's revelation they would also discover something of God. The relationship of a Muslim with God is a conscious and voluntary submission to the will of God and it provides a degree of intimacy between Creator and created. Both nature and human beings are under God's sovereignty. As described succinctly by the twentieth-century ideologue, Maulana Mawdudi, nature has no choice but to follow the laws that have been put into place by divine decree but human beings choose. In order to make the choice transparent to them, human beings are guided by revelation. The guidance of such divine intervention comes in two forms; the way of life that is commanded by revealed sacred text and the exemplary life of the Prophet.

Any ethical or moral code of conduct requires self-discipline on the part of the individual, and although Muslim religious scholars emphasize the motivation that arises from a voluntary loving and pious relationship with God there is no doubt that the strong sense of the existence of hell and its long-lasting punishments has an impact on Muslim behaviour. In addition it has to be acknowledged that many Muslim societies have incorporated Islamic moral behaviour into their judicial systems, and breaches of certain moral laws carry both legal deterrents and social stigmatization. Devout Muslims do not consider the fear of God's punishment for breaches of moral behaviour to be a negative feature of the relationship with the divine. As stated by Jamal Badawi:

> By believing in God, His Perfection and divine attributes, that He is the sole power in this universe, and believing that He is the Ultimate God Who has the full, perfect and complete knowledge, it follows that God knows what is in our hearts and minds and we can not hide anything from Him or deceive him. This results in increased self-discipline by knowing that you cannot get away with wrong-doing if you are not caught by humans because God is the All Encompassing. This self-discipline must be at the heart of any ethical or moral code of conduct.[7]

Although there is a powerful sense of the reality of the afterlife amongst Muslims, Islam is not a world-rejecting religion. The reality of judgement should not create an attitude of dismissal regarding the significance of this life. On the contrary it is the intention and the actions performed here that determine one's final destiny. Nor is Islam a religion solely confined to individual spiritual or moral development. There is an urgent appeal to community well-being, social justice, and communal religious identity. Muslims are told in the Qur'an to prepare themselves for divine judgement and the afterlife by striving to right wrongs and to establish justice and peace here on earth. Muslim ethics are therefore a divine imperative binding on both individuals and societies. The question of conflict with Western humanistic-driven ethical codes arises from philosophical understandings of what constitutes good. Both Muslims and non-Muslims would probably find nothing problematic with the Qur'an's command to 'seek not (occasion for) mischief in the land'.[8] However, the predominant Muslim religious psyche would insist that something is good because God has commanded it to be so rather than because it is an ontologically right action. Muslim ethics are more about obedience to the divine will than determining correct ethical action. For example, in contemporary deliberations concerning Islamic investments and banking, a panel of three approved members of the Saudi *ulema* decide whether a company is Islamically sound for investment. Alcohol-related products are not recommended; however, investment in tobacco companies is less straightforward. Alcohol consumption for Muslims is expressly forbidden in the Qur'an but there is nothing explicit about forbidding smoking. The debate revolves around whether the two products are *haram* (forbidden) or *halal* (allowed) rather than on the intrinsic properties of the two substances and their impact on human health.

In the first instance, ethics in Islam are derived from Islamic law, which is essentially religious rather than legal. It exists as a system of dos and don'ts which express the reality that God is sovereign.[9] Flexibility is built into the system, first by the relationship of the law with local customs. In the early centuries of Muslim expansion the customs of occupied territory were fully explored and permitted to the degree that they complied with the injunctions implicit in the revelation. This combination of local law (*urf*) mixed with *shari'a* provided Muslim society with the means to accommodate local culture as it moved around the world either through conquest or migration. In addition, the early scholars of jurisprudence acknowledged that the codification had to provide the space for personal discovery and that for the system to be truly all-encompassing it had to go beyond acts that were either completely forbidden or permitted. A fivefold categorization of actions was developed as follows: (i) *Wajib* – obligatory acts that Allah has commanded and where failure to follow leads to punishment in the afterlife (such prescriptions are found in the Qur'an); (ii) *mandub* – actions that are recommended and whose performance brings reward but omission is not punished (such actions are far too many for the Qur'an to record but may be found in the *Sunna*); (iii) *ja'iz* – actions concerning which Allah is unconcerned whether they are performed or not (there can be no reward or punishment for either their performance or omission; these are probably not mentioned in the revelatory literature); (iv) *makruh* – actions that Allah frowns upon but that are not forbidden (restraint is rewarded but performance is not punished; once again such actions are more likely to be described in supplementary literature); (v) *mahzur* – actions that are prohibited (there is no reward for avoiding them but performance is punished; such actions are found in the Qur'an).

Categories ii, iii and iv allow for individuals to develop their personal conscience and thus bring a journey of personal discovery to the world of *halal* and *haram* prescribed in the *shari'a*. Rahman points out that this system came to be known as 'resoluteness and relaxation' (*azima* and *rukhsa*) and provided the vehicle for Muslims to search in their own hearts.[10] Thus, a comprehensive system of law was developed and became the norm and the ideal for Muslim societies, providing the flexibility for both cultural difference and individual conscience, but also at the same time supplying a code of behaviour for all Muslims to be certain that they were obeying the will of God. Muslim family law, criminal justice, business and trade obligations, and rules of warfare were all developed on the basis of revelation. Thus a unique form of government was developed, and if not always implemented strictly, in theory it existed as an exemplar. Rulers were not considered to be legislators, or even custodians of divine law, although ideally they should be the latter.

From its very inception, Islam was associated with ethical reform of Arab society. Muhammad preached against what he saw as the social evils of his day, and the Madinan verses of the Qur'an are concerned with social reforms in areas such as family structure, slavery, the rights of women, and social injustices. Bernard Lewis states that Islam 'from the first denounced aristocratic privilege and rejected hierarchy'[11] and John Esposito mentions the condemnation of female infanticide, exploitation of the poor and powerless, usury, murder, false contracts, and theft amongst the pagan Arabs.[12] The Constitution of Madinah drawn up by Muhammad to establish the ground rules of the new city-state was groundbreaking and attempted to bring to an end the intertribal fighting between the Arab clans of the Aws as well as instituting a number of rights and responsibilities for the Muslim, Jewish and pagan communities of Madinah. These were concerned with security, freedom of religious practice and belief, the role of Madinah as a sacred place where violence was forbidden, a taxation system to support the community, and a judicial system for resolving disputes. Although slavery was not banned outright, slaves were granted social status, religious freedoms and quasi-legal rights.[13]

Within a few centuries Muslims had taken the fundamental principles of Islam as practised in Madinah and revealed in the Qur'an and transformed them into a body of law that could rival the best of Christian canon law or the ancient Jewish Halakhah. For its time it was advanced and helped to establish one of the world's greatest civilizations, underpinning a number of empires, sultanates and kingdoms. Muslims were proud that they possessed an ethical and legal system that they believed had been entrusted to them by God. It was not until the rise of Europe coincided with the aftermath of the Enlightenment that Muslims had reason to doubt the efficacy of an ethical and legal system based upon revelation. The development of European legal systems that were based upon a human-centred 'rights' discourse and linked with democracy, rationality, reason, secularism, superior education, and science was used discursively to demonstrate the superiority of the European nations over the Muslim world. Most Western commentators or colonial administrations would have been unaware of the intricacies and complexities of the *haram* and *halal* categories. Instead they focused on issues of concern where human rights discourse was presented as superior to the rights granted by Muslim legal systems. The differences were highlighted around philosophical and religious debates over freedom versus responsibility.

The issues of concern were to be the rights of women, gender issues, religious freedom, religious violence, criminal justice (*hudud*) and punishments handed out for offences, freedom of the individual and expression, and governance. In all these, Muslims were to be perceived by the West as backward, archaic and even branded by certain elements of the popular media as 'barbaric'. Muslim nations formed in the twentieth century after the retreat of European colonialism were themselves unsure of their Islamic heritage and began to replace religious laws and ethical codes with those borrowed or adapted from the West. However, the failure on the part of many Muslim governments to bring about significant improvements in the well-being of their populations or to match the democratic rights given to citizens of Western Europe or North America, combined with a growing dissatisfaction with a continuation of colonial relations in a modified form, led to a renewed interest in Islam and Islamic solutions. As more Muslims became literate and began to become familiar with the history of their societies and the teachings of Islam as revealed in its inception, they began to see the solution as a return to Islamic principles and distinguishing them from the cultural or political realities that existed in their respective societies. However, although Islamic ethics may be seen to be superior to the existing norms of Muslim societies, it remains a fact that seventh-century religious laws would still appear to be antiquated and sometimes lacking consideration for human rights as compared to privileges and freedoms granted to the citizens of Western liberal democracies.

The consequence was at first a proliferation of apologetic writings that defended Islam against European reason and attempted to reform Muslim societies on European lines. This was soon followed by a new type of literature that was more aggressive and asserted that the laws of God were superior to the man-made laws of Western governments. These already fraught debates would be stretched to crisis point when some Muslim opponents of the West became prepared to use violence to remove both their own governments and to attack Western civilians whose governments were perceived to be hostile to Muslim interests. Religious violence would undermine the fundamental Muslim understanding of their faith as a religion that promoted individual and social peace and harmony through surrender to a merciful and just God. In addition, new crises such as the environment and ethical dilemmas arising from medical and scientific discoveries were to foster the demand for creative thinking and interpretation of already stretched intellectual and spiritual resources.

A number of authors have picked up the issue of the environmental crisis and attempted to argue that Islam is uniquely placed to offer a solution. There are writings in Islam that would suggest an early concern for the environment. These may have resulted from resource scarcity in many Muslim nations. Traditions of preserving land and early urban planning were expressions of strong social obligations to stay within the capacity of the land and to preserve the natural environment as an obligation of khalifa or 'stewardship'.[14] Muhammad is also cited as a pioneer of environmentalism.[15] His Hadith on agriculture and animal husbandry were compiled in the 'Book of Agriculture' of the Sahih Bukhari, and Hadith such as 'There is none amongst the believers who plants a tree, or sows a seed, and then a bird, or a person, or an animal eats thereof, but it is regarded as having given a charitable gift [for which there is great recompense]'[16] are often used as evidence of primal Islam's concerns for a holistic and caring environmental ethic. Contemporary Muslim writers also point towards the evidence of early medical treatises by authors such as al-Kindi, Qusta ibn Luqa, al-Razi, Ibn Al-Jazzar, al-Tamimi, al-Masihi, Avicenna, Ali ibn Ridwan, Ibn Jumay, Abd-el-Latif, Ibn al-Quff, and Ibn al-Nafis as dealing with air pollution, water pollution, soil contamination, and municipal solid waste mishandling.[17]

Several statements found in the Qur'an are claimed to concern the environment, for example: 'And there is no animal in the earth nor bird that flies with its two wings, but that they are communities like yourselves.'[18] More often than not environmental interpretations of these verses in the Qur'an point towards the sacred text's doctrine of *khalifa* or vice-regency, and are keen to separate it from the notions of dominion over creation found in Genesis. It is here that we find the competitive rather than cooperative approach to the issue. The comparison with Genesis demonstrates the need of Muslim commentators to remain in the mode of proving Islam superior to earlier monotheistic revelations. At stake here is the issue of the innate value of other life-forms. These authors are well aware of Lynn White's provocative article which blames the Judaeo-Christian tradition for environmental problems, and they attempt to distance Islam from it. However, the quotations from the Qur'an used to defend Islamic environmentalism are often very selective, choosing unproblematic passages that appear to endorse the argument and avoiding those that appear to confirm the more exploitive relationship established by Genesis; for example Qur'an 80:24–32, which seems to suggest a partnership between humans and other creatures:

Then let man look at his food: how We pour out water in showers, then turn up the earth into furrow-slices and cause cereals to grow therein – grapes and green fodder; olive-trees and palm-trees; and luxuriant orchards, fruits and grasses ... as Provision for you as well as for your cattle.

The key issue is whether the Qur'an has a sufficient content in its understandings of nature, in particular human relations with the environment, to construct an environmental ethic. Many of the authors of Muslim environmentalism feel that it does, acknowledging the orthodox position that the Qur'an must contain answers to all questions faced by humankind, as it is the final and complete revelation of God. However, to a more sceptical and agnostic mind, the Qur'an omits any explicit reference to the issue, the ecological balance of nature and human beings not being central to the book's main themes. It is true that the Qur'an on numerous occasions urges human beings to observe nature as a 'sign', but the central reason is not to point towards nature in itself but rather to see in nature evidence of a divine creator. The Qur'an's references to nature are to do with a quest for ultimate meaning, not for securing the environment. The references are there as a 'finger' pointing to the Absolute and, if anything, they encourage a move away from creation to a renewed focus on the Creator. Any concern for nature in itself is always secondary to the quest for God. The Qur'an does suggest that each creature has its own relationship with the divine (Qur'an 20:50), thus providing evidence for the argument of their ontological existence, but, on the other hand, Islam is one of the last of the world religions to maintain animal sacrifice on a large scale.

A more promising line of enquiry, pursued by many authors on ethical issues, is provided by the Qur'an's imperative for justice. It is a fact that a disproportionate amount of the world's poor are also Muslim, and it is the poor who suffer more direct consequences of global degradation of the environment.[19] Thus Muslims are in a position to use the Qur'an's defence of those who suffer at the hands of the 'godless' powerful or greed-obsessed, to develop a religion of resistance to globalization of corporate capitalism, but so far there is little sign of Muslim nations warming to such an ideal or its subsequent activism. The main problem for both Muslim states and religious activists is balancing the need for development against environmental concerns, and up until now, the religious activists have been more concerned with issues of political and social inequality between the West and Muslim nations within a post-colonial framework than with ecological issues. For a Westerner such as myself, who once questioned deforestation to a group of international Muslim activists and was told that I had no right to morally lecture the world's poor for wanting to improve their standards of living when I myself belonged to a nation that had benefited from exploitation of nature on a grand scale, it is difficult to critique such arguments without the counter of subaltern attitudes.

The problem for Muslim environmentalists lies in persuading the rest of the Muslim world to share their concerns and to convince the traditional leaders of religion, the *ulema*, to reinterpret Islam's message in an ecological framework and to make it a central concern of their preaching. It is imperative that the Islamic activists on the environment can distinguish between text-based approaches that focus on enlightened beings or special persons and the mass of credulous believers. This is particularly important in Islam where there is a conscious and articulated division between the ideal and the real. All too often, Muslim environmentalists focus on an ideal based on contemporary hermeneutics of sacred texts which were probably never meant to carry such meanings pertinent to ecological issues in post-industrial society rather than the practices of Muslims worldwide. Too many of the articles that appear on the environment are presented as apologetics in defence of a religion that has said little about ecological issues, and rightly so, as the crises faced by the contemporary world did not exist at the time of the production of the Qur'an, Hadith and the development of *fiqh*. Neither sacred texts nor spiritual traditions of Islam's past may have sufficient context to deal with the future's ecological crisis.

This challenge also arises with the issue of medical ethics. The ethical standards of Muslim physicians were first laid down in the ninth century by Ishaq bin Ali Rahawi, who wrote the *Adab al-Tabib* (*Conduct of a Physician*). In the book, 20 chapters on various topics are related to medical ethics, including what the physician must avoid and beware of, the dignity of the medical profession, the examination of doctors, and the means of removing corruption from the medical profession.[20] Even so, the early writings of Islam have been outstripped by the rapid advances in medical technology and knowledge and displayed in twentieth- and twenty-first-century debates between religion and science taking place in the West. Islam is not the only religion to feel the impact of ethical crises resulting from genetic advances, artificial insemination, and scientific knowledge that impinges on questions of sanctity of life and even definitions of life itself. The main difficulty is that although many of the Islamic scholars concerned with such ethical issues acknowledge that the present is imperfect, the solution for a believing Muslim is to seek perfection in the past, for if the religion is the 'truth' then it is the past that contains the ideal. Muslims believe that Muhammad, like other prophets before him, was sent by God to remind human beings of their moral responsibility and challenge those ideas in society which opposed submission to God. Muhammad was primarily concerned with the care for one's near kin, for widows, orphans and others in need, and for the establishment of justice, but within the framework of establishing and endorsing strict monotheism. For so many conservative Muslims, their defensive discourses continue to look back to his examples as exemplars for our time. The challenge is not so much to exhort the Prophet's standard of ethics in the seventh century but to demonstrate that the wider principle of monotheism and submission to deity can still challenge issues of moral responsibility that arise in a very different context. However, environmentalism and medical ethics pale in significance compared to the attacks on Islam's record of human rights. These were to focus on gender, religious violence and criminal law, but underlying the fierce critique was the foundational issue of humanism (regarded as modern) and religious worldview (regarded as anachronistic).

Jihad was to become associated with religious warfare and linked in the public consciousness with terrorism. In vain Muslims defended their religion against accusations of violence. Scholars and commentators attempted to demonstrate that Islam had a body of military ethics that set out the conditions under which war could be carried out. The Qur'an is clear that jihad is only permitted when Muslims are prevented from the worship of God and that Muslims should not fight against each other. Certainly others cannot be forced to embrace Islam, for the Qur'an famously declares that 'there is no compulsion in religion'.

Jihad has certainly become both the most misunderstood and disturbing aspect of Islam, now inextricably associated with the catastrophic events of 11 September 2001 (commonly known as 9/11), suicide bombers in Palestine, Iraq or Afghanistan, and all other acts of violence performed with a religious or political motive in any part of the Muslim world. It has been linked with an ongoing campaign by certain segments of the Muslim world to declare war on Western lifestyle in general, especially where secularization and consumer capitalism impact on Muslim societies through globalization. This has led to a 'clash of civilizations' thesis where the Islamic world replaces communism as the enemy of 'enlightened' and liberal democratic values. Muhammad Sirozi, picking up on this limited understanding of jihad, cites some Western critics of Islam, for example Daniel Pipes, as interpreting jihad as a 'holy war', 'to extend sovereign Muslim power'.[21] He goes on to accuse the Western media of being guilty of referring to jihad only in the context of 'terrorist attacks organized by so-called militant fundamentalist Muslims'.[22] Many devout Muslims have claimed that jihad has been misrepresented not only by the Western media but also by a minority of Muslims, who interpret it only in the narrow sense of religious war.

The Qur'an in Sura 22:39–40 refers to the expulsion of the Muslims from Makkah and gives them permission to take up arms against aggressors, remarking in verse 41 that if the Muslims were 'given power in the land' then they would establish regular prayer and charity. The verses are significant in that, along with 2:190, they provide the justification for 'defensive jihad'. However, there is a suggestion in the above verse (41) that power should be actively sought in order to establish true religion in the land. The verses justifying a defensive jihad are as follows:

> To those against whom war is made, permission is given to fight, because they are wronged – and verily, Allah is Most Powerful for their aid. They are those who have been expelled from their homes in defiance of right – for no cause except that they did say, "Our Lord is Allah."[23]

In 2:190 and the following verses, defensive war is once again permitted where there is oppression and 'tumult' but there are restrictions and limitations. These limits on taking up arms were later developed into a charter for legitimate jihad by Muslim jurists. 'Fight in the cause of Allah those who fight you. But do not transgress limits for Allah loveth not transgressors.'[24]

Muslims, then, can legitimately turn to violent struggle for the defence of religion or even move on the offensive in certain circumstances when the onslaught of their enemies is perceived to be imminent – a type of pre-emptive strike. Only these circumstances make war morally justifiable. The war must be fought under the following conditions, according to the *shari'a*:

1. It cannot be fought for material gain or possession.
2. Non-combatant rights must be protected (lives, property and freedom).
3. No devastation of crops.
4. Old people, women, children and invalids cannot be harmed.
5. No place of worship can be demolished, nor priests of any religion be killed.
6. Prisoners of war must not be tortured or punished.
7. The war can only be fought for the defence of the faith.

Muslims argue that not only does the religion of Islam itself signify peace through surrender or submission to the will of God but that early Islamic treatises from the ninth century onwards dealt with the application of Islamic ethics to military matters such as the law of treaties, the treatment of diplomats, hostages, refugees and prisoners of war, the right of asylum, conduct on the battlefield and protection of women, children and non-combatant civilians. As early as the period of the first Caliph, Abu Bakr, ten rules were issued to Muslim combatants.

> Stop, O people, that I may give you ten rules for your guidance in the battlefield. Do not commit treachery or deviate from the right path. You must not mutilate dead bodies. Neither kill a child, nor a woman, nor an aged man. Bring no harm to the trees, nor burn them with fire, especially those which are fruitful. Slay not any of the enemy's flock, save for your food. You are likely to pass by people who have devoted their lives to monastic services; leave them alone.[25]

Typical of the type of quotations found on Islamic websites is the anecdote that refers to the crusader Oliverus Scholasticus after his defeat by Muslim forces praising the Islamic laws of war:

> Who could doubt that such goodness, friendship and charity come from God? Men whose parents, sons and daughters, brothers and sisters, had died in agony at our hands, whose lands we took, whom we drove naked from their homes, revived us with their own food when we were dying of hunger and showered us with kindness even when we were in their power.[26]

The literature on warfare has to be viewed as apologetics, a defence and justification of Islam in its present state of relative decay compared to an imagined golden age and a demand for a return to a more ethically correct past. However, the advances made by modern Western states may have progressed beyond the rights and responsibilities established in pre-modern Muslim societies. The recognition of this may also drive the motivations of Muslim apologetic writers.

Islamic gender discrimination plays a significant part in this liberal humanist critique. There is a discrete chapter in this book on the issue of female equality and the oppression of women.

Islamic views on homosexuality are influenced by the rulings prescribed by the Qur'an. Both Qur'anic verses and Hadith are opposed to sexual acts between members of the same sex. Islam rejected homosexuality from the religion's beginning. Muslim opponents of homosexual acts cite the Qur'an's reference to the story of the 'people of Lot' (also known as the Sodomites) who were destroyed by the wrath of Allah because they engaged in homosexual acts. *Shari'a* law forbids homosexual acts, and legal punishment for sodomy usually consists of capital punishment. However, the application of criminal sentences is not uniform. Islamic countries such as Saudi Arabia, Sudan and Iran are more likely to legally punish homosexuality whereas secular or multireligious Muslim countries such as Turkey or Indonesia are much more lenient. Homoerotic themes have been present in Muslim poetry and literature and in some Muslim societies sex between men has been unofficially tolerated until marriage. Some have argued that this literary tolerance for chaste male love affairs was prevalent from the ninth century but was eroded in the nineteenth by the adoption of European Victorian attitudes by the educated middle classes. The Al-Fatiha Foundation accepts homosexuality as natural and regards Qur'anic verses as outdated, or alternatively points out that the Qu'ran speaks out against homosexual lust but is silent on homosexual love.[27] Others argue that the divine anger against the 'people of Lot' is because they were guilty of male rape.

Prohibitions against homosexuality in some Muslim countries where *shari'a* law is applied more rigorously are an example of where moral and criminal law overlap. This is likely to occur where God's injunctions in the Qur'an totally forbid an act or prescribe penalties. In such circumstances Muslims are likely to find themselves endangering their fate in the afterlife and being placed in jeopardy with regard to imprisonment or even death sentences for breaking the law of the land. Western perceptions of Muslim law tend to dwell on such prohibitions as archaic and barbaric.

One example of tension between human rights discourse and Qur'anic injunctions has been the prohibition on conversion of a Muslim to another religion (apostasy). The penalty of death on this offence flies in the face of religious freedom deemed to be an international or universal human right and even appears to contradict the Qur'an's more tolerant verses on the individual's right to choose their mode of worship. The Universal Declaration of Human Rights of 1981, Article 13, states, 'Every person has the right to freedom of conscience and worship in accordance with his religious beliefs' and this is translated into a Muslim framework by the Universal Islamic Declaration of Human Rights of 1981, Article 10 (Rights of Minorities), which states that the Qur'anic principle of 'there is no compulsion in religion' should govern the religious rights of non-Muslim minorities in Muslim nations. However, this application of the universal rights is not offered to Muslims who might wish to convert to another faith. It is in this context that apostasy emerges as a challenge for some Muslim nations and individuals who live in such states. The Qur'an, on one hand, secures the rights to religious freedom and, on the other, imposes the punishment of death on apostasy.

In a penetrating work on the historical context of Islam's laws on apostasy, Abdullah and Hassan Saeed argue that because early Muslim communities were under threat from the Makkan 'idolaters' and Jewish tribes who collaborated with them, conversion away from Islam was not seen in the same light as conversion to Islam (the latter governed by the laws of 'no compulsion'). Conversion away from Islam was perceived as betrayal of the fledgling community and religious apostasy was regarded as akin to treachery. This was formalized in law when various Muslim empires arose in competition with Christendom or in India. This understanding of religious apostasy as treason would have been reinforced by the medieval concepts of *dar al-Islam* (the territory of Islam) and *dar al-harb* (the abode of war). The apostate living in Muslim territory would have chosen to adopt the faith of the enemies or rivals of Muslim states engaged in struggle or territorial competition with other empires whose religion was different and this was regarded as being guilty of treason.

The above authors argue that such contexts no longer exist and in today's world, where Islam is regarded as a religious commitment, millions of Muslims live within Muslim-majority nations with only nominal allegiance to Islam. Such Muslims seriously challenge the concept of apostasy as understood within traditional or orthodox circles. In addition, the movements of population created by globalization further complicate the old classical understanding of *dar al-Islam* and *dar al-harb*. Around 15 million Muslims live in Western Europe, 3 million in the USA. Religions need to get used to a world where their practitioners live side by side with each other. Finally, the authors state that Muslims wish to compete on equal terms with other religious faith allegiances with regard to conversion and proselytizing but there must be an equal platform. If Christians, Hindus, Jews and members of other faiths are being targeted by Muslim missionaries

successfully, then there must be a level platform for the missionaries
of such faiths to target Muslims.[28] In today's world, apostasy is no
longer an issue of treason or betrayal of a state but a choice concerning
how the individual wishes to worship God. However, the twentieth
century gave rise to a number of fundamentalisms that linked religious
identity to national or supra-national loyalty. Such conservative
religio-political movements within Islam will insist upon perceiving
conversion as treason whilst other kinds of conservatism will regard
any attempt to contextualize the Qur'an historically as endangering
the Book's authority as the final word of God.

Abdullah and Hassan Saeed identify a number of positions with
regard to the issue of apostasy but these could be generically grouped
to cover a number of ethical issues. There are Muslims who oppose
universality as enshrined in the Declaration of Human Rights and
insist that Islam has its own understanding of human rights which is
incorporated in Islamic law and not founded upon the principle of
freedom as understood by Western post-Enlightenment societies.
Rather, freedom is perceived as the inner condition of the human
being who responds to the duty placed upon individuals to be obedient
to the divine will. For such believers, the Qur'an and the laws derived
from it are not pre-modern and archaic but sacred and immutable.
For such traditionalists or followers of orthodoxies, the laws founded
upon human understanding of universal ethics are a product of socio-
historical contexts and susceptible to change.[29] Indeed the more
discerning and educated may well argue that these so-called universal
laws are no more than post-imperialist and neo-colonialist attempts
to demonstrate the superiority of secular liberal worldviews over the
Muslim world and religious worldviews.[30] A more moderate form of
Islamism attempts to seek out the existence of the 'universal values'
associated with Western humanism in the origins of Islam itself. These
can be divided into two categories: those who wish to reach a
consensus between Islam and the West in the interests of integration
and those who wish to show the superiority of Islam by demonstrating
that Muslims were given such rights when Christendom struggled in
darkness under feudal despotism. Some will argue that Christian
Europe only achieved advances in human rights because it came into
contact with superior Muslim societies.

Amongst the latter are found examples which claim that Islamic
jurists anticipated modern human rights. An example of such claims
is found in the work of Christopher Weeramantry, who states that the
Islamic world displayed:

early notions of the charitable trust and the trusteeship of property; the notion of brotherhood and social solidarity; the notions of human dignity and the dignity of labour; the notion of an ideal law; the condemnation of antisocial behaviour; the presumption of innocence; the notion of 'bidding unto good' (assistance to those in distress); and the notions of sharing, caring, universalism, fair industrial relations, fair contract, commercial integrity, freedom from usury, women's rights, privacy, abuse of rights, juristic personality, individual freedom, equality before the law, legal representation, non-retroactivity, supremacy of the law, judicial independence, judicial impartiality, limited sovereignty, tolerance, and democratic participation.[31]

He goes on to claim that many of the above found their way into medieval Europe through contacts with Islamic Spain and the Emirate of Sicily, and through the Crusades and the Latin translations of Muslim works undertaken in the twelfth century.[32] A similar argument is used with regard to the rights of women and it is common to hear Muslim men and women assert that Muslim women generally had more legal rights under Islamic law than they did under Western legal systems until the nineteenth and twentieth centuries.[33] Similarly Muslim laws of warfare developed in the period of the early Caliphate and based upon Muhammad's prophetic codes in which the humane treatment of combatants and non-combatants is prescribed are compared with belligerents in the Great War or other European wars.[34]

Other Muslim approaches to the challenge of human rights ethics are various types of apologetic discourse. For example, even though it is admitted that Islamic criminal law penalties seem to be harsh compared to contemporary secular liberal societies, it is argued that Islamic lawyers place multiple conditions and stipulations, such as the poor cannot be penalized for stealing because of poverty, noting that during a time of drought in the period of the first four Caliphs capital punishment was suspended until the people were no longer experiencing the consequences. The loss of such high moral principle from Islamic law is blamed on various factors such as the codification of the *shari'a* by the Ottoman Empire in the early nineteenth century after a series of military setbacks. Such processes replaced the scholars of Islam with a Western-type set of rules.[35] Others claim the loss of the Arab empires at the time of the Mughal invasion or even earlier when the Umayyad Caliphate replaced the *rashidun* (the first four

Caliphs) was the beginning of the loss of Islamic humanism and democratic institutions.

It is certainly true that the Muslim heritage from the time of the European medieval period demonstrates the search for knowledge and values, the love of poetry and philosophical thinking, attempts at early scientific discovery, and a general tone of humanist individualism that rival anything that the West would achieve during the renaissance. Some Muslim defenders of Islam also point towards the existence of freedom of speech and early attempts at democracy within the social structures of early Islam. Contemporary writings and online apologetics attempt to demonstrate that amongst Sunni Muslims the Caliphs were ideally elected by the people or their leaders. However, it is certainly true that this was lost very early on in Islamic history even though there were many examples of benevolent Muslim rulers who held public consultations and permitted direct audience for individuals with grievances.[36] Others argue that the institution of *shura* or *Majlis ash-shura* (consultative assembly or consultation of the people) consisting of tribal elders or religious scholars was significant in advising Muslim rulers. Qur'anic verses that refer to the *shura* are used by contemporary Muslim democrats to argue that the Islamic revelation extols the virtues of participative leadership. For example, 'those who answer the call of their Lord and establish the prayer, and who conduct their affairs by Shura [are loved by God][37] consult them (the people) in their affairs. Then when you have taken a decision (from them), put your trust in Allah.'[38]

Yet more conservative ideologues for the creation of an Islamic state, such as Sayyid Qutb and Taqiuddin al-Nabhani who are perceived by movements that struggle for a revival of the Caliphate as their founding inspiration, argue that Islam requires only that the ruler consult with at least some of the ruled (usually the elite) within the general context of God-made laws that the ruler must execute. For such Islamic revivalists it is essential that Muslims draw a clear distinction between the governance of the West and the God-revealed institutions of Islam, and choose the latter. Others seek resolution of difference. Tariq Ramadan, a Western Muslim theologian with an exalted Egyptian background,[39] argues that there is enough common ground between Islamic civilization and the values of Western secular democracies. He calls upon Muslims to avoid a bipolar view as typified by the 'clash of civilizations' argument expressed in phrases such as 'Whatever is Western is anti-Islamic' or 'Islam has nothing in common with the West'.[40] However, active citizenship in a democracy, he argues, does not mean assimilation but rather maintaining a critically constructive advocacy of social justice, freedom of conscience and worship, joining with partners in committed activism. He states that the Qur'an explicitly calls upon Muslims to side themselves with all that humanity has produced that is good, just and humane in all fields of human endeavour – the political, economic, social and cultural – and must consider the attainments of societies to advance the good as their own, even when such societies are not Muslim.[41]

It is clear that the battle lines are being drawn, both in the Muslim-majority world and where Muslims live as a minority. These disputes are taking place between various elements amongst the devout, who show a wide range of views displaying rigid conservatism and traditionalism as opposition to liberal humanism. These debates are joined by Muslims who are loyal to the idea of Western-style secularism and liberal-humanist democracy and see it as the future for Muslim societies. For those who remain loyal to the truth of the Islamic revelation, interpretation of sacred text and Muslim history becomes crucial. The foundational source in the gradual codification of Islamic ethics was the Muslim understanding and interpretations of the Qur'an and practices of Muhammad. The motive force in Islamic ethics is the notion that every human being is called to 'command the good and forbid the evil' in all spheres of life. The ideal Islamic society is one where all Muslims work in harmony through Islamic institutions to further 'the good and forbid the evil'. In principle then, it is command ethics that dominate Islamic understandings. But the belief that humankind has been granted the faculty to discern God's will and to abide by it underpins the reality of revelation. This God-given faculty marks out the human being as crucially involved in reflection over the meaning of existence. Humans, both men and women, have a moral responsibility to submit to God's will. At all costs, a condition of heedlessness or inability to reflect must be avoided. A focus on the material dimension of life to the exclusion of the spiritual can only lead to disaster for the individual and society. The imperative to comprehend the will of God leads Muslims to reflection upon the truths of revelation. Understanding the Qur'an is crucial.

In spite of a number of claims to literalism with regard to interpretation of the Qur'an arising from conservative understandings of Islam, the historical reality is that since the ninth century the exegesis of the Qur'an (*tafsir*) has been an important subdiscipline of *ulum al-Qur'an* (the sciences of the Qur'an). Although *tafsir* has maintained much the same form and method, this has not in any way diminished the creativity of Muslim scholars, who have diverged in opinion, worked with different hermeneutical approaches and developed various interpretations of the sacred text. Many of these have been written by scholars with an awareness of historical context. Added to traditional *tafsir*, the modern era has witnessed attempts at interpretation by commentators who operate outside the parameters of traditional scholarship and its methodology. There are two significant challenges for the contemporary understanding of ethics and the process of interpretation of inviolate sacred text. The first is new engagement with Islamic thought as an evolution responding to historical and cultural circumstances. The second is a more acute awareness of the need to consider reform and Islamification of knowledge in the context of accommodation of cultural value-systems. As Muslims adopt the science and technology that comes with modernity there will be pressures to become modern in their thinking. The balance between command ethics and situational ethics will require sensitive negotiation and care not to become marginalized as globalization brings with it the pressures to accept a dominant universal value system.

Chapter 4

Islam and Gender

Treat your women well and be kind to them for they are your partners and committed helpers.[1]

Anyone wishing to understand Islam must first separate the religion from the cultural norms and style of a society.[2]

Introduction

Any discussion of the position of Muslim women and their status within Islam has to be undertaken in the awareness that here lies one of the deepest divides between most Muslim opinion and the dominant Western conception. It is reasonably safe to assert that Islam receives more negative criticism concerning the role of women than any other religious tradition. Muslims are suspicious that outsiders maintain uninformed views influenced by the prejudices of the popular media, which stereotype Muslim women as victims of male oppression, usually veiled, segregated, and perceived as passive and invisible.

The Western media has focused on *hijab* (veiling), *purdah* (female segregation) and cultural practices such as 'honour killings', 'forced marriages' and female circumcision. In such sensationalist reporting the attitudes of individual movements such as the Taleban in Afghanistan are written about as typical of Muslim female experience. However, there are Muslim women who remain highly critical of discrimination and oppression of women in certain Muslim nations. Ruqaiyyah Waris Maqsood asks:

> How can anyone justify Islam's treatment of women, when it imprisons Afghans under blue shuttlecock burqas and makes

Pakistani girls marry strangers against their will? How can you
respect a religion that forces women into polygamous marriages,
mutilates their genitals, forbids them to drive cars and subjects
them to the humiliation of "instant" divorce?[3]

On the other hand, many Muslim women argue that their religion
safeguards women, and that the Qur'an provided rights to seventh-
century Arabian women that were not given to British women until
the nineteenth century. Very often the same women who ask the
questions posed by Maqsood are the ones who are convinced that
Islam gives unrivalled rights to women. Maqsood is in such a category
and states:

> The Koran is addressed to all Muslims, and for the most part it
> does not differentiate between male and female. Man and woman,
> it says, "were created of a single soul," and are moral equals in the
> sight of God. Women have the right to divorce, to inherit property,
> to conduct business and to have access to knowledge.[4]

The debate both within and without the Muslim communities is
intense. The situation is complicated by considerable media coverage
arising from the presence of significant Muslim populations in the
West. Many of these articles must be read in the context of right-wing
political views on migration and racist polemical discourse. Yet
Western feminists also tend to regard Islam as hopelessly misogynistic
and perceive Muslim women to be oppressed by pre-modern
patriarchal cultures that need to be overhauled and brought in line
with modernist or post-modernist Western cultures. Many Muslim
women would regard their Western 'sisters' as corrupted by secular
materialism, unprotected by the laws of God, seeking freedoms that
are not permitted by God's revelation and horribly exploited by sex
and fashion industries and consumer advertising that use women to
sell products.

Certainly, since the beginning of the twentieth century, women's
issues and gender relations within Islam have generated a vast
literature in which religion is presented as both the cause of female
subjugation and the solution to all her problems. Ziba Mir-Hosseini
makes the point that 'the whole literature has been ideologically
charged, and has become an arena for polemics masquerading as
scholarly debate'.[5] Attempts to classify the body of literature written
on or by women in the Muslim world are provided by Mai Yamani,

writing a year earlier in 1996, and are further developed by Mir-Hosseini. Between them the two writers have identified a number of genres amongst the books that attempt to defend Islam against a perceived attack by the West and by Western feminists in particular, yet defend the right of Muslim women to full participation and equality within Muslim society. However, these are not always written from the same perspective and can be divided into: (i) those that locate their feminism in Islam and seek new meaning in the sacred texts; and (ii) those that distance themselves from any Islamic association and expose the patriarchal bias of Islamic texts.[6] Mai Yamani, defining Islamic feminism as 'empowerment of gender within a rethought Islam'[7] provides further classification of the first category. She states that these can be categorized as women who: (a) explore religious texts and Islamic jurisprudence seeking evidence for equality in areas of family law and civil rights but recognizing that there is no uniformity of Islamic law across Muslim countries; (b) those who attempt to provide new Islamic discourses that challenge the domination of male interpretation of the Qur'an;[8] and (c) those who study Muslim history, rereading Islamic religious texts with attention given to the female figures of the formative years of Islam.[9]

The common argument of all the above positions is that women have been discriminated against by social practices and economic realities rather than by Islamic principles which in themselves functioned as tools for emancipation. The conclusion reached is that Muslims need to be made aware of the position of women by an exploration of patriarchy which has circumscribed or restricted the Islamic rights of women.[10] However, this significant position on female gender discrimination also needs to be further categorized, dividing works of Muslim academics, such as Leila Ahmed and Fatima Mernissi, from the Muslim apologetic literature, which typically provides traditional arguments illustrating the pitiful conditions of women in various ancient cultures and then providing an analysis of the superiority of the Qur'an's rights and obligations. This latter category is typified by such writers as Fatima Naseef (1999).[11]

Male writing on Islam now needs to consider the voice of women, and failure to do so is likely to elicit criticism, especially from the vocal voices of Western Muslim activists. Such criticism is aimed at Humayun Ansari by the representative of Jamait al-Nissa Women's Group, who notes that his book entitled *The Infidel Within*, describing the history of Muslims in Britain, relegates women to just one chapter.

However, it should be noted that the Qur'an itself follows a similar pattern, providing a single chapter dedicated to women in Sura 4 entitled *al-Nisa* (Women). However, it is this very chapter that is affirmed by the emic voice of young activist Muslim women, who argue that the Qur'an not only has a complete chapter devoted to women, unlike other sacred texts, but also asserts their complete equality with men. However, women operate in a complementary but different arena of life (the family), with their own qualities suited to that sphere, whereas men are suited to operate in the public realm.

Others have built upon the assertion that the Qur'an offers gender equality by arguing that it was the first generations of Muslims coming into contact with already established civilizations that watered down the Islamic revelation's commitment to women. For example, Leila Ahmed argues that the adoption of the veil by wealthy Muslim women was part of the assimilation of 'the mores of the conquered people', pointing to its usage in the Christian Middle East and the Mediterranean region, whose women were themselves influenced by the older female dress customs of the ancient Babylonian, Mesopotamian and Egyptian cultures.[12] Similar arguments of acculturation can also be put forward for the practices of *purdah* and the harems of the ruling classes.

A similar chronological focus is provided by Barbara Stowasser, who also notes transformations in the attitudes to women in various historical periods. She argues that medieval Muslim society was far more patriarchal than the early communities established in Makkah and Madinah; that is, those who first received the Qur'an's revelation and followed the Prophet of God. Stowasser appears to agree with the assertions of many Muslims, both male and female, that the original equality was lost as Muslims conquered territories inhabited by earlier religions such as Zoroastrianism or Orthodox Christianity and consequently came under their more sophisticated cultural influence.[13] Ahmed agrees, arguing that the Qur'an provides no account of the creation of the first human pair in which one is favoured over the other, in spite of its incorporation of so many Jewish biblical stories. As with Stowasser, she asserts that the story of the creation of Eve from Adam's rib only occurs in Muslim traditional literature in the period following the Muslim conquests.[14]

It is thanks to Leila Ahmed, Barbara Stowasser and others that we possess groundbreaking work that has tackled the gargantuan task of 'unearthing and piecing together'[15] the history of women in Middle-Eastern cultures and the articulation of gender in Muslim societies.

These were 'areas of history largely invisible in Middle-Eastern scholarship'[16] as any trawl of the major works of Middle-Eastern history will demonstrate, even in recent texts. However, it still remains necessary to provide accurate research that looks at the conditions of women in Mesopotamia, Egypt, Greece and Persia before the arrival of Islam, as well as local conditions in the Hijaz when Islam was formed.

This becomes more urgent in the face of a contemporary Islamist argument, which maintains that the establishment of Islam improved the conditions of women. Both defensive apologetics written by men and critiques of male patriarchy in Middle-Eastern societies written by Muslim 'feminists' uncritically affirm the above premise. The past, especially the formative period of Islam, has become the crucial period used to defend Islam's position on women. As stated by Ahmed: 'Throughout Islamic history the constructs, institutions, and modes of thought devised by early Muslim societies that form the core discourses of Islam have played a central role in defining women's place in Muslim societies.'[17]

However, the contemporary Islamic position offers up a religious narrative that asserts a situation in pre-Islamic Arabian culture which consisted of corrupt paganism devoid of the values required by God. The existing Middle-Eastern monotheisms had lost their way, corrupted the message of their respective prophets and fallen into decay, and were ripe for divine renewal. However, this position is open to the criticism that it reveals a simplistic view of both pagan and theistic realities, especially with regard to women. The position of women in pre-Islamic Arab culture was probably not as patriarchal as described, neither were their women as subservient as the upholders of the view of the 'emancipated' ideal of the Muslim woman freed by God's revelation would like to think. The stereotype of the pagan Arab women liberated from the tyrannical yoke of the godless is unable to bear too close scrutiny and the Qur'an certainly provides images of fearless women who stand their ground against the immorality of their menfolk.

Although large numbers of Muslim women are satisfied with the current or historical place of women in Muslim societies, an increasing number of women from within Islam are challenging the overwhelmingly male voice of religious authority, and reassessing the roles of prominent women in early Muslim development, most notably the women of the Prophet's household. Both the Qur'an and the Hadith are under close scrutiny in order to discover what they say about women. Although the experience of a Muslim woman will be influenced by class and family background, age, rural or urban locality, national identity and her place within the wide variety of religious understandings of Islam, it is to the revelation of the Qur'an and the subsequent rendering into everyday life through the example of Muhammad and his companions that her understanding of her place in society is finally made authoritative. Unlike her Christian feminist compatriots, who have recognized serious imperfections in the way women are treated in the religion itself even in its sacred histories and texts, many Muslim women who seek to change their position in society perceive Islam as the ideal to which their menfolk, both historical and contemporary, have failed to match.

However, the Qur'an's proclamation of equality is in regard to woman's individual capacity to attain God's rewards and punishments, to follow the revelation of Allah's will. In this respect, the text is clear that men and women are equal.

> Lo! Men who surrender unto Allah, and women who surrender, and men who believe and women who believe, and men who obey and women who obey, and men who speak the truth and women who speak the truth, and men who persevere (in righteousness) and women who persevere, and men who are humble and women who are humble, and men who give alms and women who give alms, and men who fast and women who fast, and men who guard their modesty and women who guard (their modesty), and men who remember Allah much and women who remember – Allah hath prepared for them forgiveness and a vast reward.[18]

However, in other areas equality is not so assured. For example, the testimony of a man is equivalent to that of two women, suggesting that women are less trustworthy. But the Qur'an does provide assertive statements concerning a woman's rights in marriage and divorce, the status of her property and the maintenance of her dignity. Women also have a number of Qur'anic models for both right and wrong behaviour. Four women – Asiyah, the wife of Pharaoh, Mary, the mother of Jesus, Khadijah, the first wife of Muhammad, and Fatimah, his daughter – are regarded as perfect role models, whilst the wives of Lot and Noah provide a warning of wrongdoing. These women of the Qur'an are archetypes of virtue or vice, but they are, at least in one respect, free agents, able to choose to obey both God and God-fearing husbands. On the other hand, they can oppose unrighteousness in their menfolk and independently strive to bring their men to the right path. Barbara Stowasser notes: 'many of the Qur'an's women's stories bear the lesson that a woman's faith and righteousness depend on her will and decision, and that neither association with a godly man nor a sinner decides a woman's commitment to God'.[19]

In addition, Muslim women do not have to deal with the stigma placed upon their Christian and Jewish counterparts, who are blamed for the fall of 'mankind' through the actions of their primal ancestor. Both Adam and Eve share the guilt of disobedience equally in Islamic narratives but their weakness did not result in a permanent rift between God and humanity. Human nature remains intact with no lasting defect. Both Adam and Eve are restored to Allah's mercy and forgiveness and this is celebrated by all Muslims who attend the annual Hajj in Makkah. Human beings, regardless of gender, are weak and forgetful but remain always in the vicinity of God's forgiveness. In addition, Islam rejects celibacy and monasticism in favour of married life. Sexuality is celebrated within the confines of marriage and there are Hadith that proclaim the importance of foreplay and sexual fulfilment for both men and women.

The formative years of Islam's beginnings provide a number of high-profile women from amongst Muhammad's wives and descendants. Young Muslim women looking for female role models are likely to cite Khadijah, the Prophet's first wife, who managed her own affairs and successfully traded in the Middle-Eastern world, or Ayesha, his youngest wife, who after his death led men into battle and played a public role in Muslim leadership. Such role models are needed as economic change in the Muslim world brings more women into full-time paid employment and challenges the prominent discourse that curtails women to the domestic sphere. Increasing employment opportunities bring women into the public domain and some will achieve leadership roles in professions and government. The Qur'an has little to say on women in such roles and the Hadith are ambiguous and contradictory. For every individual Hadith that positively endorses female equality, including even their rights to sexual satisfaction, there will be another that denigrates women as weak and foolish.

Fatima Mernissi, in an important and controversial book *Women and Islam*, looks at the most authoritative Hadith on women and included in both al-Bukhari's and al-Muslim's collections. It states: 'those who entrust their affairs to a woman will never know prosperity'. The Hadith appears to be a damning indictment of women operating in public life and leadership roles. Mernissi does not challenge the content but uses the traditional Muslim science of contesting Hadith by analysing its *isnad* (chain of transmission). She successfully rediscovers the cultural and political context of the chain's main contributors and seeks out their hidden motivations for taking up a misogynistic position.[20]

Certainly the content of the Hadith could be accused of appearing to be critical of the Prophet himself, who entrusted his affairs to Khadijah when he was appointed her caravan manager. She was, after all, an older widow with children from two previous marriages. Khadijah traded in her own right and even asked Muhammad to become her husband. Yet there is a problem with pushing Khadijah forward as an example of female independence and leadership. Muslims like to believe that the position of women in pre-Islamic Arabia was one of atrocious exploitation and lack of rights only corrected by the implementation of revelation of Allah. Although Khadijah was the first to embrace Islam, her independence and assertiveness was achieved in the pre-Islamic period, suggesting that women were not as badly treated in pagan Arab society as Muslims would ideally like to believe.

After Khadijah's death the Prophet married several women, and certainly the young Ayesha and Umm Salama were not passive women restricting themselves to the domestic sphere and blindly obedient to their husbands and menfolk. Mernissi points out that the Qur'an's revelation concerning women's equality with men, cited above, came about after Umm Salama asked the Prophet why the Qur'an did not speak about women as it did about men.[21] Certainly this early period of Muslim history provides a number of examples of powerful women, some of whom opposed the Prophet from amongst his enemies in Makkah, once again challenging the Muslim myth of the oppressed 'pagan' woman.

After the Prophet's death, the young Ayesha became a public figure of some authority. Known as Muhammad's favourite wife and called the 'Mother of believers', she was immensely respected and even led Muslim armies into battle during the first civil war, when she challenged Ali, the fourth Caliph, over his failure to bring the murderers of the third Caliph to justice. Yet, once again, A'isha is a double-edged sword as a role model. On the one hand, she provides an example of a woman leading the community, but on the other hand, she could be accused of causing the first division in the Muslim community and thus providing men with a justification to cite the Hadith's message concerning entrusting one's affairs to women.

Mernissi, like Stowasser, agrees that the independent assertive desert Arab woman of the early period gradually disappears as patriarchy reasserts itself into the expanding Muslim world. Mernissi believes that the turning point arrived with the dynastic absolutism of the Umayyad dynasty founded by Mu'awiyya, which finally ended the Prophet's experiment in equality and destroyed the democratic tendencies of the desert Arabs. She states that early Muslim women were 'not going to accept the new religion without knowing exactly how it would improve their situation. The critical spirit on the part of these women towards the political leader remained alive and well during the first decades of Islam.'[22]

All of the above narratives are strategically used by Muslim female gender activists to argue that early Islam promoted the rights of women. The story of women being liberated by Islam but oppressed by patriarchal Muslim cultures, historically influenced by the conquest of non-Muslim territory, has become a powerful tool to activate Muslim women. But the idea that Islam liberated women was not always the dominant narrative for emancipation in the modern period, although it has come to supplant other voices that drew heavily upon more familiar European feminism.

The Colonial Period

From the mid-nineteenth century, Muslim women were once again in the forefront of debates arising from contact with other cultures. But this time the claim that Islam had provided new rights and freedoms to women was to find itself under threat from the advances made in women's emancipation in Western Europe. Although it might have been possible to argue that Muslim societies had provided the impetus for new attitudes towards women in the formative period of Islam, it now seemed that Western societies had surpassed anything achieved by the Muslim world. Thus the West became implicated in contemporary Muslim gender politics.

Muslim nations such as Turkey, Egypt and Iran were heavily influenced by colonial self-definitions of the backwardness of the East. Reformers in the Muslim world also insisted that there was a need to transform their societies in the light of contact with the West. As a part of colonial social reform women's rights and their role within the family, and beyond in the spheres of education and employment, came under close scrutiny. Often the focus was placed on dress codes and the traditional emphasis of the Muslim world to ascribe to women the domestic realm. Challenged by the critique of 'backwardness', Muslim societies had to begin to deal with modernity, where the ideal of 'being modern' became the dominant self-image of the Western world.

Many middle-class elites and educated Muslims were to respond to the challenge by embracing Western values. Thus the West was imitated and translated in the process of 'remaking women',[23] leading to a number of Muslim women taking up the cause of emancipation in the wake of their European sisters. The late twentieth-century rediscovery of women's writings in nations such as Egypt demonstrates the influence of Western education and values. Certainly attitudes towards women began to change in the cultural meeting between Muslims and the West. Anne Roald argues that these placed into an oppositional framework the cultural patterns of the Arab world, which were patriarchal, and the Western cultural base fixated on equality.[24] Such polarity exists through to the present time. Roald notes that where Islam and the West have closely encountered each other in the Muslim world, the Qur'anic notion of *qiwama*, where men are placed in charge of women, becomes transformed into men having paternal responsibility for women.[25]

The Post-colonial Period

The most marked change in the aftermath of colonialism has been women's redefining of their roles in the Muslim world by a repudiation of Western values and a reassertion of Islam's superiority. The idea of the 'backwardness of the East' and the advanced civilization of the 'modern' West has been challenged by the new defenders of Islam. Many women have provided a critique of both Western values and their own patriarchal societies, insisting that Islam needs to be rediscovered and implemented in its original purity in order to resolve the current world crises and fuel a renaissance of the Muslim world.

In the twentieth century, Muslims have had to deal with the reality of their political decline and the prevailing threat of Western culture and secular consumer values that focus on the material acquisition of possessions as the means to human fulfilment. The more that Muslims have felt their own cultural and religious way of life threatened, the more the onus has been on women to protect and nurture 'authentic'

Islamic values and behaviour. Stowasser writes in this context: 'the images of female spiritual, mental and physical defectiveness were being replaced by those of female nurturing strength and the female's importance for the struggle for cultural survival'.[26] Although the modern era has resulted in a male-led discourse on the importance of women in maintaining Islamic values, women too have embraced the role, defending it staunchly as their own special domain. This has led to considerable self-reflection on the rights of women within Islam and the search for truly Muslim role models of womanhood rather than the *isra'iliyyat* (the Jewish women of the biblical period mentioned in the Qur'an).

Thus the theme of women's weakness or women as a threat to men and society began to dominate scriptural-based arguments on gender. These attitudes continue to prevail in traditional Muslim societies, which remain highly influenced by medieval interpretation of the Qur'an and Hadith. Thus today it is common for Muslim men to place the onus of maintaining the virtue and honour of the family and wider society on their womenfolk, punishing them sometimes for lapses that bring shame and dishonour. Leila Ahmed argues that the discussion of women in the contemporary period is about far wider issues of identity and power.[27] Abu-Lughod supports this view, stating that 'in the post-colonial world women have become powerful symbols of identity and visions of society and the nation'.[28]

Contemporary attempts by Muslim women to redefine their roles seem to be marked by two overriding concerns. The first is the question of how to be 'modern' but not to become 'Western'. The second is connected to the first, and seeks to find ways of transforming women's lives that are indigenous rather than borrowing from Western feminism. Gisella Webb notes that by this tactic they are able to counter the charge made by conservative elements in the Islamic community, which attempt to silence their activities by labelling them as 'followers' of secular Western feminism.[29]

Thus in the latter half of the twentieth century we saw the phenomenon of many women moving away from aping the West's struggle for female emancipation to a renewed interest in Islam and the rights that it offered women in the original revelation. The central thrust of the argument is that Islam had liberated women but male patriarchy has refused to let go and grant the privileges given by God in the revelation. Consequently contemporary Muslim life had become more the product of ethnic and cultural patterns than the manifestation of Islamic principles. Women began the process of textual interpretation, providing a female-centred reading of the *shari'a*, and harnessing their personal experience. The result was a renewed religious awareness and the emergence of an Islamic feminism that separated religion from culture in the quest for actualizing women's rights. Ziba Mir-Husseini notes that 'one paradoxical outcome of the rise of political Islam in the 1970s was that it helped to create an arena within which Muslim women could reconcile their faith with their new gender awareness'.[30]

One other additional factor influencing gender relations was the arrival of significant Muslim communities in North America and Western Europe. The West was to feel the impact of this reverse movement of populations. Muslim women were to have much closer contact with their Western sisters and decide whether they wanted to follow the same road towards emancipation. On the other hand, as commented on by Anne Roald, non-Muslims, both male and female, were to react with hostility to the increasing Islamic presence in Europe.[31] The effect of this was a concentration on the negative aspects of female experience such as female circumcision, polygyny, divorce and child custody, forced marriages, segregation, Islamic female dress, and honour killings. In the West little attempt was made to distinguish the ethnic or cultural aspects of these from the teachings of the religion, or to note that many Muslim feminists were also attacking the same practices as being not part of Islam but rather various male patriarchal elements brought into Muslim cultures from elsewhere or belonging to pre-existent tribal societies. For example, female circumcision is almost obligatory for Muslim women throughout sub-Saharan Africa but is also widespread amongst Christians or those who follow indigenous tribal religions in that region. Although endorsed by Muslims its practice is not mentioned in the formative sacred texts nor is it practised in other parts of the Muslim world. It is not in the scope of this chapter to provide detailed analysis of all the above-mentioned features. However, we will explore further both the phenomenon of veiling and female segregation, as these seem to have become particularly closely identified with Islam and provide the frontline criticism that posits the 'backward' condition of Muslim women.

The Discourse of the Veil

There is no doubt that the veiling (understood as 'head-covering) of women is the *bête noire* of Western feminists. Leila Ahmed argues that the veil has come to represent the 'quintessential symbol of Islam'.[32] Western feminists and even policy-makers have become fixated on it as representative of female oppression. The Western media will often represent Muslim women as veiled figures and offer up stories of young girls barred from school because they insist upon conservative forms of Muslim dress. In 2003, the French Government banned the wearing of the veil in public institutions such as state schools, to the alarm of the Muslim community who saw it as an obvious act of religious discrimination. The action of the French can be seen as another example of a European nation's conception of the backwardness of the East as opposed to the enlightened attitudes of modern secular nations. To further complicate matters, ideas of citizenship and loyalty in France since the Revolution have been dominated by *laïcité*, a particularly vigorous form of secularity that insists upon total separation of state and religion, and upon conformity to such an ideal marking out French identity. Some Nordic nations have barred veiled women from public professions such as law, teaching or medicine.

The negative fixation on the veil is born out of the understanding that it is an outward marker of female oppression by men; however, the idea that all Muslim women are forced or pressured to wear the veil by either their fathers or husbands is far from the truth. Although there are some Muslim nations – usually those where Islamic governments have been installed that insist upon the veil in public – in most places it is not obligatory. The irony is that whereas once Muslim women removed their veils as an indication of their emancipation, since the latter half of the twentieth century many – especially those amongst the young and educated – have adopted the veil as a symbol of resistance and cultural authenticity or as a conscious symbol of their Islamic identity. This process of re-veiling has also extended to older women, who may have discarded it in their youth. Ahmed argues that the wearing of the veil may be a conscious rejection of the values of the West and even a conscious resistance to the former European colonial project of de-veiling, now continued in the post-colonial era and extended to Muslim minorities in Europe.[33]

She also makes the point that Western feminists misunderstand the use of the veil and 'devalue local cultures by insisting that their own road to emancipation is the only one'.[34] Certainly Muslim women who have consciously taken to wearing the veil or covering their heads often defend their decision by arguing that it provides freedom and dignity. They will often assert that women should not be perceived as sexual objects or consumers of fashion, as is dominant in the West, and that Islamic dress in general frees them from such exploitation. Such women should not necessarily be perceived as traditional. It is more than likely that they will be active in challenging their men's understandings of Islam and demanding their full rights as given by Qur'an, Hadith and *fiqh*. On the other hand they can be equally critical of the freedoms gained by their Western sisters, seeing them as exploited by consumer capitalism and reduced to the sexual objects of male lust. Traditional rural Muslim women or urban working classes are more likely to be less self-conscious in their dress codes and to wear what they wear because it is the norm to do so.

The discourse of the veil is complex, and certainly many of the sometimes heated discussions that take place in the Arab world between the defenders of veiling and the secularists who advocate its removal have little to do with the rights of women but are more concerned with scoring points in contemporary debates about the political futures of Muslim societies where Islamists and secularists face each other in opposition. In addition, any conception of the use of the veil must take into account Muslim women's own understandings of why they have adopted it or, alternatively, removed it.

In an investigation of the veil undertaken in Cairo, Sherifa Zuhur (1992) noted various reasons for adopting the veil. Whereas some interviewees spoke of the safeguarding of honour and status and the attitudes of men to unveiled women in public places, others referred to their embracing of their religious practices. Although some older women did defer to parental or male pressure, the younger ones asserted that their families reacted badly to them adopting the veil. For women under thirty the process of taking on the veil was seen as a symbol of change resulting from introspection and involving a personal moral decision. Some, however, were keen to point out the practicalities of wearing the veil in public and how it facilitated being in employment. Of interest to women's movements was the assertion by most of the young women that the veil gave them feelings of sisterhood and solidarity.[35] Such field studies demonstrate that simplistic conceptions of the veil by Western commentators on the condition of Muslim women should be avoided. On the contrary, the veil may be a symbol of freedom and emancipation to those that wear it.

Segregation of Women

Most Muslim societies maintain segregation of males and females in the public domain. This is also generally found in the mosque, which remains a quintessential male domain. Many mosques do not permit women to enter for public prayer and others provide a segregated space for them. However, it is true that the majority of Muslim women pray at home. This has led to a critique that women are denied the religious equality that is central to the Qur'an's message and are not permitted to participate in the public ritual life of Islam. Some Muslim women have argued that this was not the case at the time of Muhammad where both men and women sat before the Prophet when he preached.

However, care needs to be taken with this analysis of the participation of women. Not only will it vary from society to society, but there is also evidence to suggest that where Islamicization takes place there is more debate on the rights of women in the religious domain. Far more fieldwork needs to be carried out in individual Muslim communities by those with sufficient access to discover the reality. In one such study of Iranian women carried out by Zahra Khamalkhani it was noted that whilst women continue to maintain the integrity of the household, they simultaneously took part in wider social activities and participated in their own religious meetings where men were denied access.[36] Such studies challenge the classic conception by Western feminists that the home is the sole institution for engagement in religious life by Muslim women. Khamalkhani argues that their studies fail to take into account the 'Islamic core and organizational patterns of the Muslim domestic arena' and suffer from a bias in that they are informed by studies of mosques and theological schools.[37] Khamalkhani concludes that such studies show that women are no less concerned than men with religious performance, piety and duties.[38]

Saifullah Khan argues that the term 'Muslim' needs to be problematized, in that we need to remind ourselves of 'the power that the term "Muslim" holds in our imaginations' and that we need to recognize both the wide variety of meaning that is contained in the term 'Muslim women' and the increasing fluidity of cultural expressions of Muslim belonging.[39] Faizia Ahmad argues that: 'Historical and contemporary encounters continue to embody Muslim women through cultural and religious frameworks as essentialised oppressed figures of victimhood and despair.'[40] The danger of essentializing will remain as long as the Western 'gaze' continues to focus on *hijab* and 'arranged marriages', projecting onto Muslim women an image of passivity and powerlessness and thus severely limiting the scope of debate. It may surprise many interested in the subject that neither of these two high-visibility issues are prominent on the agenda of contemporary Muslim female liberation discourse. The reasons for a Muslim female to wear a head covering are varied. It may be tradition, simply the way that it is done and unquestioned; it may be practicality; it may be religious or cultural reasons; or it may be because her family insist upon it. On the other hand, she may have decided to cover herself from her own conscious decision independent of her family's views and they may even disapprove of her action. If so, she may intensely defend her reasons for doing so as liberating, not binding. These arguments need to be seriously assessed, as they constitute the attitudes of millions of young Muslim women around the world who are voluntarily taking up Muslim dress codes and contributing in their own unique way to the phenomenon known as 'Islamicization'.

Arranged marriages are rarely a major issue for unmarried women although forced marriages do constitute a problem in places where they continue to thrive. As long as young women and men are provided the opportunity of refusal or acceptance they generally appear happy with the arrangements by their parents even in Western minority communities. In fact, they remain critical of the imperfections that they perceive in romantic liaisons as motivation for marriage. Once again cultural differences have to be acknowledged; arranged marriages are far more likely to impact on the Muslims of South Asia than, for example, the younger generation of Palestinians, whose marriages are rarely arranged these days.

The other minefield to be avoided is the trap of setting ourselves up as an elite voice, somehow more knowledgeable or enlightened than Muslim women, who will need our assistance to liberate themselves from the innate patriarchal structures of their religion and culture. This raises wider questions already discussed concerning who claims ownership of feminism itself. Western feminists need to be careful that they do not place themselves in the position of protectors and liberators of their silent but suffering Muslim sisters. In this regard, the Algerian-born sociologist Marnia Lazreg argues that the Western feminist emancipatory project has failed, as it continues to impose one social standard onto another.[41] She powerfully asserts that it is essential to respect the rights of women to express their lives through their own constructs.

The sources cited above provide a small sample of the writings of Muslim women and indicate the level of interest that exists on the issue of gender in Islam. It is important, as noted, to avoid stereotyping the worst experiences of women in the Muslim world and assuming that they represent all attitudes to women or that Islam is incurably misogynistic. It is important also to recognize that class, education, nationality, economy, and urban or rural backgrounds will all impact on women's experiences. Not all Muslim nations are the same with regards to the legal rights of women. Women's experiences vary enormously across even the Arab states, let alone countries on the periphery of the Muslim world such as South Asia or sub-Saharan Africa where other cultural influences may come into play. Tunisia bans polygamy and has the region's most progressive legislation for women whereas attempts to ban polygamy in neighbouring Morocco have been adamantly opposed. Libya's leader is famously protected by female bodyguards, whereas Saudi Arabia enforces strict segregation and forbids women to drive. Egyptian women have been allowed to vote since the 1950s whereas Kuwaiti women still cannot. A number of Muslim nations have had female leaders who have taken a prominent role in encouraging women's rights. In 2003, for example, two thousand female delegates from across the Muslim world met in Cairo, hosted by Suzanne Mubarrak, the wife of the Egyptian President. Queen Rania of Jordan, Suha Arafat, wife of the Palestinian leader Yasser Arafat, the Sudanese President's wife, Fatima Bashir, and Lebanon's First Lady, Andree Lahoud, were among nine First Ladies who took part.[42]

Activity is not confined to such elite groups. In Iran, women have campaigned successfully for the right to lead prayers, albeit that the right was only finally granted, in the summer of 2000, by the Islamic government out of concern that there is declining interest in Islam among young Iranians, particularly young women.[43] In 2001, the parliament passed a bill giving permission for unmarried women to apply for scholarships to study overseas, despite the fact that Iran had originally banned state scholarships for studying abroad in 1985 and the bill was resisted by Islamic conservatives.[44] Women are highly active in both the conservative and reformist sides of the political divide and many participate in higher education. In the 1997 and 2009 elections women voted in their millions for reformist candidates, and a record 513 women stood in the 1997 elections. They made up about 7 per cent of candidates nationwide, and nearly 15 per cent in the capital Tehran. The Islamic Iran Participation Front campaigns for equal pay and the abolition of forced marriages. Certainly the restrictions imposed on women in Iran are less severe than in some of the Gulf Arab states, especially Saudi Arabia which bars women even from driving. The Islamic law in force in Iran since the 1979 revolution does, however, place women under male supervision and requires them to follow a strict dress code. The Iranian clergy have generally stressed the traditional family role of women and the majority of conservative clerics still believe men are superior to women. A woman is rarely granted custody of children unless they are very young, and if her husband dies, his father usually gains authority over the couple's possessions and assets.[45]

In Egypt, it is one hundred years since Qassem Amin wrote his book entitled *The Liberation of Women* and caused uproar amongst the nation's conservative Muslims. Women can now vote and, in many places, go out to work, and the twenty-first century opened with two women in the Egyptian cabinet. Women, however, are not allowed to travel abroad without the permission of their husbands[46] and it was not until January 2000 that an Egyptian mother of two became the first woman to file for divorce after parliament approved a new law allowing women to divorce their husbands for incompatibility.[47] Unlike in Sudan, Yemen and Syria, all conservative states, women in Egypt cannot become judges. However, in 2000 the Egyptian cabinet decided to cancel a law that allows a rapist to walk free if he marries his victim, but the liberalization of divorce laws contained the condition that women who divorce lose the right to their marriage dowries or alimony. Even though the laws were approved as religiously sound by Al-Azhar, the leading Islamic university, many conservative men were distressed at the changes. Many women activists consider that since the Islamicization of society in the late twentieth century, the rights of women in Egypt have lost ground. However, in 2000 a National Council for Women was formed under the leadership of President Mubarrak and his wife.[48]

In Morocco, women have been campaigning for changes to the traditional family law (*moudouana*) for years and in 2000 the ruling monarch, Mohammed VI, announced reforms to the law regarding women's position in the home. Until these changes, men had been able to divorce wives easily whereas women struggled to get out of even abusive relationships. The changes to the law involved women obtaining property rights within marriage, and both spouses having equal authority in the family. Divorce was made easier for women and the age of marriage for girls was raised from 15 to 18. Polygamy was not outlawed but was made more difficult, in that a man will need to get consent from his existing wife before marrying another. The king acknowledged that changing the laws was fraught with difficulty, as many conservative and traditional Muslims were opposed to the reforms.[49]

In Syria there has been an Islamic revival that has seen the resurrection of the ancient tradition of Sheikhas, women who are qualified to be religious scholars. This increased religious activity of women is part of Syria becoming more religious and adopting a more Islamic identity. Women are in the vanguard of the Islamicization process and defying years of government encouragement towards secularization. The growth of girls' religious colleges (*madrasas*) has outpaced that of those for boys. At the turn of the century there were about eighty such *madrasas* in Damascus alone, serving more than 75,000 women and girls.[50] The girls learn to commit the Qur'an to memory but are also taught the principles of Qur'anic reasoning and it is this that sets them apart from previous generations of women who learned the meaning of their faith from husbands and fathers. The interpretive process is teaching the young women of Syria their rights according to Islam and as one female principal of a Syrian *madrasa* declared, 'People mistake tradition for religion. Men are always saying, "Women can't do that because of religion," when in fact it is only tradition. It's important for us to study so that we will know the difference.'[51]

Yet the situation is not quite so straightforward as religious women activists declare. Islamicization takes many forms and is not always conducive to women obtaining rights and freedoms. The Taleban in Afghanistan remain notorious for their repressive attitudes towards women, forbidding education and sometimes even medical treatment during pregnancy and childbirth. In Algeria, during the civil war between Islamist movements and the secular government forces, the treatment of women raised serious questions concerning the capacity of conservative Islamists to improve the status of women. Women found themselves targets from both protagonists in the conflict. Women wearing the *hijab* were killed by government forces whilst those in professions and who insisted upon 'being modern' were slaughtered by the fighters of the Islamic resistance. Old women had their throats cut in their own homes and students, veiled and unveiled, were shot down in the streets, kidnapped or raped. Wall posters threatened women with death if they went to the *hammam* (public baths for women), frequented beauty salons, worked, played sports or studied music or art. The *hijab* was enforced.[52] The treatment of women in Algeria by Islamic movements raises serious concerns about the relationship between faith and the rights of women in Islam and suggests that women would be no better off under Islamically guided legal systems managed by Islamic movements than they are in traditional Muslim societies where cultural norms determine attitudes and behaviour.

Certainly in the conservative Islamic environment of Saudi Arabia progress is slow. Saudi women are now more highly educated than Saudi men as a result of King Faisal overruling the powerful Muslim clerics in the 1960s and allowing women to enter universities. They currently represent 58 per cent of university students though only 2 per cent of the workforce. The policy of *ikhtilat* or the public banning of mixing between men and women in public places remains a significant obstacle to women working, as does the ban on issuing driving licences.[53] In January 2003 a number of women signed a petition calling for reform to curb the control of conservative Islamic forces over the everyday life of Saudis and requested more popular participation in decision making. The petition was not unusual but it was the first to which women had penned their names.[54] However, the involvement of Saudi women in business is increasing. At the beginning of the twenty-first century around 10 per cent of Saudi private companies were run by women and some are prepared to flout the rules.[55] Change is taking place in spite of the resistance of the legal and official representatives of Sunni Islam in the kingdom. It is in part coming from within but the Saudi Government has had to respond to increasing homegrown Islamic militancy and the pressures from the international community to reform its society since 9/11.

Conclusion

We have observed that the most potent movement for change in the Muslim world comes from female activists, who insist it is not rejection of Islam that will lead to their liberation but rather an attempt to struggle for the restoration of the rights given to them at Islam's inception, affirmed by the revelation and lived out in practice by the early generation of Muslim women. However, there are difficulties with the proposition that Islam liberated Arab women in the seventh century. Although many Muslims may assert that the Qur'an provided rights for women that were not achieved by Western women until many centuries later, many Western feminists will point out that the newly achieved rights and freedoms of the twentieth century have far surpassed anything that the original Muslims could have conceived. Even if Muslim women were given the privileges granted by the revelation they would still be playing catch-up. Comparisons with the rights of Western women enjoyed in the nineteenth century or before are no longer valid arguments. Modern Western societies now thrive on change and transformation to a degree unknown in traditional cultures. Although it is true that Islam provided rights and duties to women that may have improved their lot in the Middle East, they cannot be compared with the emancipation achieved since the twentieth century in the West. Many Muslim women may not be satisfied merely with a return to the rights of the Makkan and Madinan period.

There is also an ironical contradiction in the attempt to reclaim the rights and freedoms of the first generation of Muslim women. In doing so those women who choose to follow their religion seriously make the distinction between the Islam practised by the first generation, believed to be unsullied and true to the revelation, and that of those who came after, corrupted by innovation created by contact with other cultures. In doing so they find themselves allies to various revivalist and reform movements that also believe the same narrative but apply it wider than the field of women's rights. Often these are the very same movements that seek to create Islamic states based on complete application of Muslim religious law or that even wage jihad against the West. Thus these women find their natural allies amongst the men of the twentieth-century revivalist movements who may well champion their right to wear the *hijab* but not necessarily their right to leadership and independence. In addition, the forces of re-Islamicization often lack tolerance of pluralism and are intolerant of opposition that could cause problems for the diversity of opinion amongst Muslim women.

As in the West, the future of women's rights will be closely tied to economic fluctuations, education and employment opportunities. In this respect, the traditional Islamic segregation of women can be advantageous as it provides unique employment opportunities for women such as teachers in girl's schools and female doctors and nurses. In such cases the veil, the symbol of the West's understanding of Islam as repressive to women and restricting their freedoms, can come into play as a means to greater mobility.

Muslim women will need to take care that decisions regarding their freedoms and rights are not made by men immersed in patriarchal attitudes or safeguarding their own honour and status. A number of authors have argued that the emphasis on women in the twentieth century has more to do with the political environment in colonial and post-colonial periods than with a genuine concern for women themselves. Certainly the renewed interest in Islam and the emergence of Islamic feminism has to be seen in the light of Muslim attitudes towards the West and an attempt to reassert the supremacy of God's revelation over secular values. In such an environment, the earlier attempts by women to liberate themselves by adopting the mores of Western culture become suspect. In this context it should be observed that Islamic feminism does not show a united face to the world. There are competing variations to be noted. On the other hand, there remain prominent voices that are not convinced of the claim that Islam is liberating. Some question the conventional idea that Islam even improved the status of women in the formative period. In such debates, the icons of the Islamic feminists, Khadijah and Ayesha, were independent not because of a change in attitudes created by the new religion but because they were permitted to be that way by matriarchal values that pre-existed Islam. Others have suggested that the Qur'an did little to challenge the prevailing attitudes that women should be under the protection of men. Although such women critics may remain true to the practice of their religion they demand that the Qur'an should be studied in its historical and social context. More conservative voices amongst women insist that the Qur'an must be liberating, as it is from God, and persist in the traditional view that some inequalities between men and women are justified as each possess distinct differences attributed to their respective natures.

Many case studies written on Muslim gender issues do take into account the vast range of cultural factors that impact on Islamic values within the variety of nations that belong to the Muslim world. This is crucial, as the experiences of a Muslim woman in urban India, for example, are unlikely to be the same as those of her counterpart in a Turkish village. Increasingly, studies of Muslim gender experience explore within one cultural milieu rather than generalizing. However, in spite of that rich heritage of cultural difference, the teachings of the Qur'an and Hadith concerning women's roles and their rights and responsibilities are shared by all. Yet the interaction between religion, culture and the hermeneutical process applied to sacred texts does produce a significant variety of conclusions. Overall, these discussions and differences of opinion are no less than the shades of difference that exist among Western women but we need more study of the actual conditions of Muslim women to demonstrate the variety of experience in the Muslim world and help to overcome the stereotypes existing in the West. In the words of Gisella Webb, 'May Muslim women speak for themselves please?'[56]

Chapter 5

Islam and Fundamentalism

A pattern of many contemporary socio-political movements that share certain characteristics in their responses to a common globalisation process which can be described as secularisation.[1]

Defining Fundamentalism

Islamic movements prepared to engage in religiously justified violence have done much to bring Islam to public attention and to increase the propensity of the Western media to resort to stereotyping when reporting anything concerning Muslims. But not all such movements advocate violence though they may share in the ideological and religious goals of those who use violence as a means to achieve these goals. The following chapter will assess such movements, the similarities and differences between them, the significance of jihad, and the various justifications that such movements put forward for their activities.

Such tendencies within a religion are often labelled as 'fundamentalist' and religious violence is often regarded as an extreme form of fundamentalism. Unfortunately the term 'fundamentalism' is often used in a very loose way by the general public and the media. Any informed discussion of 'fundamentalism' in the context of Islam, or for that matter any other religious tradition, must endeavour to go beyond both the popular usage of the term by the public and the closely connected media depictions of certain typologies of religion, which portray them as anti-modern, traditionalist, intolerant and reactionary. In addition, there are academic divisions amongst scholars with regard to whether it is more useful to speak of 'fundamentalism' or 'fundamentalisms'. The former would define certain types of Islamic reaction to modernity as part of a religious phenomenon across traditions, where a 'family likeness' of common features can be defined as 'fundamentalism'. The latter would suggest that we need to look more closely at the unique features of Islam that mark it out as different from any other religious tradition.

Underlying this difference of opinion are two quite different perspectives. In the first, perhaps most clearly represented by the ambitious 'Fundamentalism Project' edited by Martin Marty and R. Scott Appleby (1994–6), is an application of the term as an umbrella appellation describing a common phenomenon that is manifest in a number of different religious traditions.[2] This approach leads to an analysis that seeks to uncover global causes that create the same religious reaction worldwide. The approach, unfortunately, also suffers from a Christian-centric analysis that seeks to impose, upon all religions, a model for the development of 'fundamentalism' and its causes that imitate certain developments in Protestant Christianity. Even as far back as 1987, Lionel Caplan was criticizing such an approach as 'glib use of concepts whose roots lie in Western tradition'.[3]

On the other hand, Partridge takes the view that 'fundamentalism' does not do justice to the diversity of religious traditions and their own unique historical development, practices and beliefs, and although he acknowledges enough common features to identify similar patterns, he prefers to speak of a family of correspondences with unique aspects that is better understood by the term 'fundamentalisms' than by the singular 'fundamentalism'.[4] This approach avoids the inherent dangers of simplification and imposing upon other religions a term whose roots lie in a particular historical and theological development in contemporary North American Christianity.

Muslims are rightly suspicious of the term, arguing that it imposes upon their religion a Christian terminology that is laden with theological baggage that cannot be successfully transferred to Islam. On the other hand, they argue that it is implicit within devout or 'correct' Muslim practice to refer back to the Qur'an for understanding and direction. The dependence upon scriptural revelation is the norm of Islam, and thus any Muslim who chooses to take his or her faith seriously is likely to be branded as 'fundamentalist'. This critique has been taken up seriously by a number of scholars who study contemporary Islam and its manifestations, and alternative terminology has been utilized to describe the phenomena of a number of *jamaats* or movements that have arisen around the Muslim world with certain common features that have been compared with fundamentalism. Rather than use the term 'fundamentalist', such scholars have chosen to speak of revivalists (Esposito, 1988), reformists, jihadists (Choueiri, 1997), Islamists (Huband, 1995; Kepel, 2002) and Islamic militants (Hiro, 1989).[5] Since the events of 9/11, the vocabulary of the media and politics has added the new and even more pejorative and perfunctory term of 'terrorist'.

In this chapter I have chosen to draw upon Hadden and Schupe's definition of fundamentalism quoted at the beginning of this chapter. The definition has been used because it provides a useful analytical boundary of 'political' to describe fundamentalism. Therefore any religious movement cannot be called 'fundamentalist' unless there is a 'coherent ideology which seeks to bring religion back to the centre stage of public life as well as private life'.[6] However, this may or may not be in response to secularization. The secularization thesis has come under criticism even in the West but it is certainly not the necessary pattern of response to modernization throughout the world. Moreover, Hadden and Schupe do not mention the link between fundamentalism, nationalism and the tensions that can exist between loyalty to nation and loyalty to God or the 'unholy' alliances that can be created between the two, as in India or Sri Lanka.

In order to understand the contemporary manifestations of 'fundamentalisms' in Islam it is necessary to realize that the historical formation of a religion and its development of unique patterns of behaviour arising from both interpretation of its sacred texts and the founding of tradition will have an impact on the present situation. It is my contention that once certain social and cultural forces impact on societies with a strong religious allegiance, then the shape of the religious response will be dictated by the unique past of the faith tradition. In this respect, any observers of Muslim fundamentalism need to be aware of certain factors as outlined below before going on to explore the contemporary politico-religious scenarios.

The Qur'an describes history as a linear struggle between titanic forces of good and evil that originated with the creation of human beings. The battle is fought out between the forces of Shaitan (Satan) and Allah for the hearts and minds of human beings. The example of the prophets of God and successive divine revelations become the main vehicles to maintain human beings on the 'Straight Path' that leads to surrender and servitude to the divine being. In this cosmic battle, there is no plane of existence that is not effectively involved in the struggle for obedience to the divine will. Shaitan's divine imperative to be the tempter of men and women manifests both within the human personality and in the various social, political and economic activities of human societies. Muslims perceive Islam as the last and final revelation, the vanguard of the cosmic struggle, to be maintained in its purity and totality, in order for it to provide the means for human victory over evil and the vehicle for God's final vindication at the last days.

Although initially applied to the pre-Islamic world of the Arabs, the concept of *jahiliya*, signifying a condition of idolatry, godlessness, social injustices, immorality and a dependence on the self as opposed to obedience to the divine will, can be applied to all societies throughout history that have failed to obey the messengers of God and the message, or, alternatively, appear not to have received any such guidance. Past examples of this mentioned in the Qur'an would be Sodom and Gomorrah and Egypt under the pharaohs. The condition of ignorance exemplified in the term *jahiliya* offers the opportunity for some Muslims thinkers and activists, since first articulated by Sayyid Qutb, to find a framework to criticize Western society and the condition of contemporary Muslim societies.

The doctrine of 'Manifest Success', in which the signifier of God's covenant with his chosen people is demonstrated by worldly achievements, contains within it a pattern of religious revival and reform. Any major worldly failure is likely to be perceived as a sign of divine displeasure and a marker to Muslims that they have left the 'Straight Path', not so much as individuals who may have maintained their own state of piety, but as the final religious community entrusted with revelation. Thus a pattern of religious revival as a response to political or social decline is established.

The attempt by Muslims, both as a community and as individuals, to maintain and promote 'the Straight Path' can be defined as jihad. Thus jihad is about far more than holy war; however, war is permitted to Muslims in certain circumstances. In a wider sense, jihad is the response to the cosmic conflict scenario and the immediate struggle to overcome *jahiliya*. It is more likely to be called for at all levels, both individually and collectively, when political or social decline is identified. If the political decline is perceived to be influenced by outside forces, the emergence of powerful enemies from outside the world of Islam, it is likely to provoke calls for military struggle as a defence against their oppression. Thus religious revivals call for a return to personal piety, the reform of Muslim society and possibly violent struggles against perceived external oppressors, all of which are likely to appear simultaneously when Islam is perceived to be in danger.

As we have seen, the doctrine of 'Manifest Success' leads to a pattern of religious revival as a response to external crises. In addition, the Muslim worldview of Islam as the final revelation gives an urgent need to protect the 'purity' of God's revealed practices and beliefs. For Muslims there can be no replacement of their revelation, as they believe happened to Judaism and Christianity (the revelations that were given before the advent of Muhammad and the Qur'an) for it is believed that Muhammad was the 'seal of the Prophets' and the Qur'an is the co-eternal Word of God in its entirety. Thus, as mentioned earlier, it has come to be a part of traditional Muslim belief that Allah sends a reformer every hundred years to maintain the revelation and destroy any innovatory departure from it. Any movement with a new charismatic leader endowed with personal piety and the energy to impact on the world around him can claim that their leader is the *mujaddid*. A special *mujaddid* is also believed to appear every thousand years.

Historically the various Kharijite movements that formed after the death of Muhammad provide a number of significant features that supply a model for those who would struggle against perceived injustices and political corruption of the Muslim *umma* in the contemporary period. Although the Kharijites were ultimately unsuccessful in their struggles to establish leadership based on personal piety rather than hereditary dynasties, and eventually disappeared from the spectrum of sects in the Muslim world, the Kharijite critique of nominal allegiance to religion remains as a powerful symbol of resistance. In particular, their redefinition of who is included within the Muslim fold to exclude those who are only nominal Muslims becomes a potent justification for modern revivalist movements to categorize as non-Muslims those who submit to governments perceived as secular or oppressive. In addition, the Kharijite understanding of the Muslim *umma* as a righteous and active remnant, rather than the totality of all Muslims, gives the impetus for *jamaat*-style movements to revive Islam and ferment revolutionary change within Muslim nations.

Later in the thirteenth century the invasion of the Mongols and the subsequent sacking of Muslim centres of culture, political administration and religion led to considerable self-questioning; in fact, a perfect example of the conditions that lead Muslims to seek to reform and renew their covenant with Allah. Ibn Taymiyya lived through the traumatic period after the Mongol sacking of Baghdad in 1258 and the fall of the Abbasid Empire and he sought to discover reasons for the inconceivable; the defeat of the Islamic world by apparently barbaric and polytheistic infidels. As a learned scholar of the Hanbali school of law, the most conservative of the four schools of law, he called for a literalist interpretation of the Qur'an and *Sunna* and the observation of Islam based on the period of the Prophet in Madinah and continuing through to the end of the first four Caliphs who had been Companions of the Prophet. Thus the first generations of Muslims are promoted as the ideal for Islamic belief and practice. Linking religion to statecraft, he called for a return to the values of Madinan Islam, the first Islamic state, rather than the later Islamic empires centred on Damascus or Baghdad. Finally and significantly, noting the failure of the Mongol converts to Islam to leave the legal codes created by Genghis Khan and embrace the *shari'a*, he followed the Kharijite precedent and branded them as non-Muslims (*kafir*), no better than the polytheists of the pre-Muslim Arab *jahiliya*.[7] Ibn Taymiyya takes on a special significance in the contemporary period as the foremost inspiration for all of the revivalist movements and their founders. Emmanuel Siven describes him as 'the model for revivalists and vigilantes, for fundamentalist reformers'.[8]

The eighteenth century was marked by the acceleration of European expansion and colonialism begun in the seventeenth century, and although it reached its zenith in the nineteenth century, the Muslim world began to feel a distinct sense of unease at its own decline and the emergence of the European powers. This time it appeared that divine providence had rewarded the older people of God – the Christians – with 'Manifest Success', resulting in a number of European victories over Muslim forces and the subjugation of Muslim nations. Whereas in previous eras, the revival and reform of Islam were to appear in localized contexts, responding to local crises, the eighteenth century witnessed Muslim revivals along similar lines across the gamut of the Muslim world. From Southeast Asia, Arabia to Africa, significant Muslim figures created movements to reform Islam. Out of these simultaneous revolutionary responses, perhaps influencing each other through significant meetings at the Hajj, the most important has to be the radical attempt to reform the original heartlands of Islam – Arabia – by Muhammad ibn al-Wahhab. The successful cleansing of Arabia of its countless shrines, tombs and sacred objects associated with popular Sufism was linked to the Prophet's cleansing of the pagan gods from the Ka'aba and was achieved by joining the religious zeal of Muhammad Wahhab with the temporal power of Muhammad ibn Saud, a local tribal chieftain. The combination was to create the first Islamic state, to be henceforth known as Saudi Arabia, but more significantly a global religious movement that to this day remains influential as it promotes the ideals of its founder throughout the Muslim world as the 'authentic' and 'pure' version of Islam. This movement was to become known as al-Wahhabism, but is more often invoked by the enemies of such revivalists, extending it beyond the actual heirs of Muhammad ibn al-Wahhab to include any movement or ideologue that espouses similar ideas or promotes renewal and reform.

Although the jihad (in this case literally meaning armed struggle) movements that appeared in the various parts of the Muslim world during the eighteenth and nineteenth centuries generally disappeared as a viable response to colonization because of the superior firepower of the various European forces, the ideal of reform and renewal based on the ideal of a return to Islam's pristine past did not. Invariably the eighteenth-century movements turned to education of their own local Muslim populations, attempting to safeguard them from popular Sufi practices and contamination from Western culture and ideas. Even the Wahhabi regime of Saudi Arabia saw more mileage in spending its new-found oil wealth on education of Muslims worldwide than promoting revolution through armed struggle.

The twentieth-century revivalist movements are much more explicitly political. Although earlier reformers, for example Ibn Taymiyya and Muhammad Abdul Wahhab, had called for a symbiotic relationship between religion and politics based on the paradigm of the first Muslim community in Madinah and the early Caliphate, they were not so explicit in their challenge to Muslim governments nor did they regard the West as complicit in maintaining such regimes, for quite simply they both pre-dated the colonial era. The connection between religion and governance, however, is promoted by Ibn Taymiyya, who asserted that government is one of the most essential requirements for Islam. In his view, the ongoing struggle and obligation to 'command the right and forbid the wrong cannot be achieved without power and authority'.[9]

The Social and Political Context

Any discussion of Islam and fundamentalism has to take account of the wider political, social, economic and cultural contexts framed within the context of both recent and more distant history. It is necessary to examine a number of issues such as secularization; the rise of modernity and modernism since the Enlightenment, and the subsequent industrialization of the West; the alternative consequent worldview of scientific discovery and its implications for religion; the rise of the nation-state as normative for the political organization of human society; globalization of consumer capitalism; and the continuing post-colonial dominance of the West, increasingly transferred from old European colonial powers to the new post-colonial economic and military dominance of the USA.

The relationship between these factors is complex. Very often modernization has arrived in the Muslim world dressed up in the clothes of secularization (defined here as the separation of religion into the private sphere of life and its removal from the public domain) and Westernization. This process has marginalized Islam from the processes of state and society in both the colonial and post-colonial periods. Many Muslims have rightly insisted that this is imposing a Christian model on Muslims (render unto Caesar that which is Caesar's) and ignoring the unique nature of Islam's revelation, where governance and God are interwoven through *shari'a* and the fundamental issue of Allah's sovereignty and humankind's intended response of submission to God's will. Thus many Muslim thinkers have called for modernization to be sifted out from Western models of secularization and given a uniquely Islamic mode of expression and development. However, such a project becomes increasingly difficult as the world becomes smaller and more interconnected through technological advances, and corporate capitalism with its emphasis on consumerism takes hold everywhere.

The Iranian revolution in 1978 first shattered the composure of those with faith in the paradigm of modernization being linked to the secular nation-state and since then the world has seen a revival of Islamic religious alternatives entering the political international arena. Although this phenomenon of religious nationalisms has been observed across the spectrum of religions, John Esposito points out that 'the discrediting and, in some cases, dethronement of secular paradigms has been particularly vivid in the Islamic world'.[10]

It is my contention that in the case of Islam it is necessary to explore and understand the relationship of religion in the role of nation-building in the post-colonial era and to place 'Islamic fundamentalism' within the framework of liberation movements. In addition it is important not to oversimplify Muslim reactions by focusing only on high-profile jihad movements.

The significance of these movements goes far beyond high-profile and notorious acts of violence undertaken against the Western world. The recent attacks on the West exemplified by the iconic but terrible success of the events of 9/11 are significant in that they appear to demonstrate a move away from the pattern of national resistance movements seeking to find local solutions to the perceived crises towards a concerted internationalization or globalization of the conflict.

The degree to which this is true can be measured by comparing Huband's book, *Warriors of the Prophet*, written in 1995, and Esposito's *Unholy War*, published in 2002 after the events of 9/11. Huband's book provides chapter-by-chapter case studies of revivalist movements in the Muslim world located within their unique local situations.[11] On the other hand, Esposito focuses on the 'Muslim world' and why it hates 'the West'. In it, Osama bin Laden is described as a 'global terrorist'.[12] Esposito states that: 'The twenty-first century will be dominated by the global encounter of two major and rapidly growing world religions, Christianity and Islam, and by the forces of globalisation that will strain relations between the West and the rest.'[13] There are a number of problems with this approach, not least the juxtapositioning of Islam and Christianity as adversaries. Certain kinds of Christianity, most commonly those found in the Bible Belts of the USA, do seem to be at odds with the Muslim world, especially over the issue of Israel/Palestine. It is common to find Muslims being demonized as the army of Satan prior to Armageddon in the literature of such types of Christianity. These types of popular belief are paralleled in the Muslim world, where there are also some imminent millenarian expectations of the end of the world. Although Esposito insists that globalization will strain relations between Islam and the West, it is also true that such forces obscure traditional boundaries and will not only bring Westernization to the Muslim world but also bring Islam into the West itself. In many European nations it is already the second largest religion after Christianity. As will be seen in Chapter 6, this also brings with it tensions between rival sets of values.

Certainly 9/11 and other incidents alert us to the globalization of the conflict and a paradigm shift away from national and regional struggles. This has been accelerated in the meetings of various Islamic movements in Afghanistan, where individuals from around the world fought alongside each other against the Russian occupiers and then dispersed to various more localized struggles. However, their new-found camaraderie with each other gave them an international dimension. Thus volunteers from various radical Islamic movements have been found in Bosnia, Palestine, Chechnya and Iraq and have now returned to Afghanistan via strongholds in the northwest frontier territories of Pakistan. However, it would be wrong to oversimplify the globalization of the Islamic jihad movements. To a large degree they remain national and regional movements and the presence of international fighters is not always welcomed by local leaders and people.

Tensions may also exist ideologically between local homegrown movements that came into existence through the desire to create Islamic regimes out of an existing secular Muslim nation and international Muslim fighters who may insist that the very idea of a nation-state is not Islamic and that Muslim activists should be struggling for a universal Caliphate that would represent and embody the ideal of the *umma*.

Politically, a number of world events in the years since the collapse of the Soviet Union – namely the failure to resolve the Palestinian issue, the apparent lack of support by the West for Chechnya's struggle for independence, the ethnic cleansing of Muslims in the Balkans, the invasion of Iraq and Afghanistan, and the presence of American troops in Saudi Arabia – have reinforced conspiracy theories amongst young Muslims in particular and led to the popular view on the streets of Muslim cities worldwide that the USA and its allies have declared war on Islam itself. It is clear, however, that the election of Barack Obama as American President and the removal of the neo-conservative regime of George Bush and the Republican Party has changed the rhetoric of a 'War on Terror' directed primarily against various Muslim regimes and movements to a new softer tone in an attempt to repair the damage done to the US's reputation in the Muslim world.

The Western media's focus remains on global terrorism, and the supposed ability of al-Qa'eda to strike anywhere around the globe or recruit others locally to the same end still remains the tone of police, intelligence forces and government spokespersons. The public is informed via the media that the threat of global terror remains and vigilance is essential. New anti-terror laws are brought in and crucial debates set up concerning the importance of national security over and above human rights and individual liberty. We are told that the justification for the invasion of Iraq and Afghanistan was to ensure that the terrorists cannot use such places as bases for operations against the Western world and its way of life. However, the significant impetus of such conflicts still remains local, either as continuing various national or regional struggles around the world to establish Islamic states or to give Muslim communities in multicultural environments such as Indonesia, Malaysia or the Philippines more authority in the legal frameworks of the nation or autonomous control over territory. Thus the relationship between religious fundamentalism and nationhood remains an essential aspect of any attempt to understand the former.

Fundamentalism and Nationhood

In a scathing article, John Shepherd does not spare the scriptures of the three 'Abrahamic' religions and demonstrates that any literal approach to their content will justify the use of violence, in spite of the attempts by liberals and modernists in each of them to issue sets of apologetics that rationalize violent incidents or teachings in the face of contemporary criticism and human rights discourse.[14] However, more significantly Shepherd points us to the linkage of a religious people chosen by God to a 'promised land'. The origins of such a phenomenon, of course, lie in the promise of God to the ancient tribes of Israel. Shepherd writes:

> Thus the Jewish tradition celebrates, as in good measure foundational, what is euphemistically termed the 'entry into the promised land' – an event that in practical terms is described as a bloody conquest with periodic divinely sanctioned massacres and would-be genocide, inaugurating a history of intolerance and persecution of idolaters and deviants.[15]

Shepherd provides us with an analysis of Jewish fundamentalism that links certain forms of contemporary Jewish orthodoxy with the campaign to re-establish a Jewish state consistent with biblical borders and governed by the implementation of the *Halakhah*, a religiously inspired legal system that governs every aspect of life according to God's revelation to the Jews. Shepherd points out that certain forms of Christianity have also possessed self-perceptions of themselves as the new chosen people with rights to a new promised land.

This link between nationhood, identity and religion can also be found in the other forms of religious fundamentalism. Shepherd cites the examples of the Afrikaner state of South Africa and the 'Calvinist emphasis on "the elect" fused with inspiration drawn from the Hebrew scriptures to engender a sense among the Scots settlers in Northern Ireland that they too were a chosen people sent to redeem the land from idolaters'.[16] He makes the link to the original Puritan settlers in America, who also perceived themselves as a chosen people with a new promised land and equally had no regard for the non-Christian original occupants. He argues that to this day the USA retains a strong sense of identity based on a sacralized 'manifest destiny' as 'God's own country'. Although this is generally benign, the tendency of the Protestant right – dominant in the Bible belts of the American South – to exert pressure and make alliances with conservative Republicans does reassert the old promise of the Puritans and a role for a cleansed America in the final days and the struggle with Satan. Sacred soil is not a foreign concept to the populations of India and a variety of communal movements have organized themselves around religious identity and the recovery of a 'sacred territory'. Thus the Sikhs struggled in the Punjab throughout the 1980s to create a separate state of Khalistan; more significant in terms of contemporary Indian politics is the concept of Hindutva, which has created the ideal of Hindu India.

Certainly an early form of globalization significant in the Muslim perception of world history was the transformation of 'Christendom' into a collection of more or less secular nation-states. Although the religions of the world had struggled with each other for the hearts and souls of human beings, sometimes spilling over into violence especially when religion was linked to imperial powers, it was nothing compared to the threat offered to their hold on human loyalties provided by the new allegiance to nationhood. Fazlun Khalid acknowledges this when he says that the secular nation-states 'succeeded in persuading or coercing the rest of the human community to organize their lives in a like manner'.[17] Khalid argues that the resolution made by the League of Nations in 1920, asserting that the nation-state was the only legitimate form of government recognized by the world, directly contradicted the Qur'an's perception that humans were organized into large religious collectives whose ultimate aim was to transform and even encapsulate the entire world.[18] If Khalid's view is held by Islamic activists then the Muslim world cannot help but be dismayed by the proliferation of nation-states and the loyalty that their citizens can display towards them.

The nation-state needs to be seen in the context of a particular ideology that had become increasingly identified with the Western world since the Enlightenment. As such it was not a neutral phenomenon but part of a highly successful new paradigm where societies, governments and nations centred themselves on rational organizational structures and developed a philosophy of endless progress through the fruits of scientific discovery. In other words the 'modernity' project of industrialization, secular education, the privatization of religion, and technical innovation took place alongside the ever-increasing numbers of the new nation-states, each competing with the other for scarce resources.

But there have been two major issues for Muslims in this new paradigm for the organization of human society. First, not all the new states were able to compete on a level platform with each other. Many of the new states were disadvantaged by recent histories of colonial domination and many Muslim nations fitted this category. The odds seemed to be stacked towards the old colonial powers of the West maintaining a relationship of dominance through economic and military superiority. Secondly, the Muslim nations were uncomfortable with the new paradigm on religious grounds. The humanist project that underlay the new secularism put humanity rather than God at the centre of the world. Human rights discourse replaced revelation as the new moral and ethical high ground. The rationalism and humanism that was to become dominant after the Renaissance gradually desacralized the cosmos.

The success of the European nations in the colonial projects they pursued resulted in what Zygmunt Bauman described as a climate of superiority where the rest of the world was perceived to be in a state of arrested development.[19] This appeared to apply particularly to Muslim nations, which were not only often poor, but were also attached to tradition and religiously conservative when it came to innovation. Khalid states that the same movement that developed the modernist project also 'ushered in the age of the nation-states, deployed nationalism in the service of state authority, and promoted national interests as the criteria of state policy'.[20]

He also points out that Muslim elites produced by the modernizing project came to desire what the West had achieved.[21] A new middle class began to develop for those who had taken advantage of the education facilities on offer by the colonial powers. Generally, the opportunities were provided in order to train a middle-level administration that could work under the new authorities in ruling colonized territory. Some of the most successful of these new elites were educated in the universities of the Western nations and came to be firm believers in the educational, legal and political structures they observed in Europe. However, their education did not convince them that their colonization was just and it also provided them with the resources to campaign for freedom.

Ironically, it was those trained in Western values who led the way to independence, often at the helm of resistance movements. Once freedom from the colonial power was achieved they became the rulers of the new nation, which they determined should follow the modernist paradigm, competing with others in a global market and politically structured on either socialist or capitalist models borrowed from the influence of non-Muslim nations. However, as it has been pointed out, these new Muslim nation-states were rarely on level terms with their Western counterparts and often could not succeed in a world where the rich and powerful were determined to maintain and increase their prominence. Where economic success was achieved it was often with the loss of local culture, benefiting only the new elites and failing to carry either the religious elites or the common people along with its goals. Resistance or non-cooperation with the regime was often greeted by repressive measures. Corruption became rife as wealth was gathered into the hands of the Western-trained elites and increasingly there were those who came to believe that the modern secular nation-state had failed as a project in the Muslim world.

However, the first attempts to seek an Islamic solution for the Muslim world instead of the imported Western systems of social and political organization did not seriously consider an alternative to the nation-state and that remains true to the present day despite the creation of Islamic movements that seek a return to the Caliphate model of political organization. Rather, the newly formed Islamic movements influenced by the ideas of Maulana Mawdudi or Sayyid Qutb attempted to establish within their respective nations an Islamic solution based on the imperative to restore Islamic law in its entirety. A number of options were used to reach out and gain support from the people. These involved preaching, printing tracts, education, political activism, social welfare, and armed struggle where governments were intransigent or repressive.

Thus within a few decades of the second half of the twentieth century, many Muslim nations were involved in a prolonged struggle concerning how they should be structured and the debate was framed within concerns as to whether the state should be secular or religious. However, the criteria of success and competition being the goals of the nation-state were rarely challenged. To the revivalist or jihad movements, this success would come as a result of submission to God rather than turning to the essentially godless humanism embraced by the West since the Enlightenment.

Islam and Fundamentalism

Any analysis of fundamentalism within Islam has to take into account both of these vertical and horizontal approaches to the study of the Muslim world. Factors in the historical development of Islam will influence the shape of Muslim responses and reaction to certain political events in the present moment and the recent past, especially where Islam is perceived to be threatened by either internal or external forces or a combination of both. The most significant factor in the history of Islam that is likely to shape contemporary Muslim responses is the identified pattern of reform and renewal (*Islah* and *Tajdid*) that is seen to periodically occur whenever Muslim society or civilization is under attack or in decline.

A number of postures and attitudes towards the West have developed in response to Western hegemony, and, from a Muslim point of view, the domination of the world by the wrong authority. Since most of the Muslim world remains part of the poorest sectors on earth Muslims are also drawn towards Islamic rhetoric borrowing from the Qur'an's powerful voice concerning social injustice and divine retribution for the offenders. For the last hundred and fifty years the Muslim world has been overly concerned with how to react to Western domination; its economic, military, technical, scientific and educational superiority continuing over from the colonial to the post-colonial eras. As succinctly stated by S. Nomanul Haqq, 'the control of the world fell into the wrong hands'.[22] The responses range from Muslim apologetics, sometimes very naively expressed, through to bitter and violent antagonism towards anything perceived as Western. However, revivalist and reformist responses are not necessarily lethal to Western interests, nor do they always contemplate violent overthrow of their respective regimes, many instead seeking more peaceful methods of transformation through education and legitimate political processes. The danger is the temptation of various Muslim governments, often tainted by corruption and supported by Western interests, to heavily repress Islamic opposition.

Yet the most common response of Muslim rulers and governing elites to the domination of the West has been to duplicate as effectively as possible the Western paradigm for material success, and it is in reaction to such imitation that we find the more radical responses.

Robert Pope has written, 'politics is the place where fundamentalism becomes public',[23] but I would go further and argue that it is the combination of certain religious responses to political situations that actually defines fundamentalism as opposed to merely taking one's religion seriously or its sacred texts literally. However, caution has to be exercised when attributing the causes of Muslim revivalism in the twentieth and twenty-first centuries to 'common globalisation processes that can be attributed to secularisation', as quoted from Hadden and Schupe at the beginning of this chapter. The shortcomings of any such attempts to provide a universal causal analysis of 'fundamentalism' is that they do not acknowledge sufficiently the unique features or characteristics of religious beliefs and practices within a particular 'faith' community. As we have seen, a kind of secularization – as defined by models of nationhood that separated religion and governance – entered the Muslim world as their nation-states proliferated in the twentieth century. However, the claim by Muslim revivalists that Islam and politics are always inseparable is disputable. Even before the influence of the Western world, most Muslim rulers had made compromises with the *ulema* regarding the implementation of *shari'a*, often employing it no further than the laws concerning worship and private family law. Generally speaking, with the exception of certain jurists such as Ibn Taymiyya, this had been accepted pragmatically by the vast majority of Muslims and their religious leaders.

Thus any attempts to analyse the causes of Muslim revivalism, especially when linked to the ideology and pursuit of Islamic states, must be rooted in an anti-colonial and post-colonial discourse combined with attempts to redefine nationhood in uniquely Islamic terms. New narratives that interpreted original sources, namely the Qur'an and *Sunna*, were therefore required and a new generation of Muslim ideologues such as Mawlana Mawdudi and Sayyid Qutb responded to the *zeitgeist*, creating both new frameworks of understanding and activist movements.

In spite of the growth of organizations that are prepared to use violence against their own regime's accommodation with the West or to strike at Western interests or even attack Western nations, it would be too narrow a focus to describe only such organizations as 'fundamentalist'. In addition, it would not be helpful for the analysis of such movements, because organizations such as the Taleban in

Afghanistan and al-Qa'eda, although linked with each other for mutual benefit and seen by the Western media and the British and US governments as virtually identical 'terrorists', are very different phenomena and deserve to be treated as such if we are really going to understand their origins and objectives. Similarly, to label as fundamentalist any Muslim who takes his or her religion seriously, adhering to the *shari'a* where possible and living by the words of God as transcribed in the Qur'an and the Prophet's example, is ludicrous, and provides support to the views of those Muslim critics who argue that the term cannot be transferred from Protestant Christianity to Islam.

Contemporary revivalist movements in the Muslim world have certainly sought to advocate or create social and political changes based on scriptural authority; in fact it could be argued that they have overemphasized socio-political and cultural issues to the neglect of other aspects of religiosity in their interpretation of the Qur'an. In this respect they could be accused of selectivity in opposing certain aspects of modernity. Indeed, they have also opposed the vast majority of Muslims, perceiving their position as a compromise with modernity. Certainly, they claim that their interpretation of the scriptures is the authentic one, using it to develop a consistent ideology to bring religion back to the centre of public life. But it is also problematic to define Islamic fundamentalism as a modern phenomenon, as it has been shown that certain patterns of behaviour have occurred as a response to socio-political conditions since the first centuries of Islam, traditional or nominal allegiance to the religion having always been condemned by the advocates of reform and renewal. In addition, the characteristic looking back to an ideal past to be reconstituted in the future often discovered in fundamentalisms would seem to be logical behaviour for Muslims, in view of the religious core beliefs. Once one accepts that the present is imperfect then it is beholden on the devout to remain loyal to the religion's original truth claims. In such religious scenarios the past is seen to hold perfection. The hope then is that the past ideal can be resurrected in the future by either piety or activism.

Abdul Said and Nathan Funk argue that there are at least four paradigms for understanding the complexity of the contemporary Muslim world. They list these as: (i) the power political paradigm; (ii) the reformist paradigm; (iii) the renewalist paradigm; and (iv) mystical Islam.[24] The first paradigm describes the present condition of most Muslim nations, arguably borrowed from the Western conception of the nation-state but with a historical heritage of triumphalism left over from the old Muslim empires. It is this paradigm that I have argued provides the well-spring of contemporary Muslim revival in all its forms. Those who pursue revival and criticize the power/ political paradigm need not be militant. The reformist paradigm seeks to re-establish Islamic values through the twin processes of seeking the essentials of Islam and transforming social practices and belief in accordance with the spirit of the religion. Although critical of the contemporary Muslim political situation, the reformist paradigm may well harmonize with Western human rights discourse, issues of social justice, rights of women and ecological concerns.

The renewalist paradigm, however, tends to reject the idea that anything good can be found in the West in favour of Islamic solutions discovered by a return to an ideal primordial Islam found not only in the Qur'an and the *Sunna*, but also in the earliest Muslim communities. Only by a return to a pristine Islam and a rejection of the materialist, consumer societies of the West can Muslim fortunes be restored. It is further complicated by the very recent globalization of Islamic movements, where national 'liberation' movements concerned with radical transformation by the creation of Islamic states are intertwined with newer movements that see the conflict in terms of a universal *umma* struggling against a worldwide conspiracy to destroy Islam.

Lastly, Said and Funk mention mystical Islam, commonly referred to as Sufism, which advocates spirituality as the way to transformation, both individually and socially. However, the focus on Islam as an internal process and state of being in relation to God does not lessen the importance of the message of the Qur'an, and will further encourage the insistence upon a life of religious piety and rejection of materialism.

The popular press and, since the invasions of Iraq, the US Government, have conflated the power politics paradigm and the militant variations of the renewalists or revivalists to present a negative image of the Muslim world, even though the two groups are often bitterly opposed. It is certainly true that the more radical revivalists have come to dominate Islamic discourse in the last fifty years but there are signs of a revival of Islamic spirituality taking place. Certainly any analysis of the contemporary Muslim world would need to consider that millions in the Muslim world are in some way considering the possibility of religious solutions to questions of identity and purpose, and as dissent over the problems aggravated by industrialization and globalization of consumer culture.

To do so will require a renewed understanding of the Qur'an, for it is axiomatic that Muslims will need to work within a worldview that takes scripture as both guide and authority. But, even so, the Qur'an remains as not so much an elaborate and consistent set of doctrines as a 'rich and subtle stimulus to the religious imagination'.[25] As pointed out by Haqq, no reconstruction can claim 'epistemological finality on the part of the reader'[26] even though most Islamic movements will claim the privilege, not only amongst the revivalists but also amongst the more esoteric mystical movements.

While Islamic politics may claim to possess the authentic interpretation of the sacred texts it does so for expediency, a way of resistance against perceived Western hegemony set within a context of post-colonial power relations, globalization of consumer capitalism, fear of the success of secular values, but above all the context of discovering how to be Muslim within the competing arenas of ethnic and national identity. However, in the process of discovering how to have an Islamic renaissance in the twenty-first century, Muslims will need to remember, and millions of them already have, that the Qur'an is above all else a text to be used for guidance on submission to, and intimacy with, God. The central purpose of the *shari'a* in all its manifestations is to foster piety and godly living, not to create governments and nations.

Muslims are called by their religion to activism. As Yasin Dutton reminds us, the Qur'an's imperative voice insists that they should 'actively establish justice and combat injustice wherever and whenever possible'.[27] It would be too easy to place such a struggle into a dualistic framework that pits two worldviews against each other. Again as expressed by Dutton: 'We have thus, two world views: one that, in putting scriptural authority uppermost, declares its allegiance to a God-centred view of the world; and one that, in putting human authority of scientific discovery uppermost, declares its allegiance to a human-centred view of the world.'[28]

It need not be so polarized, for not everything in the West is bad, neither can everything that has been perceived as corrupt in the Muslim world be attributed to Western influences. That is too facile. However, I agree with Muslims that fundamentalism as broadly defined cannot be a useful category for Islam. The term is all too often used negatively to denote bigotry, irrationality, militancy and a pre-modern worldview. However, the analysis provided by sociologists such as Hadden and Schupe can provide us with a more narrowly defined usage of fundamentalism that does appear to describe certain kinds of Muslim revivalism manifesting since the second half of the twentieth century with definite political aims.

There are two religious revivals happening across the Muslim world: one that my Muslim friends label 'political Islam' and could accurately and usefully be defined as 'fundamentalism', and the other that they call 'faith-based Islam'. The causes of each phenomenon may be entwined with each other but to those who are returning in such large numbers to the practice of their religion, it is the desire, above all, to have a concrete living experience of God that is foremost. It does not help us to define such people as fundamentalists although they may seek fundamentals, nor does it help us to understand the recent rise of politicized religion in many traditions that may more accurately be called 'fundamentalisms'.

In the context of terrorism and the fear that it brings to both governments and civilian populations, perhaps the term 'fundamentalism' no longer resonates in quite the same way as it once did in the past. There is no doubt that it has negative connotations but since the rise of Islamic militancy and its readiness to use violence against both Muslim and non-Muslim populations, jihad has taken over as the predominant misused and misunderstood term. Jihad has certainly become both the most misinterpreted and disturbing aspect of Islam, now inextricably associated with the catastrophic events of 9/11, suicide bombers in Palestine, Iraq, Afghanistan and Pakistan, and all other acts of violence performed with a religious or political motive in any part of the Muslim world. It has been linked with an ongoing campaign by certain segments of the Muslim world to declare war on Western lifestyle in general, especially where secularization and consumer capitalism impact on Muslim societies through globalization. This has led to a 'clash of civilizations' thesis where the Islamic world replaces communism as the enemy of 'enlightened' and liberal democratic values. Muhammad Sirozi, picking up on this limited understanding of jihad, cites some Western critics of Islam, for example Daniel Pipes, as interpreting jihad as a 'holy war', 'to extend sovereign Muslim power'.[29] He goes on to accuse the Western media of being guilty of referring to jihad only in the context of 'terrorist attacks organized by so-called militant fundamentalist Muslims'.[30]

On the other hand, many devout Muslims have claimed that jihad has been misrepresented not only by the Western media but also by a minority of Muslims who interpret it only in the narrow sense of religious war. However, it is necessary to remind ourselves once again that the Muslim world is represented by a wide range of political and religious expressions, each of which may place a very different emphasis on the significance of jihad. It literally means to 'struggle' or to 'strive' and at first glance there appears to be a contradiction between this injunction to fight and the meaning of Islam itself usually understood by Muslims to signify 'peace'. Peace is commonly understood as the cessation of struggle but not in the context of Muslim understanding of the relationship with God. Instead 'peace' is synonymous with obedience, an act of surrender to Allah's will, a process that requires effort maintained throughout life to the final moment.

The idea of jihad then is built into the Muslim conception of the origins of humankind. From this perspective jihad is inextricably part and parcel of the Last Judgement when all human beings will receive divine justice according to their deeds. However, it is the present life of the believer where jihad is played out. There can be any number of differing emphases in the everyday application of jihad, from the general attempt to live a moral life according to the principles of the final revelation; the struggle to achieve a more just society based on God's precepts; utilizing one's time and energy in preaching or teaching in order to establish Islam in the world; inner transformation of the self (all defined as the greater jihad); and finally armed struggle in defence of Allah's last revelation, which might lead the believer to the blessed goal of martyrdom (lesser jihad). As stated by John Esposito: 'The Quranic notion of jihad, striving or self-exertion in the path of God, was of central significance to Muslim self-understanding and mobilization.'[31]

For the majority of Muslims, *jihad akbar* (the greater jihad) is of far more significance in their lives than *jihad asghar* (lesser jihad). Most will pass their lives without being involved in a 'holy war' to defend Islam. For the pious, jihad 'simply refers to a spiritual striving to attain nearness to Allah'.[32] The call to jihad, to participate in a cosmic struggle against evil, involves everyone, Muslim or non-Muslim, but for the believer it goes beyond the confines of only individual transformation. The Qur'an frequently calls upon Muslims to 'enjoin what is right and forbid what is wrong'[33] and Islam demands an active participation to forbid evil in the world, especially placed upon the hearts, minds and actions of Muslims who, as the recipients of final revelation, are the 'best of peoples, evolved for mankind'. This understanding of jihad is invoked by the Qur'an in the verse that states: 'Those who believe fight in the cause of Allah, and those who reject faith fight in the cause of Evil. So fight against the friends of Satan: feeble indeed is the cunning of Satan.'[34]

Thus, at the most inclusive definition of jihad, most Muslims would agree that it is 'the use of the powers, talents, and other resources of believers to live in this world in accordance with God's plan as known through the Islamic Scriptures'.[35] In this understanding, it can include social action, financial support, or private endeavours to live as a good Muslim and will utilize spiritual, physical, moral and mental resources.

However, it is the mission of the Muslim community as the trustees of Allah on earth to promote his final revelation to all human beings, and in the act of doing so, to defend the territory that has been reclaimed for God. Islam is more than individual piety; it has strong community awareness, an imperative from God to be His last community, a sacred people.

In the context of the Muslim community as the last people of God allied to jihad lies the idea of *da'wa*, literally 'to call', or 'to invite', in other words, the promotion of Islam to both non-Muslims and Muslims. *Da'wa* activities to non-Muslims take place mostly through preaching activities; however, such activities are directed at fellow-Muslims in order to bring them back into the practice of the faith. Thus the word 'revert' rather than 'convert' is more often heard in Muslim circles. The archetypal form of *da'wa* belongs to God, and involves his prophets and messengers communicating his revelation to believing people. This activity is then picked up by the conscientious believers in imitation of God's messengers. Muhammad Sirozi defines *da'wa* as 'a call or invitation to an individual, family, and others to take Islam as a way of life, to live in accordance with Allah's will, with wisdom and consciousness, nourished by His blessings'.[36]

There are a number of *da'wa* organizations around the world, including 'Tabligh-i Jamaat', which, although originating in Saharanpur in North India, has become truly international. The 'Tabligh-i Jamaat', a non-political organization, uses a tried and tested formula of sending out groups of volunteers on preaching tours. They base themselves in local mosques from where they conduct a campaign to bring Muslims back to communal prayer, going out from the mosques to knock on doors of households, in non-Muslim nations utilizing the resources of the local mosque officials. Other organizations may fulfil *da'wa* activities through preaching at university Islamic societies, setting out street stalls in city centres, or promoting their tracts and leaflets, utilizing the mosques as outlets. However, it needs to be noted that such organizations may also possess a political agenda and will usually represent their own strand of Islam even though calling upon the rhetoric of a 'universal Islam'.

For radical Islamic movements, *da'wa* is very often framed within a particular context in which Muslims are seen as having fallen away from the ideal practice of their religion and are called back to a purer form supposedly practised by Muhammad and the early Muslim community. Radical leaders who have called for a purification of the community from un-Islamic influences see the promotion of Islam at the individual, family and political levels as the means to provide Muslims with the renewed power of God that they need to take over leadership of the world once again. In Muslim countries, *da'wa* activities, especially by such organizations and individuals who call for the creation of an Islamic state, are more likely to include very successful social welfare programmes. It would be hard to ascertain the impact of such organizations in the recent Islamicization of the Muslim world. The return of countless Muslims throughout the world to the practice of their faith is a complex phenomenon, with local variants added to its causes. However, while not all Islamicization has a political dimension, there can be no doubt that the activities of the *da'wa* movements have been part of the process of the return to faith. The support for such movements can be measured by their successful social welfare activities on behalf of the urban poor, their incorruptibility compared to many Muslim secular officials, and the piety of their ranks.

To such movements jihad may be perceived to be the sixth pillar of Islam and therefore beholden on all believers. Muhammad al-Farag, an Egyptian member of 'Jamaat al-Jihad' (Organization of Holy War), argued that the decline of Muslim nations had been made possible by the lulling of the people into a state where they no longer knew that violent jihad was permissible against injustice and tyranny. He wrote the influential *The Neglected Obligation* in which he claimed that jihad was the forgotten sixth pillar of Islam and armed struggle was the duty of every Muslim against a decadent or corrupt society.

This ideal of a 'holy war' is not exactly a Muslim concept but rather a very loose translation of jihad borrowing on the Christian concept of 'crusade', used to refer to the act of liberating the Holy Land from Muslim possession and originating in Medieval Europe. The idea is that Muslims can legitimately turn to violent struggle for the defence of their religion or even move on the offensive in certain circumstances when the onslaught of their enemies is perceived to be imminent – a type of pre-emptive strike. In 1979, the Western world was shocked as the people of Iran rose up under the guidance and leadership of Ayatollah Khomeini and overthrew the powerful and autocratic regime of the Shah of Iran. Ayatollah Khomeini's justification for Islamic revolution and the overthrow of corrupt or tyrannical regimes was framed within a series of writings and speeches that outline the case for legitimate use of jihad. First and foremost, Khomeini did not see the mobilization of the people in the name of Islam as offensive but rather as a defence against oppression and tyranny that was particularly manifested through the exploitation of Iran's resources by the West.

> This misappropriation of wealth goes on and on: in our foreign trade and in the contracts made for the exploitation of our mineral wealth, the utilization of our forests and other natural resources, construction work, road building, and the purchase of arms from the imperialists, both Western and communist.[37]

In calling for jihad, Khomeini did not lessen the resolve of the Muslim people to pursue all the means for establishing Islam, such as the promotion of Islamic social, economic, moral and spiritual values, but he indicated that it is legitimate for devout Muslims to remove oppressive regimes. Citing various Hadith, for example, 'a word of truth spoken in the presence of an unjust ruler is a meritorious form of *jihad*' or 'there is no obeying the one who disobeys God', Khomeini called for a select band to withstand injustice and then to ignite the Muslim masses. 'Address the people bravely; tell the truth about our situation to the masses in simple language ... The entire population will become *mujahids*' (i.e. those who engage in jihad).[38] Khomeini particularly associated his call for a struggle against tyranny with US imperialism.

The method of jihad is twofold; first that the people should turn against oppression, and second that they should be led to a true Islamic society by a righteous minority 'who are just and ascetic and who fight in God's way to implement the laws of Islam and establish its social system'.[39] The solution was to be the establishment of an Islamic government: 'A government whose form, administrative system, and laws have been laid down by Islam.'[40] Such a state will not only provide protection for Muslims against the 'tyrannical regimes that imperialism has imposed' upon the Muslim people,[41] it will also provide the example that will stir popular revolutions throughout the Muslim world.[42]

Usually such calls to the lesser jihad are made in the defence of territory perceived as under threat from non-Muslim aggressors such as the armed struggle of Hamas to re-establish Palestine as liberated territory from Israeli occupation. This justification for jihad is repeated in Kashmir and Chechnya. These are primarily nationalist struggles concerned with perceived occupation by an outside power but given religious credibility by the old concept of *dar al-Islam* (territory of Islam) and *dar al-harb* (territory of war). The jihadist groups, such as 'The International Islamic Front for the Jihad Against Jews and Crusaders' led by Osama bin Laden, 'Laskar Jihad' led by Ja'far Umar Thalib in Indonesia, 'Harakat ul-Jihad-i-Islami' in Kashmir, 'Palestinian Islamic Jihad, Egyptian Islamic Jihad', and the 'Yemeni Islamic Jihad', are different in that they wage war to protect a particular vision of Islam according to their understanding of the original vision of the Qur'an and *Sunna*. They see this 'pristine' Islam of the Prophet under threat from 'corrupt' or 'tyrannical' Muslim regimes aided by the West. They either fight against those regimes in a particular locality or internationalize their campaigns by including the West, especially the USA, as part of a Judaeo-Christian conspiracy against Islam.

It might be difficult for the Western world to understand the violence that can erupt explosively from some of these groups, especially since the enormity of the events of 9/11, or to understand how such groups within Islam can justify their actions as defensive. However, the jihad movements still operate, in their terms, within the paradigm of a defensive war. Ba'asyir, the Indonesian ideologue for the Islamic movements, jailed for four years after the Bali bombing, insists that these were appropriate self-defensive actions in response to the violence of the United States against the entire Islamic world.[43]

Chapter 6

Islam and the West

English Muslims have adopted the faith not for personal advantage but because they believe it to be true, and the world will then know how to appreciate these courageous men and women who have boldly made a stand for truth.[1]

Islam in the West

A recent study has highlighted that the Muslim population in Europe is over 38 million. A further 3 million can be found in North America. If the 16.5 million who are found in Russia are included under the definition of 'West' the total Muslim presence in the West is around 60 million.[2] Germany, France and Britain have the largest populations in Western Europe. Germany with 4 million, mostly of Turkish origin, has the largest population (5 per cent of the total) – a larger number than Palestine, Lebanon or Kuwait. France's population, predominantly North African, is around 3.6 million (6 per cent)[3] and the UK has 1.6 million, predominantly South Asian Muslims (2.7 per cent).

Not all European Muslims are of migrant origin. Six million live in Bosnia (40 per cent), Albania (79.9 per cent) and Kosovo (89.6 per cent), the latter two countries being the only Muslim-majority states in Europe. These populations are long established, beginning when the territories were part of the Ottoman Empire. Conflict between Muslim Arabs and the Byzantine Empire began soon after the establishment of Islam, with conquest of the Syrian, Armenian, Egyptian and North African provinces of the Christian Empire. Although Constantinople was besieged twice and the Caucasus conquered, it was not until the fall of the capital of the Byzantines in 1453 that its European territories came under the sphere of Islam.

However, even before that significant date the Volga Bulgarians had accepted Islam as the state religion in the tenth century and much of European Russia and Ukraine had come under Muslim rule when the Mongols accepted Islam as their state religion in the early fourteenth century. The rise of the Ottomans brought the Crimea into their empire in 1475 and they began their expansion into Europe by capturing the Byzantine territories on the other side of the Bosphorus. By the mid-seventeenth century most of Eastern Europe was under Ottoman dominion and it was only in 1699 that they lost territories in central Europe at the Treaty of Karlowitz. Even though by 1922, when the Empire finally collapsed, most Eastern Europeans were no longer under the control of the Ottomans, many territories remained with large Muslim populations.

Muslim armies had also captured large territories in Western Europe. Sicily had been invaded in 652 and Spain and Portugal (Al-Andalus) became effectively Muslim nations by the tenth century. From bases in Spain they pushed into Aquitaine in Southern France in the eighth century, where they met with defeat at the Battle of Tours in 732. Southern Italy was gradually conquered by the Arabs and Berbers from 827 onward, and the Emirate of Sicily was established in 965. They ruled the region until their expulsion by the Normans in 1072. There is strong evidence to suggest that the Muslim presence in Southern Europe influenced the Renaissance of the twelfth century, when it is argued that many aspects of Muslim culture were introduced into Western Europe; however, Muslim rule in Western Europe was more short-lived than in Eastern Europe and, from 1238, only endured in the Emirate of Granada as a vassal state of the Christian Kingdom of Castile until the completion of La Reconquista in 1492. The Moriscos (converts to Christianity) were finally expelled from Spain between 1609 (Castile) and 1614 (rest of Spain), by Philip III during the Spanish Inquisition.

The tide turned and from the seventeenth century the European powers gradually established supremacy through expansion overseas and the creation of their various empires. At their heyday during the late nineteenth century and into the twentieth, European colonial empires (British, French, Dutch) colonized regions in the Muslim world such as North Africa, the Horn of Africa, the Malay archipelago, the Indian subcontinent and sub-Saharan Africa. It is during this period that small but significant populations of Muslim sailors, wealthy travellers and students came to visit or stay in the ports and capitals of the colonizing nations and some Europeans came into contact with Muslim populations and Islam. After these colonies achieved their independence in the middle of the twentieth century, they were in prime position to feed the demand of Western European countries for cheap labour as the latter half of the century provided opportunities for postwar reconstruction followed by economic expansion.

Today most of the Western European Muslims are descendants of these mid-twentieth-century migrants and new arrivals come only as asylum seekers or as part of family reunification. If these 38 million Muslims living in Europe are taken as a bloc it forms the ninth largest Muslim population in the world. It is surely the most diverse, and although various Western European nations are dominated by single regional groups all contain smaller populations from other parts of the Muslim world. It can be safely surmised that Western Europe contains populations from most Muslim-majority nations. The present chapter will look briefly at the Muslim populations of Germany, France and Britain.

Germany

As in most Western European nations, Islam is the second largest religion in the country, 4.3 million Muslims comprising 5.4 per cent of the population. The majority of Muslims in Germany is of Turkish origin (63.2 per cent), followed by smaller populations from Pakistan, countries of the former Yugoslavia, Arab countries, Iran and Afghanistan. The last three would be mainly of refugee origin whereas Turkish and Pakistani migrants are predominantly labour-migrants. Around 1.9 million Muslims have become German citizens (2.4 per cent)[4] and, as of 2006, it is estimated that around 15,000 are converts of German ancestry.[5] The populations are mostly concentrated in Berlin, Frankfurt, Hamburg and other large cities. There are relatively few Muslims in the former East Germany but, unlike France and Britain, Germany has significant populations in some rural areas of Bavaria and North Rhine-Westphalia. The population is religiously diverse, with the majority being Turkish Sunni (75 per cent) and a small population of mostly Iranian Shi'as (7 per cent), but there is also a significant Turkish Alevi population (possibly 20 per cent), a heterodox Muslim community whose religious life is difficult to ascertain as they often maintain *taqiyya* (a Shi'a practice that permits hiding one's faith in the face of persecution).

Most debates in Germany revolve around the question of Muslim religiosity and its impact on integration and citizenship issues. As in other Western European nations these revolve around the wearing of the *hijab* (head-scarf) by female Muslim teachers in schools and universities. Many of the German federal states have introduced legislation banning head-scarves for teachers and some German federal states have gone further and introduced legislation banning head-scarves in all professions. However, there are no laws banning the *hijab* from being worn by students. The controversial issue of the *hijab* is thorny on two counts. First, it raises questions about the oppression of women, rigorously denied by most European Muslim women, and second, it brings into sharp focus the German state's position that it is neutral on the question of religion. The issue of mosque construction in German cities has also aroused some animosity in the neighbourhoods concerned. There has also been concern about the level of qualification for mosque religious leaders (imams) with recent attempts to introduce a university qualification for German imams. In schools, religious education has also been problematic. In German schools the religious communities concerned organize their own curricula as part of an elective subject taught in state schools. Catholics, Protestants and Jews have successfully achieved this goal but Muslims have not been able to create a unified Islamic religious education due to there being no single religious organization that represents the interests of all Muslims in the country. It is being discussed whether alongside the Catholic and Protestant (and in a few schools, Jewish) religious education that currently exists, a comparable subject of Islamic religious education should be introduced. However, efforts to resolve this issue in cooperation with existing Islamic organizations are hampered by the fact that none of them can be considered as representative of the whole Muslim community.[6]

As with other Western European governments, Germany is concerned about Islamic radicalism and banned two Muslim organizations in 2002 as contrary to the nation's constitution. These were Hizb ut-Tahrir and the so-called Caliphate State founded by Cemalettin Kaplan and later led by his son Metin Kaplan. However, Germany's main concern has not been political Islamic radicalism and its implicit threat of terror. Its government may feel that the country's minimal involvement in the US-instigated 'War on Terror' and Germany's lack of a colonial past in Muslim regions of the world has lessened the threat of homegrown Muslim terror. More significantly,

Germany has been caught up in regional North European concerns relating to the protection of freedom of speech and the rights of religions to defend themselves against blasphemy. In the Netherlands, the homosexual movie director Theo van Gogh was killed by Mohammed Bouyeri, a Dutch Muslim, who claimed that he was responding to the blasphemous nature of some of the scenes in the film *Submission*, which criticized Islam's treatment of women. Van Gogh's partner in the production, Ayaan Hirsi Ali, had to leave for exile to secure her safety against extremist factions. In Denmark, the Danish newspaper *Jyllands-Posten* published cartoons representing Muhammad as a suicide bomber to highlight the issue of Islam's lack of tolerance. The cartoons caused an uproar in the Muslim world leading to attacks against Danish and Norwegian embassies. Several newspapers across Europe, including Germany, reprinted the cartoons as a way of taking a stand in the debate. It was inevitable that such controversies taking place in neighbouring countries with similar cultural values would impact on German attitudes towards their Muslim populations.

France

With the second largest Muslim population in Western Europe (3.6 million) France has the largest concentration (6 per cent) and nearly half are French citizens.[7] The vast majority of the Muslim population originates from North Africa (Algeria, 1,550,000; Morocco, 1,000,000; Tunisia, 350,000). There are also significant populations from Turkey (315,000), sub-Saharan Africa (250,000), the Middle East (100,000) and South Asia (100,000).[8] France also has a significant problem with illegal migrants, whose numbers are estimated at 350,000.[9] Surprisingly France claims that there are 40,000 converts and this may be explained to some degree by the higher levels of intermarriage in the country compared to Germany. Interestingly, a study carried out by the Institut Français de l'Opinion Publique (IFOP) showed that only 36 per cent of French Muslims described themselves as 'observant believers', with only 20 per cent attending *juma* prayers on Fridays. However, in common with other Muslim communities, a high percentage maintained the fast at Ramadan (70 per cent).[10]

Regardless of the numbers that claim observance, France has been affected by the growing demand of young Muslims to assert a Muslim

identity over and above their various ethnic identities. The desire for
a primary religious identity has clashed heavily with the dominant
French ideological position with regard to citizenship and religious
allegiance (*laïcité*). The term signifies the strict separation of Church
and state and the closest approximation in English is secularism. In
2003–4 the Stasi Commission, set up by Bernard Stasi to investigate
the application of *laïcité* in France, and the resulting law of February
2004, forbade school students to wear any conspicuous religious or
political signs or symbols, such as the Islamic headscarf, the Jewish
skullcap or large Christian crosses. The law took effect at the
beginning of the 2004–5 school year and has been seen as an attack
on Muslim women and their right to wear the *hijab* and other forms
of Muslim dress in a public space.[11]

The challenge for the French state is one of how to understand
'Muslim'. The precise meaning of the term remains contested between
those who perceive it as referring to an inherited culture and therefore
accessible to public negotiations and those who see it as the practice
of a religion and therefore existing only in the private realm of
individual life. In 2002, Nicolas Sarkozy, then Interior Minister,
helped to create the French Council of the Muslim Faith (*Conseil
Français du Culte Musulman* – CFCM) on the former understanding
of Muslim as a cultural identity. The involvement of the Paris Mosque
led many to challenge the existence of the organization as a compromise
of the principle of *laïcité*.

More problematic for the French Government has been the issue
of integration. Several political parties, such as far-right leader
Jean-Marie Le Pen's *Front National* and Bruno Mégret's *Mouvement
National Républicain*, believe that large numbers of immigrants with
non-Western European cultural backgrounds destabilize France and
insist that there is a clear danger in Islamist behaviour among the
immigrant Muslim population. In 2004, the French Government
responded to the claims of Islamicization by expelling several foreign
imams for preaching hate. France has suffered from terrorism but the
series of attacks in 1995 were linked back to Algeria and were far
more to do with very tight ties between France and its former colony
Algeria, and the internal conflicts in that country between Islamic
movements and the secular government vying for power, than they
were with the US-led 'War on Terror' post 9/11. Islamist activities are
more likely to be directed towards secular-orientated Algerians living
in France as part of ongoing campaigns to create an Islamic state in
Algeria.

France's main problems with its Muslim communities is how to integrate them into mainstream French life. This debate between integration and assimilation has become mixed up with the strong ideological commitment to French secularism or *laïcité*. The first generation of Muslim immigrants, who are today retired from the workforce, keep strong ties with their countries of origin, but most of them asked for French nationality before quietly retiring. They live isolated in housing projects, having lost their ties with their countries of origin. The second generation born in France also remain located in the housing projects in the suburbs of the major cities. Unlike other European countries, the French working classes reside outside the city centres in new dormitory towns with little infrastructure. Although most follow their religion within the French *laïcité* model it is hard for them to integrate further when kept in class/ethnic conclaves with little state assistance to aid them in such a venture. Thus the 2005 French Muslim riots – presented, especially to the foreign press, as an illustration of the problems of integrating Muslims in France – may have been more to do with French working-class suburban dissatisfaction and concerns relating to social/economic deprivation and isolation than with Islamic issues. So far, the French Government has no official policy towards making integration easier and insists upon its Muslim populations integrating into French life according to the citizenship model implicit in the concept of *laïcité*. The French Government and intelligence agencies estimate that a very low number of radical Muslims exist in the country and that the majority of French Muslims are relatively secularized. Estimates suggest that only 200,000 Muslims in France are committed to religious practices. The main concern is that French Islam is still strongly subject to outside North African influences and that this is perpetuated by the lack of French-educated French-speaking imams in the mosques and the resistance of Muslim women towards adopting European modes of dress.[12]

Britain

According to the 2001 census 1,536,015 Muslims live in England and Wales, where they constitute around 3 per cent of the population but are not evenly distributed. In England, 40 per cent of Muslims live in London, where they make up 8.5 per cent of the population. There are also large numbers of Muslims in Birmingham, Manchester, Bradford, Luton, Slough, Leicester and the mill towns of northern

England. In these cities they are concentrated in one or a few areas. Most Muslims in Britain originate from South Asia (in particular Pakistan, Bangladesh and India) but there are also substantial populations from the Middle East, Somalia, Malaysia, Turkey, the Balkans, Afghanistan, Iran, North Africa and Indonesia, while others have come from African countries such as Nigeria, Uganda and Sierra Leone.

The attacks on London's transport systems were especially shocking, as they were carried out by Muslim British citizens. The attacks aimed to induce a sense of crisis amongst British Muslims and British policy-makers concerning fundamental precepts of British democracy in the twenty-first century. A number of issues have come under the microscope, including issues of race, religion and discrimination, media depictions of Islam, the complexities of plural societies, identity formation and citizenship, cultural literacy, the quality of educational provision by both Muslim and non-Muslim providers, freedom of speech, the intellectual capacity of British Islam, and the inadequacy of religious leaders to meet modern challenges. In the aftermath, a new rhetoric concerning plurality has begun to emerge from government policy-makers in which the overemphasis on diversity in multicultural and pluralist discourses has been perceived to be at the cost of integration.

However, these events, however traumatic, should not lose sight of transformations that have been taking place amongst British-born Muslims since the 1980s, and accelerating into the twenty-first century. These changes could be summarized as a renewed focus on issues of minority citizenship in an Islamic context as opposed to the older attempts to resolve the dichotomy of regional ethnicities and belonging to the Muslim *umma* (community).[13] The tragic events of 7/7 will, if anything, accelerate the change of discourse in the Muslim communities even faster than the processes of ageing and the inevitable transferral of authority from the first-generation migrants to their British-born offspring.

It was the younger generation of British-born Muslims, especially those influenced by a modified post-Mawdudian radicalism, who provided the evidence to demonstrate a shift in the relationship between religion and ethnicity as they grappled with three major factors in their identity formation; that is British, Muslim and Pakistani/Bangladeshi/Indian etc. In fact, it went further than that, for within each national category there were intense regional identities; for example, Punjabi, Bengali, and Mirpuri.

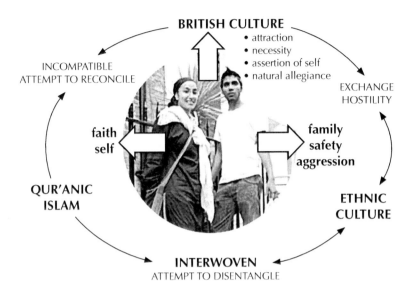

The diagram above shows the three major categories, labelled as ethnic culture, Qur'anic Islam and British culture. The three identities are in a state of dynamic tension with each other resulting in positive and negative exchanges as they interact. In the first stages of migration, the major interactions take place between British culture and ethnicity. Islam principally plays a functional role as a marker of identity as first-generation Muslim engage in micro-politics focused on community-building.[14] However, the second generation find themselves drawn towards British identity as a natural allegiance of birth and as a result of socialization processes. However, the tensions that can exist between the loyalties of parents towards ethnic identity at the place of origin and the social norms of the new culture can be very difficult to negotiate. Thus we find British-born Muslims beginning to move away from the engagement between ethnic cultures and to develop a discourse based on religion as their primary identity. The term 'British Islam' was beginning to gain currency amongst the generation born and raised in Britain even back in the early 1990s and had found institutional expression with the advent of the Islamic Society of Britain. In this position, Islam is paramount and moderates over and determines the content and shape of ethnic and national identity. The debates of the 1990s were to set religion and ethnicity at odds with each other and resulted in attempts to discover an Islamic identity that could resolve these tensions. The advantages of such an approach were that Islam was perceived as a universal identity able to be allied with any national loyalty, which, as a primary identity, provided a global ethic and code of behaviour that transcended locality. Today the picture is changing again. As young British Muslims have moved into negotiating Islamic identity with British identity, issues of religion and citizenship have become paramount.

Successful negotiation of these three strands of identity can lead to a British Muslim being able to enjoy the best of all worlds, integrating Britishness and Islam, but with ethnicity weakening or taking on new hybrid forms. However, imbalance can result in identity crises that can lead to the pathological in extreme cases. Too much focus on maintaining ethnicity can lead to isolation and living in a past that becomes increasingly difficult to hold on to. Too much focus on scriptural Islam can lead to fundamentalism and a literalism that is not fluid enough to cope with living in a non-Muslim environment. Too much emphasis on Britishness at the expense of Islam, with an accompanying loss of ethnicity, can lead to an assimilation that leaves the individual isolated from community roots and origins.

The efforts of the new generation to shift the debate away from ethnicity towards citizenship were to be complicated by the worsening international political situation. Many had been attracted to the teachings of the most influential Islamicists of the twentieth century, Maulana Mawdudi and Sayyid Qutb. Both these activists offered two very powerful ideas. The reinterpretation of the *shahada* to focus on the sovereignty of Allah led to a powerful critique of Western society and institutions as *shirk* (idolatry) and the emergence of Islam as a political ideology. In such thinking, the ills and imbalances of the contemporary world order could be righted by embracing Islam and its political, legal, social and economic institutions wholeheartedly and rooting out from Muslim societies the man-made compromises with Western systems that were the consequence of the recently past colonial relations. The objective in the Muslim world was the foundation of Islamic states. The second potent idea was connected to the first and posited that any Islamicization, whether individual or communal, required the purification of Islam from any cultural innovations that had been added historically to the religion as practised in some ideal past (either in Madinah or by the first three generations of Muslims). Although the majority of British-born Muslims essentially rejected the idea of an Islamic state in Britain as hopelessly utopian, the idea of an Islam that existed free from cultural accretion was a powerful symbol for a generation trying to carve out an identity that released them from the requirement to maintain the cultures of their parents. If Islam could exist in a pristine state, it could provide its own independent cultural identity but one flexible enough to integrate with other systems of identity where there was a symbiosis with Islamic norms.

New movements appeared that offered British Muslims the organizational avenues to make concrete these two idealizations. For those who adopted both visions, the dream of a pure Islam manifested in an Islamic state led to the advent of radical 'rejectionist' movements such as Hizb-ut Tahrir and al-Muhajiroun. The majority of British activists, however, embraced the ideal of a pure Islam as a strategy for working with British institutions in partnership without losing sight of Islamic values. The result was the creation of the influential 'participationist' movements such as ISB (Islamic Society of Britain), MAB (Muslim Association of Britain) and MCB (Muslim Council of Britain).[15] These 'participationist' movements have travelled far from the original radical positions of Qutb and Mawdudi, moving towards mainstream politics and integration, framing their discourse within citizenship issues and Islam's compatibility with democracy. The minority who have remained loyal to the radicalism of the two ideologues continue to proclaim loudly that democracy, founded on the tenet of the sovereignty of the people, is at odds with the rule of Allah and constitutes an enemy to be struggled with and overthrown by the law of God and the triumph of Islam.

However, the old reformist argument of removing cultural accretions to find a 'pure Islam' can result in a loss of richness and diversity that generations of tradition have established as part of the religion. At worst it leads to forms of fundamentalism and primitivism, even aggressive radicalism that has plagued Islam in the last twenty years. On the whole, the varieties of British Sufism were not prone to such forms of primitive Islam but they were open to criticisms of cultural accretion as long as they were unable to discern where tradition and ethnicity separated. On the other hand, they retained an inner piety and aura of spirituality that appeared to be absent from the more politicized reform movements.

Recent voices are emerging that appear to take account of these factors and are prepared to draw upon the new reform rhetoric of moderation, citizenship and participation in Western democracies and also realize the value of Muslim piety and spirituality. Whilst on one hand encouraging British Muslims to participate actively in British democratic institutions from a standpoint of Islamic values and to reassess their position as citizens of a non-Muslim society through creative reinterpretation of the Qur'an and Hadith utilizing the methodology of traditional Islamic sciences, on the other hand they are deeply aware of the lack of spirituality in many socio-political Islamic solutions. Tariq Ramadan calls for 'the birth of a new and authentic Muslim identity, neither completely dissolved in the Western environment nor reacting against it but rather resting on its own foundation according to its own Islamic sources'.[16]

European Islam

Tariq Ramadan has developed a profile that is European in scope and has taken the concept of 'British Islam' and developed it to provoke discussion concerning 'European Islam'. He calls for the creation of a new European-Muslim identity and demands participation of Muslims in social and cultural life in conformity with European culture and Muslim ethics, saying that Muslims should disassociate themselves from militant foreign influences.[17] He also thinks that European Muslims 'need to separate Islamic principles from their cultures of origin and anchor them in the cultural reality of Western Europe'[18] but he is equally keen to promote the idea that Europeans need to begin considering Islam as a European religion.[19] The political scientist Bassam Tibi is attributed with creating the term 'Euro-islam', referring to liberal and progressive interpretations that distance themselves from the radical voices and acknowledge the separation of 'church' and state. Western academic commentators on Islam and the West are joining the debate. Jocelyn Cesari, a French academic, also agrees that Islam should be merged into European culture and that Islamic culture should be added to Europe's educational curricula.[20] In 2007 the European Commission entered the fray, similarly arguing that the most effective way to tackle the radicals prepared to use violence is to create a 'European Islam', an Islam that is a more tolerant 'European' branch of the faith.[21]

So some Muslims who live in the West are now faced with a dilemma. On the one hand, similar to Abdullah Quilliam in the nineteenth century, they want to live out their Islamic life incorporating

Islamic values in an all-encompassing manner which includes involvement in the civil society of their new locations, but they may have to face the reality that the democratic institutions they inherit in the West arose outside of the framework of Islam and may even embrace a secular mentality that has no place for religion in public life. Even worse, secularism may be celebrated in the West as the means through which ordinary people discovered individual freedom and liberated themselves from the restraints imposed upon them by organized religious life. This is not a position that is likely to find much sympathy from the religiously orientated Muslim, who sees citizenship as more to do with divinely given responsibilities conferring certain rights that are to be enjoyed by the faithful than a human rights paradigm based on individual liberty. Rippon argues that in the face of such difference, Muslims will divide into three basic typologies: isolationary traditionalists, radical rejectionists and involved reformists.[22]

The problem here is that Islam in the West gets caught up in Islamic and Western politics. To complicate matters it will depend on where the Muslims living in the West originated and the history of the relations between religion and politics in the respective Western nation where Muslims have settled. The relations between Islam and democratic processes vary in different regional locations and according to the way in which Western modes of government integrated with Muslim governance at the end of the colonial era. Sometimes the process of integration was complementary but in other places it was contrary. A number of scholars have analysed the processes whereby democratic institutions have appeared in Muslim nations and divided them into instances where Western modes have been imposed upon a Muslim location and those where Islam has been used as a resource to commit Muslim countries to the values of democracy.[23] The process has been nowhere easy. Islamic religious revival has complicated the process even further. Democracy may be perceived as the rejection of Islamic legal systems in favour of aping the West. This may be seen as secularization and the continuation of colonial relations in a post-colonial setting. On the other hand, Islamic movements may challenge undemocratic institutions in their respective political systems and seek to develop and protest for the implementation of Islamic democratic models such as *shura*.[24]

Islam and the West

The phrase 'Islam and the West' needs to be taken with care by students of the subject area. At its worst it can be seen to represent a polarization of two irreconcilable and immutable entities that regard each other with hostility and suspicion as repositories of 'uncivilized' values. In such a scenario Muslims would typically regard the West as a moral desert in which citizens have moved away from the God-given laws of Christianity to post-Enlightenment man-made legal systems which replaced divine revelation with human-centred secularism. In such an analysis of Western society, secularism is often equated with atheism. There is no doubt that certain elements amongst conservative and radical religionists perceive the West in these terms and brand it a new 'jahiliya'.[25] From the other side, since the 'War on Terror' was announced by the neo-conservative government of US President George Bush, there have been a number of academics and journalists who have posited the idea of a clash of civilizations in which Islam is perceived as the barbarous 'other', outdated and outmoded in the face of democratic liberal values that are implicitly heralded as the pinnacle of human social, moral and political achievement.[26] In reality, the positions taken from both sides are far more nuanced.

Clarke, writing in 1997, believed that the 'master-myths of polarity and complementarity between East and West may be at last in the process of out-running their usefulness'. He considers that both terms, 'East' and 'West', have lost whatever coherent meaning they may once have had.[27] Promoting an optimistic version of globalization, Clarke argues that, worldwide, ideas and institutions are being transformed by 'cultural and political energy' whose origins lie in the West. In this respect, he agrees with Francis Fukuyama's position that in the post-communist era, Western institutions and political ideals will spread throughout the world.

This optimism of Clarke and Fukuyama is sometimes contrasted with Huntingdon's 'clash of civilizations' thesis. However, Fukuyama's optimism originated in the economic boom of Southeast Asia, now joined by China. So far there is little evidence of Muslim nations benefiting in the same way. Bedevilled by corrupt regimes, they remain amongst the world's poorest communities, thus providing ammunition for those who would seek solutions in conspiracy theories and external threats of a war on Islam. Huntingdon's thesis is located in tensions between the Muslim world and the West and thus contributes to the body of Orientalist literature that has historically promoted divisions. What is certainly significant is that, even when one removes the politicization of Islam, Muslims are returning to their religion and its traditions around the globe. They may well form the strongest resistance to the globalization features proclaimed by Fukuyama, for they do not tend to see them in the same optimistic light, not necessarily because they oppose the economic benefits of Western consumer society, but because they see deficiencies in the latter that all the world's great religious founders warned against.

A closer examination of 'Islam and the West' would reveal that the phrase contains a number of distinct categories that require unpacking. The first category would indeed include an understanding of the constructed realities of 'Islam' *and* 'the West', historically competing with each culturally, both politically and religiously. The second category is 'Islam *in* the West'. This category can be subdivided into (a) the historic contribution of Islamic civilization to European cultures, (b) the colonization of European territory by the Ottomans and Moors which has resulted in large territories in Eastern Europe maintaining large Muslim populations to the present day, and (c) the influx of significant Muslim populations into Western Europe and North America through the movements of people from Muslim-majority nations as a consequence of economic migration or fleeing wars, disasters or political regimes. The latter has resulted in Islam becoming the second largest religious grouping after Christianity in most European and North American nations. The present chapter addresses 'Islam *and* the West' but focuses primarily on 'Islam *in* the West', acknowledging that to some degree the reality of 'Islam *in* the West' has renewed the debates concerning 'Islam *and* the West'.

The West and Muslims have known each other for many centuries now, but often on antagonistic terms, in spite of the contributions they have made to each other's cultures. At first, it was both Eastern and Western Christianity that felt the impact of the success of Islam, and it was Europe itself that felt threatened as the Muslim empires came up to its heartland, pushing back the frontiers of its Christian heritage in Spain and the Balkans. In turn, Muslims felt the impact of the Crusades in the Holy Land, but, far more significantly, the turn of the tide and the colonization of their territory by the emergent European powers from the eighteenth century onwards. Thus the modern era builds upon historic conflicts between religions and empires and many Muslims in the twenty-first century still react to the West with memories of colonial and post-colonial domination and with fears of global capitalism and secularization, whilst the West has created new stereotypes consisting of oppressed women and 'suicide-terrorists'.

The new arrival of Muslims in the West itself has contributed to this fear of the 'other' and exacerbated old stereotypes concerning 'Muslims and the West', resulting in the relatively new phenomenon of religious discrimination against Muslims as opposed to the more typical ethnic racism usually associated with migration. The arrival of Muslims in the West has achieved little so far to eradicate ancient fears or prejudices, and in Britain this condition of suspicion has been labelled 'Islamophobia' to differentiate it from ethnic racism. Over thirty years ago Heeren suggested that the historic rivalry between Islam and the West has led to an 'ignorance of the ordinary Westerner towards Islam'.[28] However, it is equally true that misconceptions of Western culture and the teachings of Christianity are held by Muslims. This needs to be understood in the context of a historic relationship and the appropriation of the East in the colonial era that has become famously known as 'Orientalism' since the publication of Edward Said's seminal text bearing the same name.[29]

Behind it all is an essentializing of the Muslim world, with an inability to recognize that behind the stereotyping that depicts Muslims as different and dangerous is the lived experience of millions of human beings, diverse and sometimes difficult, but who seem to be able to draw upon the spiritual resources of their religion, and who are also able to recognize its shortcomings. As stated so succinctly by Bruce Lawrence:

> In the 1990s most Euro-American journalists continue to echo the sentiments that drove European kings and their subjects to launch their crusades almost a millennium ago, crusades whose enemy was Arab Muslims. In the aftermath of the Cold War the enemy, once again, has become the one Islam, the militant, unyielding, violent face of "Arab" Islam. Whether one picks up a popular book claiming to represent "Western cultures and values" under attack from Islam, or lead articles of the *New York Times*, such as the recent "Seeing Green: The Red Menace is Gone. But Here's Islam," the message is the same: Islam is one, and Islam is dangerous.[30]

It is not only the supporters of liberal secularism that have difficulties with Islam. The twentieth century has witnessed the growth of a Christian Protestant revivalism, particularly in the USA, where increasingly Millennialist and Dispensationalist tendencies once again revile Islam. Such tendencies within North American

Protestantism can perceive Muslims to be the agents of Satan and the protagonists at Armageddon. Norman Daniel, in his masterly exploration of Christian attitudes towards Islam, explains that the antipathy towards Islam amongst Christian authors arose as a result of Muslim religious beliefs concerning Christian doctrines rather than the power relations between the two civilizations. He states that: 'Western authors did not set out to shock Muslims with their sacrilege; they were themselves shocked by what they saw as blasphemy against Christian doctrines.'[31] Christians were horrified by the Muslim denial of the Crucifixion, refusal to accept the divinity of Christ, and the crude dismissal of the Trinity as polytheism. Yet they were also alarmed by the rapid expansion of Islam and the conquest of Christian territory.

It was probably the latter, the sense of the dangerous 'other', combined with a fear of being overpowered by an enemy with whom they shared many shifting borders, that, above all, helped maintain the 'deformed image' of Islam as a dogma of Christian society for many centuries. At the present time, it raises its head again, when once more the threat of the 'barbarian at the gate' is promoted by certain elements of the Christian Right in the USA and the political right in Europe. It is this which, as stated by Daniel, 'led men to prefer, sometimes nonsensical, and often unpleasant and untrue versions of the history of Muhammad and of the tenets and practices of Islam; and that they did so even when sound information was available'.[32]

Historically there seemed to be no awareness or sympathy for the range of beliefs that the religions shared with each other and this position of mutual ignorance remains.

Christian fears of Islam remain alive in the twenty-first century, especially in the aftermath of 9/11. The Reverend Franklin Graham, son of the famous evangelist Billy Graham and chosen by George Bush to deliver the prayers at his presidential inauguration, has continued in the tradition of Christian polemic against Muslims by asserting that 'Islam is a wicked and evil religion'.[33] The same school of thought was followed by the US deputy under-secretary of defence for intelligence, General William Boykin, who has described the US as being involved in a 'holy war' against the 'idol' of 'Islam's false god' and a 'guy called Satan' who 'wants to destroy us as a Christian army'.[34] The theme of a false god, possessing no connection to the monotheistic deity of Judaism and Christianity, has been picked up by the Reverend Pat Buchanan, who has claimed that Muslims worship a moon-god revered in ancient Mecca.

Early Christians denied Islam's independent status as a new religion, instead seeing it as a heretical sect of Christianity. This would appear to be echoed by the works of contemporary writers such as Michael Cook, Patricia Crone, Martin Hinds, John Wansbrough and Gerald Hawting, a group of authors whose approach has been labelled the 'revisionist' school of interpretation. Such writers develop a series of arguments based on archaeological and non-Muslim textual sources which in a variety of ways suggest that 'Islam' only slowly emerged as a new religion, and that it fabricated its early history. They argue that 'Islam' emerged out of sectarian controversies between Christian and Jews in the Middle East 'projected back to an Arabian origin'.[35] Such writings need to be placed within the history of Christian suspicions of Islam and Orientalist 'scientific' attempts to 'objectively' discover the source of Islam.

However, the position in regard to Christian understandings of Islam was to change with the European dominance of the Orient in the colonial period, when Western fears of Muslim power were diminished by the European resurgence achieved through advances in science and technology. The relationship now radically altered as the post-Enlightenment West increasingly transferred its own religious heritage to the private sphere of individual choice, removing piece by piece the role of Christianity in the public realm. From the eighteenth century onwards, Islam would be put under the microscope of a different kind of criticism influenced primarily by an attempt to comprehend religion based on the methodology of the natural and human sciences. To this day the heritage of the religious struggle to assert opposing truth claims and the rise of the secular and scientific paradigms remain as thorns in the side of relations between Muslims and Western perceptions of them.

Thus it can be seen that any contemporary negativity expressed towards Muslims, either in the contemporary news media or in acts of prejudice against Muslims, has a history arising out of both explicit vehemence against Islam originating in Christian fears and ignorance of the new religion and colonial discourse towards the East in general and Muslims in particular. Recent attempts to create negative images or reinforce stereotypes have to be seen in the context of this history. Since 9/11 there has been anecdotal evidence of an increase in racist attacks directed at Muslims but studies in 2002 by the University of Leicester show hostility towards Muslims in the city peaked whenever there was a 'terrorist' atrocity. Reported incidents included abuse hurled at children and women, insults on public transport, objects hurled in the street, and even a baby being tipped out of a pram. However, the motives for the attacks seem to indicate that they are not the direct consequence of violent activities by extremists but rather that extreme events focus negative views of Islam and allow discrimination to become public. The main criticisms of the perpetrators seem to be that Islam victimizes women and that Muslims refuse to integrate.[36] Where such attitudes persist, the question has to be asked to what degree the popular media has promoted such attitudes through a plethora of articles over the last decade putting forward such a view of Islam.

The main concern of Muslims with the Western news media is that they tend to portray Muslims as either terrorists or misogynists. In the case of the former it has disproportionately focused on the views and actions of a violent minority, thus risking stereotyping Muslims as aggressive and anti-Western and ignoring millions who are peaceful citizens of their respective nations. It is essential that perceptions are not created which endow all Muslims with the potential to become violent advocates of jihad or with feelings of alienation towards the West. Media assumptions can be clearly perceived in the hasty attribution of the Oklahoma bombings to Muslim extremists. In regard to women, they are far too often presented as passive victims of male dominance and exploitation. The overriding focus is on Muslim dress codes, especially head covering, an issue that is of little concern amongst Muslim women themselves.

As a number of high-profile events take place around the world involving 'suicide bombers', there is often little to distinguish in media and political narratives between the liberation struggles of the Palestinians reduced to using themselves as weapons against a modern heavily armed and resourced Israeli military and the actions of the al-Qa'eda pilots of 9/11. All is too often conflated and, without a more nuanced analysis, it would appear to many that Muslims across the globe are a problem to the West that can be resolved only in a conflict scenario. Of more concern is the ability of the media to bring the horrors of tragic events into our personal space. Mark Wark has stated that Muslims have been 'inserted as close to home in the West as it is possible to go; right into the living rooms of millions'.[37] Thus powerful images, with the ability to create strong emotional impressions and provoke subsequent reactions, are projected but without any analysis or reflection on the situation that has provoked the event.

As a consequence, it can become legitimate to perceive Muslims with distrust and suspicion. Even before 9/11 and the subsequent 'War on Terror', both local and global news focused on Muslims as the 'other'. This was very apparent in Britain where the media focused on a number of key events such as Salman Rushdie, the formation of the Muslim Parliament, riots in Oldham and Bradford, and the fight to win state funding for Muslim schools. Each of these was presented in such a way as to promote the image of an irrational and alienated stranger whose values were completely at odds with those of the West. Interspersed with these global news events, continuous small items focus on dowry abuse, honour killings, estranged women, and children taken to places of origin in divorce cases, none of which are anything to do with Islam but are rather ethnic practices often condemned by the official representatives of the religion as in opposition to the tenets of Islam. In addition, since 9/11 there have been continuous news items provoked by the global situation describing various crises or conflicts in the Muslim-majority world. As the 'newsworthiness' of Muslims and Islam increases, the overall impact is to develop an imagined and distorted construct; a constructed identity increasingly at odds with Muslim perceptions of themselves and one that further alienates Muslims and non-Muslims from each other. Both polemic representations made by Muslims and Christians of each other and secular media representations of Muslims need to be examined in the context of the history of relations between the cultures of Europe and Muslim civilization and the contemporary situation of post-colonialism, especially since the events of 9/11 dramatically transformed the context worldwide.

The religious and secular media are part of this struggle for the world-soul, and very little of their output is objective or informed. In Britain, the tabloid newspapers fuel Islamophobia as part of their vociferous campaign to demonize the migrant and the outsider. On the other hand, the writers of the liberal broadsheets promote their own Orientalist fantasies, fearing accusations of being racist or Islamophobic or right-wing in a post-colonialist discourse. At its worst, this kind of writing presents Islam as the last torch of spiritual light in a world of ill-gotten comforts and atheism.

Lorraine Sheridan stated that attacks on Muslims carried out in Leicester in the UK were perpetrated by people hostile to Islam, the abuse being 'more about the religion than race'.[38] In isolating religion as the cause of discrimination she has noticed a change in the polemics of racism in Britain, where discrimination is moving away from ethnic identity to religious identity. Yet it should be noted that even in the nineteenth century in Liverpool, the mosque founded by the famous convert W. H. Abdullah Quilliam was often attacked, and Muslims were likewise victimized whenever British foreign policy resulted in conflict between Britain and regions of the Muslim world. This was in spite of the fact that British Muslims were predominantly white British middle-class converts. In 1997, almost five years before the traumatic events of 9/11, Professor Gordon Conway, Vice-Chancellor of Sussex University and chairman of the Runnymede Trust, recommended to the British Government in the Runnymede Report that changes be made to British law to make religious discrimination and incitement to religious hatred illegal. In the delivery of the final report, Conway noted that 'the media, in particular, are commonly Islamophobic. They generate stereotypes of British Muslims which serve to marginalise them in our society.'[39] He noted that British Muslims are increasingly subject to prejudice, discrimination, harassment and violence.

It has to be accepted that the European situation is unique in that Muslims are no longer merely within its borders but belong to the identity of Western Europe no less than any other populations that may have been around for more generations. It is not nationality that is problematic for young British-born Muslims but rather the degree to which they wish to share in their parents' or grandparents' lifestyle or the extent to which they wish to involve themselves with their religious affiliation. These issues are no less relevant for non-Muslim youth. But, in spite of Muslims' sense of belonging, there is no doubt that fear and hostility remain dominant features of the perceptions of those who – making no differentiation between the new diaspora communities and Muslims in the Middle East or other parts of the wider Muslim world – continue to regard Muslims in the West as a 'fifth column' or 'enemy within the gates'.

Since the seminal work of Edward Said was first published in 1978, scholars in the field of Islamic Studies have been alerted to the dangers of Orientalism. Said simply defined Orientalism as 'a way of coming to terms with the Orient that is based upon the Orient's special place in European Western experience'.[40] He argued that the European academic study of the East can be criticized as a method of dominating, restructuring and having authority over the Orient. It is perhaps unfair to accuse all the scholars of Islam in the colonial era as dominating over and redefining Muslim culture and religion in their own terms. The alternative view would be that some were colonized by Eastern worldviews, trying to ditch their European socialization and adopt the customs and religious beliefs of the Oriental, although this is more common amongst those influenced by Indian traditions and Buddhism than by Islam. Even so, Montgomery Watt would appear to confirm Said's view of Orientalism when he wrote in 1988 that:

> For Muslims unchangingness is both an ideal for human individuals and societies, and also a perception of the actual nature of humanity and its environment. Unchangingness is an all-pervading assumption which colours most aspects of the standard world-view ... It is thus very difficult for the Westerner to appreciate the outlook of those in whose thinking there is no place for development, progress, or social advance and improvement.[41]

Although Watt focused on progress as opposed to rationality, there remains the assumption of an innate difference between the Western and the Oriental mind to the degree that the one is not understandable by the other. The second assumption is implicit and not recognized or challenged. The differences are perceived as primordial or as belonging to inner nature rather than economic, social or political circumstances. It is this very primordialism that underlies the work of the current crop of Islamic scholars writing in the aftermath of 9/11 who still posit Western democracy and the values of secular humanism as the pinnacle of human achievement and, in the process, still assert the cultural, intellectual, political, economic and material supremacy of the West over the East. None of this is presented as having anything to do with relations of power; rather it is seen as an innate superiority that leads to analyses that posit Western civilization contrasted with barbarism – for example, Huntingdon writing in 2002. Recent events in which several Muslim states have been identified as 'rogue states', the invasion of Iraq and Afghanistan, the torture of prisoners to elicit information, the number of arrests without due legal process in Western Europe and the USA, have all helped to generate the growing perception that 'Islam is the new American enemy, a green menace that has replaced the red menace of the Soviet Union'.[42] The sense of Muslim beleaguerment and marginalization, especially amongst American Muslims, has been encouraged by new Islamic scholars, who in reality are ideologues for Western culture and who have spared no opportunity to present Muslims as terrorists and a threat to the United States. Haddad uses the label 'Islamophobes' for scholars and journalists such as Steven Emerson, Daniel Pipes and Bernard Lewis.[43]

The resurrection of academic media that denigrates Islam or suggests in some way that Muslims are inferior to their Western counterparts is an unfortunate corollary to the events of 9/11 and perhaps forewarns us that the reputation of academia must be challenged by informed and questioning reading. Perhaps more unfortunate is the overshadowing of the works belonging to the new generation of scholarly analysis of Islam and Muslims, which were written partly to offset the distorted images of Muslims and their cultures created by Islamic scholars coming out of an older tradition of Orientalism. Of equal concern is the impact of Edward Said and the shadow he has placed over European scholarly constructions of the Orient in the colonial period. The publication of Said's *Orientalism* in 1978 dramatically transformed the landscape in which scholars study Islam. Whereas 'Orientalism' was previously a value-neutral term connoting the study of Eastern cultures and religion, it is now deemed to be part of a larger European project to colonize the East through the creation of an imagined reality reinvented through the intellectual gaze of the colonizers. To study Islam as a Western scholar since the latter half of the twentieth century is to be a figure of suspicion amongst Muslims, and the accusation of 'Orientalist' is not one to be taken lightly. There is no doubt that some nineteenth-century scholars were deeply complicit in the colonial venture or seeking to advantage the truths of Christianity over its religious rivals. Yet this is not the complete picture. It could be argued that the fascination with the East and its religions arose out of the mixture of a Romantic sentiment and the pursuit of knowledge that arose from the values of the Enlightenment. The straightforward equation of studying the Orient and furthering the European empires breaks down, for example, in Germany, where the tradition of Orientalism was developed to a far more sophisticated degree than elsewhere in Europe but was not connected to imperialism.[44] Regardless of motive, it has to be admitted that some European minds were 'colonized' by the East and became fascinated by Indian, Chinese or Arab culture and religion. Ibn Warraq points out that it was the desire for knowledge on the part of Europeans that led the people of the Near East to recover their own past and identity, and we hear the voice of religious empathy in Goldziher's description of joining Muslims in prayer in the city of Cairo.[45]

This colonization of some Western minds has more bearing on the early relations between Islam and the West than the crude Orientalism that concerned Said. Although it was unlikely to have been his intention, Said's dichotomy of Eastern victims and Western oppressors has played into the hands of those who promote a more primitive form of Islam, but there is another story to tell. In Germany, the translation of Islamic texts reached its height in the nineteenth century. The fascination with Islam can be found in the writings of the German poet Johann-Wolfgang von Goethe, who praised the Qur'an and the Muslim poets Hafiz and Rumi, and in Friedrich Rückert, who prepared the first poetic translation of the Qur'an at the beginning of the eighteenth century. As previously stated, Germany had no colonial encounter such as that experienced by France and Britain, and its engagement with Islam is described by Gritt Klinkhammer as 'an aesthetic turn to the Orient, imagining the Orient as positive and ethical'.[46] Klinkhammer persuasively argues that Islam became the realm in which some Germans were able to find a counter-narrative or 'antidotal response' to rationalism and secularism, and was therefore part of a social, political, cultural or religious reaction to European cultural/social developments in the post-Enlightenment period.[47] The same is true of Britain, where there is a close link between Orientalism and Romanticism.

One other area of divide between the Muslim world and the liberal West concerns the privatization of religion. Seidentop proposes that the West has become unused to thinking about faith when assessing the causes of political and social change and thus may overlook its significance in the contemporary world.[48] This is certainly not the case in the Muslim world. Even in the nineteenth century, as touched on earlier, attempts to establish a Muslim community in the British city of Liverpool by the prominent convert William Henry Abdullah Quilliam ran into problems over the issue of religion, politics and dual loyalties. Abdullah Quilliam had always been interested in politics but his conversion to Islam was to determine his relationship with British expansion overseas and particularly where Muslim territory was involved in the colonial enterprise. Balancing his patriotic allegiance to the nation of his birth with his intense loyalty to the religion of his choice was never easy. His personal solution was to declare a dual loyalty to the Crown and to the Muslim Caliphate. The former represented his love and pride in the land of his birth but it did not extend to passive acceptance of the policies of government. Quilliam was a community activist and he passionately believed in the right of British citizens – a right which extended to the millions of Muslims who were part of the Empire – to protest in the cause of justice. But he was not beyond going outside the legal framework if he considered the moral imperative to be greater than the legal position. Above all, the law of God as revealed through the Islamic revelation took ultimate precedence over man-made laws when the two conflicted.

Quilliam's dual loyalties were soon to be tested in various conflicts around the Muslim world. During the invasion of Sudan in which General Kitchener fought the remnants of the forces of the Mahdi, which had earlier defeated Gordon in Khartoum, Quilliam was enraged at the recruitment of Egyptian Muslim troops to fight the campaign. He issued the first of his *fatwa*, declaring that Muslims who assisted the British Government were not only in breach of Islamic law but in danger of being excluded from the *umma*.[49]

Not all Muslims were happy with the proclamation, Quilliam himself mentioning the controversy it gave rise to in Muslim circles and a letter received from India pleading with him to confine himself to religion and leave politics alone.[50] He quoted the Prophet on the subject of Muslim brotherhood and stated that if Muslims are being set against each other to the detriment of the unity of the *umma* (universal Muslim brotherhood) by the politics of a *Giaour* (infidel) nation then it was a matter of religion. The aim of all Muslims should be to seek actively for the union of all Muslim people and Islam.[51] Controversially, he declared that the ultimate religious goal for all Muslim endeavour is the 'world for Islam'.[52] Thus in this scenario it could be posited that the religious revival impacting on the Muslim world marks a vanguard of resistance for those who perceive themselves as having no option but to stand up for their faith in the public arena.

Those who seek to maintain the position of isolation from Western culture in order to protect time-hallowed traditions imbued with sanctity face the possibility of being labelled anachronistic and out of touch with the realities of the modern world. In Muslim countries they may be seen by both reformers and radicals as too quiescent to the status quo of corruption and social ills. When they import such positions into Western diasporas they are likely to be accused of creating an isolationist critique of the new host society that forbids integration. In the new post-9/11 environment they are accused of promoting terrorism through nurturing a set of values that set Islam in confrontation with Western values and morality.

Reformists find themselves accused by traditionalists and radicals of jeopardizing the revelation of God. In addition, radicals accuse them of supporting democratic reforms only to further the domination of the West over Islam. In the West they find themselves courted by governments desperate to seek out the so-called respectable or moderate face of Islam as allies in the struggle against extremism, but as a result they find themselves unrepresentative of the traditional mainstream. To the radical rejectionists, the implementation of democracy in Muslim lands is only an attempt to colonize by subtle means. Modernism, progress, the free market and globalization are all perceived as the imports of Western powers keen to maintain historic domination of Muslim lands. Where Muslim communities live in the heart of the West, such groups will exploit any Muslim dissatisfaction with their lot. Racism, economic and social discrimination, and Islamophobia all become the backdrop to encourage Muslims to radicalize in the name of religion, to reject the values of the host nation and to embrace the cause of transnational Islamic identity over national loyalties. In the process they are duty bound to defend Muslim nations against the incursion of Western values or of an unwelcome military presence.

All of this has to be seen in the context of confidence. Each of the three groups are reacting with different strategies to the loss of confidence felt by Muslims in facing the dominance of Western civilization that began in the eighteenth century, accelerated in the nineteenth, and showed no signs of abating in the twentieth. In the twenty-first century, despite the rise of China, India, Brazil and the re-emergence of Russia as a world power, the Western paradigm of neo-liberalism appears to be developing into a world order into which the powers just mentioned owe their success to its partial adoption. Occidentalism, which appeared as a reaction to the loss of Arab authority in the colonial period, now offers some consolation to Muslims worldwide as they attempt to come to terms with neo-liberal values as an inevitability. Some will resist to the bitter end, relying upon God for final justification and victory, leading to a millennial expectation where the godless are defeated through divine intervention, but many more will attempt to find reconciliation through faith inclusion within the neo-liberal paradigm.

There will be those who will seek to reduce the perceived polarization between Islamic revelatory discourses and modernity in order to demonstrate that Islam is compatible with the West. In Western Europe this will focused around citizenship discourses, the highly politicized debates around identity and loyalty, and the ways in which Islamic values can be combined with respective 'core' national cultures to create British, French or German Muslims. These debates are politicized to the degree that various European governments are beginning to perceive that the discourses around 'European' Islam are the antidote to the far more polarized radical positions, which only focus on incompatibility. The debates are not new and, as we have seen, they build upon existing paradigms where figures such as Jamaluddin al-Afghani (1839–97), Muhammad Abduh (1849–1905) and Rashid Rida (1865–1935) introduced the idea that Islam is a rational religion and therefore could not conflict with the discoveries and application of Western scientific, technological and educational achievements. However, the weakness of the modernist argument was always that it did not recognize the self-sufficiency of Islam.[53] The dangers of such an argument were always going to be that for possibly the first time in Muslim history the referents of the Islamic revelation would become secondary to Muslims,[54] diluted as the teachings of the Bible have become in the majority in Western European nations. The issue is one of compromise. Does the acceptance of liberal values mean that Muslims in the West have to accommodate liberal moral behaviour? To identify both as inseparable and 'dangerous' to Muslim religious life offers the possibility of contamination, a drift into secularization and the weakening of the fundamental tenet of the religion that Muslims exist as a vanguard trusted by divine edict to protect the final revelation until the end-time. For such religious sentiments, the only solution is isolation. Some will take up this option as religious men and women have always done throughout history when faced with compromise with societies that are considered a threat to religious conviction.

The challenge for the West is to ensure that the isolationist option remains benign and does not lead to religious violence. It would be easy to argue that such solutions can only lead to stagnation and the emergence of primitivist versions of the religion. Yet, it is also possible to argue that out of such isolationist modes of resistance may come solutions that are truly Islamic in nature. Creativity can also be found in the new modernist paradigms, as European Muslims such as Tariq Ramadan promote a 'progressive inclusive Islam'. It is in the discursive dialogue between positions that Islam in the West will find its own unique voice.

Chapter 7

The Future

Much of this book has been concerned either implicitly or explicitly with relations between Islam and the West. Any questions concerning the future of Islam, its immense relevance in contemporary religious and political life, and its contribution to interreligious dialogue and harmony between various communities has to take account of the implications of radical movements, religious violence and the relationship between religion and politics that various elements in the Muslim world interpret in a way that predisposes a conflict scenario. Various chapters have dealt in depth with the relations between Islam and the West, and investigated the role of fundamentalism, religious primitivism, and Islamic responses to globalization, secularization and the dominance of neo-liberal models for international relations. However, the Muslim world has its own challenges, which are not always removed from contemporary relations with the Western world. There are issues of ecology, gender and equal opportunities to education, vast disparities between rich and poor, and ancient problems of religious difference to be resolved, in addition to the modern challenges of the role of Muslim nations in the international community and the relationship of Islam to modernity.

It is problematic for a scholar of religion to make too precise predictions concerning the future of any religious tradition let alone one that is as heterogeneous and as vast as Islam. When a religion influences the culture of nations as diverse as Saudi Arabia, Senegal and Indonesia, covers a geographical range that is truly global, has established significant populations in the West, and is practised by millions within political systems that range from tribal societies, monarchies, republics, democracies, dictatorships and theocracies, any assertion about the future of Islam in the twenty-first century would be scandalous essentializing. Two statements can be made with some safety. There is no doubt that Islam will be a significant factor in international relations throughout the twenty-first century and much of the activity that will be significant could be described as 'bridge-building'.

Religious Bridge-building

Any significant bridge-building will be concerned with Islam's two closest companions in the religious pantheon. Islam's fortunes have always been closely linked to Christianity and Judaism, the former because of political rivalry and the latter to a lesser degree because of their similarities and historic meetings in the Middle East after the rise of Islam in the territories now known as Iraq. However, the creation of Israel has to a large degree cancelled out the former harmonious relations between Muslims and Jews in the Middle East. The intractable issue of Palestine has dominated Jewish/Muslim relations since the creation of the state of Israel. In the Western world Islam has supplanted Judaism as the second largest religious minority and the immediate future should show signs of Islam's significance in the West as the largest religious presence after Christianity having an impact on pressure-group politics concerning the future of the Palestinian people.

Relations with Christians will always be to some degree fraught because of Islam's denial of the central elements of Christianity's doctrines of salvation. A fellow monotheistic religion that shares much of the common heritage of the Abrahamic gift to the world's spirituality but denies the Crucifixion, the divinity of Jesus and claims to supplant Christianity as the final revelation is inevitably going to be problematic. When this is added to the fact that both religions are the most proselytizing of the world's major faiths and directly compete with each other in a number of regions, especially Africa, it can be easily comprehended that relations are likely to be difficult. They are likely to remain so until Muslim-majority nations improve the conditions of their sometimes sizable Christian minorities and allow for a level platform regarding conversion back and forth between the two faiths. However, the world needs the contribution of its major ethical voices to mobilize dissent on a number of global social justice and environmental issues, and it may be that the future will see the monotheistic religions coming together to raise issues on moral and ethical concerns and crises that will impact heavily on a global scale but will affect the world's poor disproportionately.

In the West the issue of public and private will be of concern to all religious believers, whether Christian, Jewish or Muslim. But the debates over the privatization of religious belief will spill over into Muslim-majority nations. They have already done so, and the twentieth century has observed a political and religious crisis arising from the demands of a considerable minority of Muslims for a fully comprehensive, all-encompassing and holistic relationship between Islam and politics that is manifested in the idea of an Islamic state. Unfortunately the volatile mix of such non-Western solutions to the political crises of the Muslim-majority world with the historic heritage of colonial and post-colonial relations between the West and most Muslim nations complicates this significant debate and obscures the important contribution of Islam with religio/political violence.

In the Western world it has been assumed by both social scientists and political commentators and activists that the secular paradigm of keeping religion out of the public realm and confined to private life was a *fait accompli*. Religious people may not have felt comfortable with the relegation of God's revelations to the world of private morality and ethics but in Western Europe there seemed to be little alternative, and, but for small pockets of resistance that could easily be marginalized as fundamentalism and religious primitivism, a flag of surrender had been raised. Even though the battle has not been lost in the USA, where larger numbers of the population remain churchgoers, the battle for the place of religion in public life has not been able to withstand the Constitution's fundamental premise that no single religion could dominate the affairs of state, However, it became apparent throughout the final decades of the twentieth century and the first decade of the twenty-first that the voice of religion had certainly penetrated one of the USA's major two political parties.

The issue that now faces the secular democracies of the West is one of inclusion. The crucial question concerns the place of the active involvement of people of faith in the democratic process when they bring their faith with them to the political table and insist upon decisions being taken that acknowledge their religious sensitivities. Recently there have been a number of signs that religion remains both a contentious and a positive voice in world affairs and no one in the twenty-first century is under the delusion that the significance of religion is in decline. Conflict in Bosnia, Chechnya, Israel, Pakistan, Afghanistan and Iraq, or tensions with Iran, repeatedly capture the headlines, each highlighting disputes within the Muslim world. The issues appear to be irresolvable, and these conflict zones demonstrate that religion remains both highly relevant and a potential threat to world peace and international relations.

I would argue that the underlying and more significant impact of Islamic resistance to secularization and globalization of neo-liberal values is the encouragement it has given to all people of faith that the religious voice still matters in public affairs. When the Archbishop of Canterbury called for a debate on the public role of faith in Britain it is no coincidence that he drew upon the controversial example of *shari'a* and the implementation of Islamic family law within Western nations that have significant Muslim minority populations. In drawing our attention to such matters he was not attempting to argue that *shari'a* law should be adopted in Britain but rather to ask questions concerning allegiance and identity. Since the nineteenth century the dominance of nationalism has given rise to patriotism supplanting all other loyalties and subsuming familial and religious allegiances, but the twenty-first century has opened with the question of how two modes of belonging, that of allegiance to God and that of loyalty to the state, relate to each other. When national allegiance clashes with obedience to God's law, which is paramount: the identity of a believer or the role of a citizen? In Mawdudian terms this is phrased as a clash of loyalties between fealty to the sovereignty of God and acceptance of the democratic ethos of the rule of the people.

Mawdudi saw the choice in stark terms, with little room for compromise. The only solution for Muslims was an Islamic state, but the choices are in reality far more nuanced. In the West, Muslims, Jews and Christians are seeking new responses in societies traditionally dominated by the liberal secular attitude that has separated the two realms of civic and religious by developing a discourse of public and private. New discourses are appearing that challenge both civic secularism and religious totalism in favour of a model of citizenship that has a double responsibility to God and state and a sense of shared multilayered identity that permits a contextualized dialogue between faith and citizenship.[1] These debates have been driven by the attempts of Muslims in the West to establish a place for faith in their new secular homes. The debates have been noisy and have woken up the practitioners of the dominant faith, who may have sharply felt the tensions in the previous century but saw the cause as lost. The large question for the twenty-first century will be whether the solutions can be worked out in the more secure Western European democracies and imported back to Muslim-majority societies that struggle with religious totalism as the dominant mode of discourse and the chosen route for activists.

In pursuing the common concerns that religious people and their institutions share with regard to their relations with the dominantly secular, Islam, Christianity and Judaism may discover something of their shared heritage and its potential in defining common ground. Perhaps before this can be achieved a 'purification of memory' is required. This is especially true of Muslim/Christian relationships and working partnerships where civilizational or ethnic religion has led to conflicts and wars between empires and nations. Where communities have suffered over generations, the South African example of reconciliation and forgiveness will have to be mutually accepted. The Second Vatican Council's *Declaration on the Relation of the Church to Non-Christian Religions*, in which it was stated that the past needs to be forgotten in order to arrive at new relations that are formed of mutual understanding, showed its awareness of 'quarrels and hostilities' that occurred over the centuries.[2] Since then the Declaration has been built upon by the acceptance of Islam's path to God as authentic.[3] However, for such endeavours to be successful both parties have to admit their complicity in the past's conflicts and acknowledge their shortcomings.

The process will involve an increasing recognition that Islam, Judaism and Christianity consist of people who seek solutions to life's challenges through turning their faces towards the same God rather than merely the humanist paradigm consisting of the human project and the common good. In the case of Christianity and Islam, which remain dominant rivals for the world's souls and their salvation and which still predominantly consist of followers whose main connection to the religion is through the cultures and civilizations founded upon it, the challenge is considerable. Understandings of God differ greatly between their believers and in respective doctrines contained in sacred texts, but there is a shared common ground of believing themselves to be a people first and foremost able to be transformed through contact with the divine Word and the capacity of such religions to build trust, friendship and cooperation.[4]

Once these goals are achieved, Christians and Muslims will be in a position to offer support and protection to each other in times of crisis. There are moments in history when human communities are faced with mutual antagonism and suspicion. In particular such moments are faced by religious minorities, whether Muslims in the

Balkans or Christians in Iraq. These conflicts are often political rather than religious in origin but only the concerted moral voice of those who understand the religious truths of Christianity and Islam can overcome the ancient memories that re-emerge at such times. It is those who believe that the Word of God, as diversely understood by either Muslims or Christians, primarily exists to purify human nature so that it can achieve intimacy with the divine and overcome all that stands between believers and God who hold primary responsibility to be a voice to moderate the behaviour of those who perceive human relations through the lens of 'otherness'. Both traditions have their versions of the 'Good Samaritan' and the Golden Rule.

In Europe, the rights and freedoms to practise one's religion or to practise another are enshrined in the Conventions of Human Rights but these are only safely assured when religion is seen primarily as a matter of private conscience. The challenge for many Muslim countries is to balance understandings of *umma* (a community of human beings defined by religion) with that of an individual's freedom of choice to pursue their own way to relationship with the divine (there is no compulsion in religion). For the latter to predominate over the former, religion has to be seen as more than an issue of identity and as primarily a set of beliefs and practices that provide human beings with alternative modes of worship and relations with a perfect being.

It is true that groups of individuals who espouse one path as preferable over all others make unique claims and share common practices that bind them into communities. However it is the moral imperative of such communities that has to be paramount over and above claims that assert the label of 'other' upon outsiders. Islam acknowledges that difference is God-given. The Qur'an clearly states that people are made to belong to different communities so that they may know each other, and that if God had wanted it so, the world would have believed in one path.[5] Pluralism is part of the plan. It is the acknowledging of this truth that led Muslim empires to adopt the *dhimmi* system, which provided Christians and Jews with limited self-government and freedom to practise their religion.

The shared moral imperative gives religious communities the right to provide a powerful voice in the public arena, particularly as very often the ethical and moral concerns that matter to religious people are shared by non-believers. When Muslims engage in global affairs and policy-making they not only demand that society considers the values that underpin it but also send out a message of comfort to all religious people that their beliefs matter and that religion cannot exist in isolation from all other arenas of public life. Religion does not have to exist separated from the realm of politics but, as pointed out by Paul Heck, the moral authority of religion depends upon its freedom from political power.[6] Muslims in the West have discovered that democracy can be their friend, for they are permitted a freedom of practice and belief that acknowledges the full heterogeneity of Muslim religious life to a degree that many Muslim nations would not permit. If the Muslim world has to learn how to live with the full participation of its people in civil life, it can also teach the West something about the prevalence of religious values in public life.

Perhaps the greatest contribution of Islam in pursuit of religious bridge-building will be in debates and actions that contribute to the common good. Religions remain as one of the largest treasure troves for human beings to discover values that may help to overcome the crises of ecology and economy, social injustice and difference. The values of both Christianity and Islam may be divinely mandated but on many occasions they come packaged in human attempts to resolve problems and discover a wisdom that can manage human affairs with fresh insights that promote compassion and justice. The contribution of religion to these debates is not the same as the human rights debate on justice, but religious believers need to find a common voice to speak to each other.

Both Christianity and Islam build upon the Jewish concern for justice and recognize it to be one of the defining qualities of the divine nature. But even more than that, both Muslims and Christians are charged with the divinely given imperative to seek a world that reflects God's justice in human affairs. The pursuit of God's justice has given rise to a discourse of obligations in which both God and the other are represented. Yet the discourse of obligations is not always comfortable with the language of human rights and the principles of human autonomy that are espoused assertively. Problematically, the human rights discourse gives the dominion over religious authority to human law-makers when it declares that religious allegiance itself is subject to human sovereignty rather than to scriptural injunctions concerning religious orientation. Malcolm Evans argues that this is because international human rights legislators perceive themselves as creating an ethical code rather than building a means of policing the borders between the public and private spaces and making sure that the power of the state does not overreach the bounds of legitimacy.[7] He suggests that such discourses are not 'distillations of any particular form of wisdom' nor 'in any sense moral absolutes'.[8] In these spaces between the understandings of human rights discourse as 'tools in which we work' to configure the international community,[9] acknowledged as a fundamentally human process, and Islam's and Christianity's concern with moral absolutes, lies one of the greatest creative tensions of the twenty-first century.

Political Bridge-building

Although the focus of both Muslim and Western governments, reflected in the coverage of the media and its impact on public opinion, is almost certain to be on the problem of religious violence and 'terrorism', the debates within Muslim societies and their internal and external political relations will need to go beyond the immediate challenge of dealing with the crises caused by extremist or radical movements and to engage with the larger questions of civil life, governance and justice. Only a deep and committed engagement with such issues will resolve the problems that gave rise to radical politicized Islam in the first instance. Islam is a religious system that maintains the allegiance of tens of millions and shows little sign of decline or giving way to global secular values or neo-liberalism and the market economy. As a religion it remains the main focus of resistance to such values and does not accept the moral base of modernity easily. The stark dichotomy of acceptance of values that fly in the face of Islam's morality and a return to religious primitivism in reaction will do neither Muslim nor Western societies any degree of good. The Western powers need to start listening to a discourse that has inherited an ancient wisdom critiquing the values of rampant materialism; a discourse shared by most of the world's major religions and that also has something to say on social justice and the impact of greed on human well-being and tragic inequalities. Muslim nations need to understand that they cannot criticize the West on one hand, and deny their own people on the other. Blaming the West for all that is ill in Muslim societies will work as a strategy for only so long.

The peddlers of the 'clash of civilizations' thesis on both sides of the imaginary border between East and West need to be contained and refuted. Even if the divide ever existed, in today's world of rapid communication and intercultural penetration it can make no sense. Unfortunately, politicians in the old and new colonial powers seem to have inherited a new interventionism that, alongside the dominance of neo-liberalism, reeks of nineteenth-century modes of 'gunboat' foreign policy in which the moral supremacy of the 'democratic' West is heralded over the religious primitivism, social backwardness and political repressiveness of the 'East'. The paradigm of Saidian Orientalism needs to be transcended, as it is too easily recognized by most Muslims as a form of neo-colonialism and hypocritical in its lack of even-handedness.

One area of divide between the Muslim world and the liberal West concerns the privatization of religion. The concern is an issue of authority. Jelen argues that religious citizens 'may well be tempted to forgo the essentials of democratic civility and procedures and act on their belief in a higher law'.[10] The argument is not unknown in the West. John Rawls argued for a North American position which maintains that a truly fair and just society cannot allow one religion to prevail in influencing government in a pluralist society.[11] Rawls begins by equating Western society with pluralism and argues that a system of justice has to be created that all citizens may reasonably be able to endorse.[12] Therefore no one doctrine can hope to assume the role of the basis of political justice.[13] However, Segers argues that religious convictions are fundamental for many people who regard them as the root of civilization and culture.[14] In a purely functional society is it reasonable to ask religious individuals and groups to cooperate with a system of justice that is not founded upon the law of a higher power? Wolterstorff argues that such religious individuals would have to acquire the skills to translate their convictions into other forms of reasoning.[15] Many others would reason from their political convictions. He states, 'it belongs to the religious convictions of a good many religious people in our society that they ought to base their decisions concerning fundamental issues of justice on their religious convictions. They do not view it as an option.'[16] This is not an issue of East and West but one that concerns all religious people who face a globalized spread of political liberalism. In this scenario it could be posited that the religious revival impacting on the Muslim world marks a vanguard of resistance for those who perceive themselves as having no option. Hanafi sees this polarization in terms of an Occidentalism and argues that such attitudes arise from a fear of Western domination. However, he is concerned that two positions appear to dominate the discourse; those who completely reject the West and those who totally accept its values. Amongst those who reject the West are a number of individuals and movements who develop responses to modernity and Western hegemony.[17] Amongst these groupings are those who want to maintain the superiority of Islam and strengthen Islamic-based identity. Islam is perceived as the only solution to resolve all human problems. Another group in the Muslim world accepts Western traditions and values, and is perceived by the first grouping as mentally and politically colonized by the West. Many of these are in positions of power in the Muslim world and belong to governments that have close political and economic ties with the Western powers. Hanafi wrote in 1995 that, so far, Western traditions have become a main reference for Muslim awareness[18] and thus religious fundamentalism arises as rejection and resistance. To his mind this attitude is one of arrogance, which is the counterpart to the weakness of the colonized Muslims. He argues that when Islamic power was strong it was able to possess a critical appreciation of the West as expressed in Greek civilization. Hanafi argues that a more nuanced Occidentalism would break the dualism of the Muslims and 'the other' and destroy the relationship dominated by inferiority and superiority.[19] The West's claim to be the most modern, humanist and mature civilization so far developed as opposed to Islamic culture's lack of civil rights or egalitarian justice requires a new perspective that neutralizes Western superiority and removes the Orientalist paradigm of an unchanging and irrational Orient that is juxtapositioned with a modern and progressive Occident.[20]

It is clear in writing this conclusion under the two main subheadings of political and religious bridge-building that there is considerable overlap between the two categories. It is more a question of emphasis. The challenge of definition of terms also causes problems. Muslims are likely to contend that religion and politics are inseparable in Islam but it has to be acknowledged on both sides of the religious divide that this is to a certain degree a recently constructed narrative developed by those movements within the Islamic spectrum that have politicized Islam to create a challenge to the existing world order. The classical period of Islamic civilizations presents Muslims with many examples where religion and politics were indeed separated, and rulers and *ulema* sometimes clashed with each other over whose authority was primary. The first Islamic state in Madinah may provide an example for both Islamists and jihadist movements but it has to be acknowledged by Muslims that the Prophet was carving out and developing a system of religion that updated the existing religious systems in the Middle East and was above all concerned with a human relationship with the One God of the Abrahamic traditions. The challenge to salvationary systems when they become civilizational religions has been a familiar story in the study of religions and has plagued Christianity. Indeed the major divisions between Islam and its greatest rival have always been primarily concerned with power, not religious doctrine or practice.

Bassam Tibi refers to this when he argues that it is not the rival religions of Christianity and Islam that are the problems but rather the 'civilizations related with each'.[21] It is this which makes the challenge of separating religion and politics so difficult for Muslims. Western Christianity has in a sense been forced to be self-critical under the onslaught of secularism and to re-examine the relationship between 'civilizational religion', nominal belonging and committed practice of a system that purports to bring individuals and communities closer to a divine being. In spite of the census data in Britain that showed over 70 per cent allegiance to Christianity, it is a fact that most Christians in Western Europe define themselves by religious commitment, not nominal belonging. Muslims will find this process more problematic in that they do not want to accept the underlying secularism that has brought this change to the West. As long as secularism remains a thorn in the Muslim religious psyche, modernity will also be suspect, as in the European model the two are closely bound up in each other. Whilst this dilemma remains unresolved, the West will have to deal with Muslim movements that function as religio/political resistance movements. The great challenge for Muslims will be discovering the means to embrace the benefits of modernity without necessarily accepting a concomitant secularism.

Habermas has argued that the separation of the world and the divine is one of the central pillars of cultural modernity, but the Islamist movements, although they might agree, do not see it as a universal law but rather insist that it is a key factor in Western imperialism. It is inevitable from this challenge to Western hegemony that the concept of the nation-state as established at the 1648 Westphalia Treaty comes under intense scrutiny in the Muslim world. It is the way in which states are governed that determines the role that religion plays in public life. The Muslim world is discovering how to deal with the paradox that those who were instrumental in the formation of Muslim nation-states and their mode of governance were also those who had most bought into the Western paradigms of state formation. This is all very recent in history. Many Muslim nation-states were brought into existence in the mid-twentieth century and some of them artificially created as part of the European colonial enterprise. Iran, in particular, has to be treated carefully and cautiously by Western observers. The Islamic experiment in statehood is not a return to medieval or classical Islam, but a modern attempt to resolve the challenges of a post-colonial world and create a genuine Islamic alternative. Any clumsy attempt to impose a military solution on the experiment that is still trying to discover its place in the world will only further the chaos that the jihadists seek in their attempts to collapse the world order in favour of a reinvented political Islam.

The Iraq war has to be seen as a disastrous mistake by the USA and its European allies. It has not brought about the stability that was argued for by the politicians on both sides of the Atlantic. On the contrary it has destabilized an ancient religious balance of power in the Middle East. It has not reduced homegrown Muslim terrorism on European or American soil but rather provided more grievances to add to Muslim discontent. Whether democracy as defined by the Western powers is brought to Iraq or not, those concerned with world peace will have to confront the reality of the new Shi'a power block created in Iran, Iraq and Lebanon. Sunni Muslim dominance is threatened for the first time since the Fatimids ruled in Egypt, and the Wahhabi-influenced rulers of Saudi Arabia will have difficulty accepting the change in traditional power relations between the Sunni majority and the Shi'a minority in the region.

Palestinian/Israeli relations will continue to dominate the twenty-first century. Here too the situation has been complicated by the 'return of the sacred' in international relations. It is no longer a simple dichotomy between Israelis and Arabs over ownership of territory. This had been difficult enough for the international community to resolve. The Judaization of the territorial demands that occurred after the 1967 war and the increasing demands of the Jewish settler movement for a biblical Israel will place huge demands on the secular reality of the modern state of Israel. It has been accompanied by an Islamic reaction in Palestine, and the tensions between Hamas and the PLO indicate a parallel development in the fledgling Palestinian authority over governance. Even if the international powers could find a solution to the intractable problem of Palestinian sovereignty, it is likely that the first post-independence crisis would be a civil war between secularists and Islamists to determine the kind of state that Palestine should be. It is unlikely that either Israel or the USA would permit an Islamic state.

Pakistan and Afghanistan will remain a challenge. There is no doubt that this is a single geo-political region where for several decades the jihadists and Islamists have cemented a power base. The combination of Mawdudian influence at all levels of Pakistan's political and military apparatus and the various jihad movements that came into existence to defeat the Russians in Afghanistan has completely undermined Pakistan's civil society and created a very dangerous situation in South Asia. Many would argue that, for the first time, the NATO powers have discovered the real trouble spot in the Muslim world but it remains extremely problematic whether the military solution will succeed.

When Bassam Tibi states that the new global jihad expressed as a return to Islam is not so much Islam understood as a religious faith as the revival of Muslim civilization in its relation to world politics he is arguably correct in his analysis.[22] However, he also points out that the study of religion is a recent player in international relations and that vice versa is also true. Although his assertion that no International Relations scholar in Europe or the US would deny the relevance and significance of the study of religions may be true, I am not convinced that the importance of religious knowledge and understanding has yet filtered down to policy-makers, who predominantly appear to remain in the secular mode of understanding where the implications of the 'return of the sacred' have not yet been absorbed. There are massive challenges that will require the combined knowledge of both disciplines and several others. When Bibi speculates that his fellow Muslims will cease to engage in jihad, he unfortunately conflates jihad with terrorism or, as he defines it, the 'violence of irregular warfare'.[23] The deeper problem to be overcome is the innate religious *zeitgeist* that underpins the Islamic revelation and has existed for centuries, that is, the superiority of the Islamic revelation over all other human religious and civilizational achievements and the divine imperative to carry Islam to the world. When this age-old religious superiority meets with the dominance of the Western-based world order and the equal certainty that Western liberal democracy and the values of neo-liberalism are the pinnacle of human civilization's achievements, then conflict is sure to occur. Jihad incorporates *da'wa*, the promotion of Islam worldwide, within its brief, or, more accurately, jihad is only an aspect of *da'wa*. It is the means through which *da'wa* is achieved that will be the challenge for an awakened Muslim world aroused from its slumbers by a call to 'return to the sacred'.

Bibi and other moderates have called for Muslims to return to the values of the Muslim rationalists who were 'open to learning from others'.[24] But when he points out that the Muslim rationalists adopted the Greek legacy, he does not put his finger on a solution to the contemporary Islamicization of the Muslim world and its relations with others. It may make good sense for the world order based on Western values of democracy and secularism, but it does not meet the religious understanding of devout Muslims through the centuries that the Qur'anic revelation is a 'complete' and 'Arabic' solution given by God for the world. It was for exactly these reasons that Al-Ghazali had refuted the philosophers in the eleventh century.

Tibi does accurately analyse the conditions that afflict both internal conflicts within the Muslim world and its overspill into international relations with the West but the solution is far more difficult to foresee. Bridging will be the necessary process but it will require delicate handling that avoids both the Huntingdon-type analysis of permanent and irreparable fault lines and the jihadist interpretations which insist upon a collapse of the world order in favour of a revived civilizational Islamic religion. Neither will the Muslim moderates necessarily provide the solution. They have never been able to answer the criticism that they favour the West and attempt to impose European solutions onto Muslim society. The religiously devout have re-emerged in the twenty-first century and demand a re-examination of their place in public life. In the Islamic religious worldview, it is the religious solutions provided by the Qur'an and Hadith that offer the way forward for Muslims and the rest of the world.

Any solution to the challenges that religious Muslims may pose towards modernity, secularism and neo-liberalism will require not only a re-examination of relationships with the West and its political/ economic supremacy but also a process of reflection on Islam's own mechanisms for the creation of civil society. In the process, Muslim governments will not be able to ignore the religious, and the processes of interpretation and exegesis of sacred texts will be as significant as statecraft and international relations. When Tibi highlights the challenge between the call for global jihad to secure Islamic supremacy and the alternative requirement to include the world of Islam into the existing European and North American world order he neglects to inform us that this battleground will need to be partly theological.

However, the challenge of interpretation will be to find a methodology that can engage with the demands of modern life without being either a borrowing of Western understandings of exegesis or denied creativity by hidebound traditions belonging to another age of methods of interpretation. As expressed by Al-Alwani:

Renewal of religion cannot be equated simply with revival of the heritage of our forefathers which represents a summation of their thought concerning the religion and their understanding thereof. Nor can modernization be equated with imitation of the West and following in its footsteps. Rather true renewal derives its substance from the reconstruction or reformation of the Muslim mind, and restoration of its connection with the Book of God in its capacity as the sole creative source – together with the cosmos – of thought, knowledge, creed, law and method.[25]

It is this process of the Islamicization of knowledge that will require the creative efforts of the best Muslim minds of the twenty-first century. As stated so succinctly by Al-Alwani, it must not come from the West, but must first be generated by interpretation of Islamic sources and then synthesized with Western knowledge in the way that classical Muslim thinkers drew upon and Islamicized the knowledge of the Greek philosophers.

The large-scale arrival of Muslims in the West could play a significant part in this process of reflection and reinterpretation. These communities in Europe will not only bear the brunt of Western acceptance of Islam in its midst but will also provide the closest links with Muslim nations. They will be more influential than the Muslim presence in the USA precisely because the European nations in which they have settled remain close geographically to Muslim neighbours such as Turkey, North Africa and the Near East, but in addition maintain political and economic links with their former colonies. Muslims in Britain, France and Germany will continue to have strong links with their places of origin, making it possible for them to influence religious and political thinking. So far, the direction of religious influence has been more from the countries of origin and has given rise to fears of the Islamicization of Europe. There are signs that the younger generations born in the places of migration are seeking to Europeanize Islam and in the process will discover creative ways of living out Islamic values in a non-Muslim Western environment.

It is in Europe that the histories of Orientalism, colonialism, and political and military incursions from both sides complicate the transmigration of Islam and its possibility of becoming a European religion. Fukuyama has presented the argument of 'the end of history' as a more subtle response to Huntingdon's 'clash of civilizations'. He argues that the dominance of neo-liberalism and the collapse of communism have presented the cultures of Western consumerism, secularism and civic participation with no rivals.[26] Thus history as we have known it for the last two thousand years has come to an end. However, Tibi argues that the presence of Islam in Europe and the concomitant Islamicization may result in a return to civilizational and cultural competition.[27] However, Tibi may be accused of 'gilding the lily' in presenting his argument for the 'return of history'. The Muslim presence in the West remains a small minority that still faces a number of challenges such as racism, social and economic deprivation, and difficulties that arise out of the migrant experience. Only time will tell if the successful resolution of these will further the processes of an Islamic renaissance in Europe. History informs us that religion and culture flower in Muslim societies when Muslims are confident of worldly success. Loss of confidence has traditionally led to religious introspection and the revival of primitivism. However, one impact of the Muslim presence in Europe has been the emergence of debates on the role of religion in public life. Whether in the polite discourse of the Archbishop of Canterbury on the place of those who answer to a higher authority in their relations with a secular state; the religious discourse that is dispersed in the political speeches of both George Bush and Barack Obama, albeit representing different sides of the US's religious spectrum; or the political engagement of Muslim minorities in the West; religion has re-emerged as a powerful voice in public life in the twenty-first century, and in this challenge to the secular paradigm that dominated the latter half of the twentieth century Muslims have already played a substantial part.

Sandel, in a new book, persuasively argues that Obama was successful on the campaign trail precisely because he had grasped a new *zeitgeist*; a yearning for civic life to be more meaningful; and his language resonated with the need for politics to demonstrate a more moral and spiritual content.[28] Sandel states that we have accepted a notion of neutrality in issues pertaining to justice and fairness. He challenges the secular paradigm that politics is a fundamentally neutral mechanism to assist people with different ideas of what constitutes 'good' to live together peacefully, by asserting that all questions concerning justice are spiritual or moral in content and it is not possible to remain neutral on what constitutes living a 'good life' or being a 'good citizen'.[29] If Sandel is correct then we may have to question the concept that underpins secularity and accept that the revelations believed to have been given to various peoples and underpinning civilizations have to be given a serious voice in politics and may create the narratives for a serious voice of dissent, an alternative model of citizenship, that will have to be provided a place at the table of public discourse and subsequent policy-making.

Notes

Chapter 1

1 Yasin Dutton (2007), *Original Islam*, London: Routledge, p. 1.
2 The belief in three righteous or perfect generations comes from a saying (Hadith) of the Prophet Muhammad, which states 'the best of you are my generation, then the ones that will follow them, then the ones that will follow them' (al-Bukhari, iii, p. 498; al-Tirmidhi, iv, pp. 500–1; Ibn Majah, ii, p. 791).
3 Qur'an 7:12.
4 Qur'an 2:34.
5 Qur'an 23:44.
6 The detailed story of the events prior to Muhammad's birth is recounted by Martin Ling (1983), *Muhammad: His Life Based on the Earliest Sources*, Cambridge, UK: The Islamic Texts Society.
7 For example, I. Goldziher (1966), *Muslim Studies*, ed. S. M. Stern, trans. C. R. Barber and S. M. Stern, London: George Allen & Unwin, Vol. I, p. 12, and R. A. Nicholson (1966), *The Literary History of the Arabs*, Cambridge, UK: Cambridge University Press, p. 135.
8 The general view is that the Quraysh had imposed a four-month truce period in which thousands of pilgrims from the desert tribes could enter the city to worship in the Ka'aba, believed to have contained 360 tribal idols.
9 Muhammad's father Abdullah died before his birth. As was customary, he was brought up by his paternal grandfather and entrusted to a Bedouin foster-mother for several years. On his return to his maternal uncles at the age of eight, his mother Amina died leaving the young boy an orphan. His grandfather died soon after. At this point his uncle took over raising the young boy.

Tradition states that he was employed as a shepherd boy until he travelled with his uncle's caravan at the age of 10.

10 Qur'an 96:1–5.

11 Barnaby Rogerson (2003), *The Prophet Muhammad*, London: Little, Brown, p. 208:

> O my people listen to me in earnest, worship God, say your daily prayers, fast during the month of Ramadan, and give alms. Perform the Hajj if you can afford to. All mankind is from Adam and Eve, an Arab has no superiority over a non-Arab nor a non-Arab has any superiority over an Arab: also white man has no superiority over a black nor a black has no superiority over white except by piety and good action. Learn that every Muslim is the brother of another Muslim, and that Muslims constitute one brotherhood. Nothing shall be legitimate to a Muslim which belongs to a fellow Muslim unless it was given freely and willingly. Do not therefore, do injustice to yourselves. Remember, one day you will appear before God and answer for your deeds. So beware, do not stray from the path of righteousness after I am gone.

12 S. Vahiduddin (1979), *Studies in Islam*, Indian Institute of Islamic Studies, Vol. XVI, No. 2, p. 75.

13 Kenneth Cragg (1987), *Islam and the Muslim*, Milton Keynes: Open University Press, p. 7.

14 Ron Geaves (1996), *Sectarian Influences within Islam in Britain*, Community Religions Project Monograph Series, Leeds: University of Leeds, p. 24.

15 F. Heeren (1976), *Women in Islam*, Leicester: The Islamic Foundation.

16 Edward Said (1978), *Orientalism*, London: Routledge and Kegan Paul.

Chapter 2

1 Other than Tirmidhi, Ibne Maja gives three independent narrations of the same Hadith. Talking about the authenticity of this Hadith, Abu Mansur Abd al-Kahir ibn-Tahir Al-Baghdadi says:

There are many isnad (independent testimonies) for the tradition dealing with the division of the community. A number of following companions have handed it down as coming from the Prophet (peace be upon him): Anas ibn-Malik, Abu-Hurairah, Abu-l-Darda, Jabir, Abu-Sa'id al-Khidri, Ubai ibn-Ka'b, Abd-Allah ibn-Amr ibn-al-'As, abu-Imamah, Wathilah ibn-al-Aska' and others. It is also handed down that the pious Caliphs mentioned that the community would be divided after them, that one sect only would save itself, and the rest of them would be given to error in this world, and to destruction in the next.

2 Muslim voices are not the only ones that proclaim the solidarity of the *umma*. Several Western Orientalists also describe Muslims in such terms. For example Montgomery Watt (1961), *Islam and the Integration of Society*, London: Routledge and Kegan Paul, p. 174, states that 'the Islamic state had gone a long way towards becoming a genuine community'. Charles Adams (1983), 'Mawdudi and the Islamic State', in *Voices of Resurgent Islam*, ed. John Esposito, Oxford and New York: Oxford University Press, p. 120, insists that 'Islamic society is held together by ideological harmony, composed of individuals with various ethnic-linguistic backgrounds'. Finally, Hamilton Gibb (1963), 'The Community in Islamic History', *The American Philosophical Society Proceedings*, 107 (2), April, p. 173, claims that

it consists of the totality of individuals bound to one another by ties, not of kinship or race, but of religion in that all of its members profess their belief in one God, and in the mission of the Prophet Muhammad. Before God and in their relation to Him, all are equal, without distinction of rank, class or race.

3 Roy Wallis (1979), *Salvation and Protest: Studies of Social and Religious Movements*, New York: St Martin's Press, p. 188.
4 Daniel Brown (2004), *A New Introduction to Islam*, Oxford: Blackwell, p. 101.
5 The Holy Qur'an (1405AH, revised Abdullah Yusef Ali, English translation), The Presidency of Islamic Researches, Mushaf Al-Madinah An-Nabawiyah: King Fahd Holy Qur'an Printing Complex, Sura 33:33.
6 Brown, p. 101.

7 Fuad Khuri (1990), *Imams and Emirs*, London: Al-Saqi Books, p. 105.
8 Khuri, p. 107.
9 Moojan Momen (1985), *An Introduction to Shi'i Islam*, New Haven: Yale University Press, p. 66.
10 Ibid.
11 Halm Heinz (1991), *Shiism*, trans. Janet Watson, Edinburgh: Edinburgh University Press, p. 12.
12 Eric Hobsbawm (1992), *The Invention of Tradition*, Cambridge, UK: Cambridge University Press.
13 Momen, p. 45.
14 Robert Brenton Betts (1988), *The Druze*, New Haven: Yale University Press, p. 8.
15 P. 9.
16 Khuri, p. 99.
17 Pp. 40–1.
18 The Holy Qur'an 3:104.
19 Malise Ruthwen (2004), *Fundamentalism*, Oxford: Oxford University Press, p. 39.
20 Ahmed Ishtiaq (1987), *The Concept of an Islamic State: An Analysis of the Ideological Controversy in Pakistan*, London: Francis Pinter, p. 33.
21 Ahmad, K. and Ansari, Z. I. (eds) (1979), *Islamic Perspectives: Studies in Honour of Sayyid Abul A'la Mawdudi*, Leicester: Islamic Foundation, p. 20.
22 Abdul Aziz Said and Meena Sharify-Funk (eds), *Cultural Diversity and Islam*, Lanham, MD: University Press of America, p. 168.
23 R. A. Geaves (2005), *Aspects of Islam*, London: Darton, Longman and Todd, and Washington, DC: Georgetown University Press, p. 124.
24 R. A. Geaves (2000), *Sufis of Britain*, Cardiff: Cardiff Academic Press, p. 18.
25 R. Nicholson (1989), 4th edn, *The Mystics of Islam*, Harmondsworth: Arkana, p. 146.
26 A. J. Arberry (1956), *Sufism*, London: George Allen & Unwin, p. 119.
27 Gibb, Hamilton (1963), 'The Community in Islamic History', *The American Philosophical Society Proceedings*, 107 (2), April, pp. 174–5.

Chapter 3

1   Antonio Rosmini (1867), *Principles of Ethics*, trans. Terence Watson and Dennis Cleary (2nd edn 1989), Durham: Rosmini House, p. ix.

2   J. Thompson (trans.) (1984 edition), *The Ethics of Aristotle*, Harmondsworth, Penguin.

3   J. Schacht (1952), *The Origins of Muhammadan Jurisprudence*, Oxford: Oxford University Press.

4   J. Schacht (1964), *Introduction to Islamic Law*, Oxford: Oxford University Press, p. 1.

5   Fazlur Rahman (1979), 2nd edn, *Islam*, Chicago: Chicago University Press.

6   S. Nomanul Haqq (2003), 'Islam and Ecology: Towards Retrieval and Reconstruction', in *Islam and Ecology*, ed. R. Foltz, F. Denny and A. Baharuddin, Cambridge, MA: Harvard University Press, p. 139.

7   Quoted from a lecture of Dr Jamal Badawi's from his Islamic Teachings series and published on www.islamonline.net as 'The Foundation of Islamic Ethics' in September 2005. Jamal Badawi is a Professor at St Mary's University in Halifax, Canada.

8   Qur'an, Al-Qasas 28:77.

9   R. A. Geaves (1999), 'Islam and Conscience', *Religion and Conscience*, ed. R. Hannaford, Canterbury, Gracewell Books, p. 164.

10 Rahman, p. 84.

11 Bernard Lewis (1998), 'Islamic Revolution', *The New York Review of Books*, 21 January, http://www.nybooks.com/articles/4557.

12 John Esposito (2005), *Islam*, Oxford: Oxford University Press, p. 79.

13 Bernard Lewis (1994), *Islam and the West*, Oxford: Oxford University Press, chapter 1.

14 S. Nomanul Haqq (2001), 'Islam', in *A Companion to Environmental Philosophy*, ed. Dale Jamieson, pp. 111–29, Oxford: Blackwell Publishing.

15 See, for example, Nomanul Haq (2001).

16 Sahih Bukhari 3:513.

17 L. Gari (2002), 'Arabic Treatises on Environmental Pollution Up to the End of the Thirteenth Century', *Environment and History*, 8 (4), pp. 475–88.

18 Qur'an 6:38.
19 Richard Foltz, Frederick Denny and Azizan Baharuddin (eds) (2003), *Islam and Ecology*, Religions of the World Ecology Series; Cambridge, MA: Harvard University Press, p. xxxix.
20 A. Vanzan Paladin (1998), 'Ethics and Neurology in the Islamic World: Continuity and Change', *Italian Journal of Neurological Science*, 19: 255–8 [257], Springer-Verlag.
21 Daniel Pipes (2002), 'What is Jihad', *New York Post*, 31 December.
22 Muhammad Sirozi (2004), 'Perspectives on Radical Islamic Education in Contemporary Indonesia: Major Themes and Characteristics of Abu Bakar Ba'asyir's Teachings', *Islam and the West Post 9/11*, ed. R. Geaves, T. Gabriel, *et al.*, Aldershot: Ashgate.
23 Qur'an 22:39–40.
24 Qur'an 2:190.
25 'Islam', Online Etymology Dictionary, http://www.etymonline.com, accessed 14 September 2009.
26 'Islam', Online Etymology Dictionary.
27 Al-Fatiha Foundation is dedicated to Muslims of all cultural and ethnic backgrounds who are lesbian, gay, bisexual, transgender, intersex, queer, and those who are questioning or exploring their sexual orientation and/or gender identity, and their families, friends and allies (the description of the organization is taken from their website at www.al-fatiha.org).
28 Abdullah and Hassan Saeed (2004), *Freedom of Religion: Apostasy and Islam*, Aldershot: Ashgate, pp. 170–2.
29 P. 13.
30 P. 12.
31 Judge Christopher G. Weeramantry (1997), *Justice Without Frontiers*, Brill Publishers, pp. 136–7.
32 Ibid.
33 For example, Jamal A. Badawi (1971), 'The Status of Women in Islam', *Al-Ittihad Journal of Islamic Studies*, 8 (2), September.
34 H. Yousuf Aboul-Enein and Sherifa Zuhur, *Islamic Rulings on Warfare*, p. 22, Strategic Studies Institute, US Army War College, Diane Publishing Co.
35 Noah Feldman (16 March 2008), 'Why Shariah?', *New York Times*, http://www.nytimes.com/2008/03/16/magazine/16Shariah-t.html.
36 Ronald Bontekoe and Mariëtta Tigranovna Stepaniants (1997),

Justice and Democracy, University of Hawaii Press, pp. 250–1.
37 Qur'an 42:38.
38 Qur'an 3:159.
39 Tariq Ramadan is the grandson of the Egyptian religious leader, Hassan Al-Banna (1906–49), who was the founder of the Muslim Brotherhood, which is considered the forerunner of contemporary movements of Islamic revivalism.
40 Tariq Ramadan (2004), *Western Muslims and the Future of Islam*, Oxford: Oxford University Press, p. 5.
41 Ibid.

Chapter 4

1   Cited from the last sermon of the Prophet Muhammad before his death.
2   Ruqaiyyah Waris Maqsood, 'Islam, Culture and Women', in *Islam for Today*, http://islamfortoday.com/ruqaiyyah09.htm, accessed 24 August 2009.
3   Ibid.
4   Ibid.
5   Ziba Mir-Hosseini (1999), *Islam and Gender*, Princeton, NJ: Princeton University Press, p. 7.
6   P. 5.
7   Mai Yamani (ed) (1996), *Feminism and Islam*, Reading: Ithaca, p. 1.
8   P. 2.
9   P. 5.
10 Ibid.
11 Fatima Naseef (1999), *Women in Islam*, London: Institute of Muslim Minority Affairs.
12 Leila Ahmed (1992), *Women and Gender in Islam*, Newhaven: Yale University Press, p. 4.
13 Barbara Stowasser (1994), *Women in the Qur'an: Traditions, and Interpretation*, Oxford: Oxford University Press.
14 Ahmed, pp. 4–5.
15 P. 2.
16 P. 3.
17 P. 1.
18 Qur'an 33:35.
19 Stowasser, p. 21.

20 Fatima Mernissi (1991), *Women and Islam*, Oxford: Blackwell.
21 Pp. 118–19.
22 Ibid.
23 Lila Abu-Lughod (1998), *Remaking Woman: Feminism and Modernity in the Middle-East*, Princeton, NJ: Princeton University Press.
24 Anne Sofie Roald (2001), *Women in Islam: The Western Experience*, London: Routledge, p. 295.
25 P. 297.
26 Stowasser, pp. 23–4.
27 Ahmed, p. 2.
28 Abu-Lughod, p. 3.
29 Gisela Webb (ed.) (2000), *Windows of Faith*, New York: Syracuse University Press, p. xiii.
30 Mir-Husseini, p. 6.
31 Roald, p. 295.
32 Ahmed, 1992, p. 14.
33 Ibid.
34 Ibid.
35 Sherifa Zuhur (1992), *Revealing Reveiling*, Albany: State University of New York.
36 Zahra Kamalkhani (1998), *Women's Islam*, London: Kegan Paul International.
37 P. 7.
38 Ibid.
39 S. Khan (1998), 'Muslim Women: Negotiations in the Third Space', *Signs: Journal of Women and Culture in Society*, 23 (2), p. 465.
40 Fauzia Ahmad (2003), '"Still in Progress?" – Methodological Dilemmas, Tensions and Contradictions in Theorizing South Asian Muslim Women', in *South Asian Women in the Diaspora*, ed. Nirmal Purwar and Parvati Raghuram, Oxford: Berg, p. 43.
41 Marnia Lazreg (1988), 'Feminism and Difference: The Perils of Writing as a Woman on Women in Algeria', *Feminist Studies*, 14, Spring, p. 96.
42 Caroline Hawley, 20 November 2000, 'Arab Women Demand Equal Opportunities', BBC News Middle-East World.
43 BBC News, 1 August 2000, 'Iranian Women to Lead Prayers', BBC News Middle-East World.
44 BBC News, 7 January 2001, 'Iran Overturns Women's Study Ban', BBC News Middle-East World.

45 BBC News, 23 February 2000, 'Iranian Women Seek Equality', BBC News Middle-East World.
46 Caroline Hawley, 23 October 1999, 'Egyptian Women's Rights: A Century On', BBC News Middle-East World.
47 Caroline Hawley, 29 January 2000, 'First Egyptian Woman Files for Divorce', BBC News Middle-East World.
48 Caroline Hawley, 12 March 2000, '"New Era" for Egyptian Women', BBC News Middle-East World.
49 Stephanie Irving, 20 November 2000, 'Morocco Women Win Rights', BBC News Middle-East World.
50 Katherine Zoepf, 29 August 2006, 'Islamic Revival Led By Women Tests Syria's Secularism', *Islam for Today*, http://islamfortoday. com/women, accessed 1 September 2009.
51 Ibid.
52 Aicha Lemsine, 16 March 2001, 'The Suffering of Algeria's Women at the Hands of Islamists', *Middle East Times*, Cairo.
53 David Hirst, 3 August 1999, 'Educated for Indolence', *The Guardian*.
54 Roger Hardy, 30 September 2003, 'Saudi Women Join Reform Call', BBC News Middle-East World.
55 Ibid.
56 Webb (2000).

Chapter 5

1 Hadden and Schupe (1989), *Secularisation and Fundamentalism Reconsidered*, New York: New Era Books.
2 Published between 1994 and 1996, the comprehensive edited collections attempt to be the definitive collection on religious fundamentalism. The titles of the five volumes of edited contributions are as follows: *Fundamentalisms Observed* (1991), ed. Martin Marty and R. Scott Appleby; *Fundamentalisms and Society* (1993), ed. Martin Marty, R. Scott Appleby, Helen Hardacre and Everett Mendelsohn; *Fundamentalisms and the State: Remaking Policies, Economies and Militance* (1993), ed. Martin Marty, R. Scott Appleby, John H. Garvey and Timur Kuran; *Accounting For Fundamentalisms: The Dynamic Character of Movements* (1994), ed. Martin Marty, R. Scott Appelby, Robert E. Frykenberg, Samuel C. Heilman and James Piscatori; and *Fundamentalisms Comprehended* (1995) ed. Martin Marty and

R. Scott Appleby, all published in Chicago by Chicago University Press.

3 Lionel Caplan (1987), *Studies in Religious Fundamentalism*, London: Macmillan.

4 Christopher Partridge (ed.) (2001), 'Introduction', *Fundamentalisms*, Carlisle: Paternoster Press.

5 John Esposito (1988), *Islam – the Straight Path*, Oxford: Oxford University Press; Youssef Choueiri (1997), *Islamic Fundamentalism*, 2nd revised edn, London and Washington, DC: Cassell-Pinter; Mark Huband (1995), *Warriors of the Prophet*, Colorado: Westview Press; Gilles Kepel (2002), *Jihad: The Trail of Political Islam*, Cambridge, MA: Harvard University Press; Dilip Hiro (1989), *Holy Wars: The Rise of Islamic Fundamentalism*, New York: Routledge.

6 Hadden and Schupe (1989).

7 John Esposito (2002), 'Islam and Secularism in the Twenty-first Century', in *Islam and Secularism in the Middle-East*, ed. John Esposito and Azzam Tamimi, London: Hurst & Co., pp. 45–6.

8 Emmanuel Sivan (1985), *Radical Islam: Medieval Theology and Modern Politics*, Newhaven: Yale University Press, p. 96.

9 Othman Llewellyn (2003), 'The Basis for a Discipline of Islamic Environmental Law', in *Islam and Ecology*, ed. R. Foltz, F. Denny and A. Baharuddin, Cambridge, MA: Harvard University Press, p. 221.

10 John Esposito (2002a), *Unholy War: Terror in the Name of Islam*, Oxford: Oxford University Press, p. 1.

11 Mark Huband (1995), *Warriors of the Prophet*, Boulder, CO: Westview Press.

12 Esposito, p. 3.

13 P. x.

14 John Shepherd (2004), 'Self-critical Children of Abraham? Roots of Violence and Extremism in Judaism, Christianity and Islam', *Islam and the West Post 9/11*, ed. R. Geaves, T. Gabriel, *et al.*, Aldershot: Ashgate, pp. 27–50.

15 P. 31.

16 P. 37.

17 Fazlun Khalid (2003), 'Islam, Ecology, and Modernity: An Islamic Critique of the Root Causes of Environmental Degradation', in *Islam and Ecology*, ed. R. Foltz, F. Denny and A. Baharuddin, Cambridge, MA: Harvard University Press, p. 300.

18 P. 308.

19 Z. Bauman (1993), 'Modernity', in *The Oxford Companion to the Politics of the World*, ed. Joel Kriegar, Oxford: Oxford University Press.

20 Khalid, p. 307.

21 P. 300.

22 S. Nomanul Haqq (2003), 'Islam and Ecology: Towards Retrieval and Reconstruction', in *Islam and Ecology*, ed. R. Foltz, F. Denny and A. Baharuddin, Cambridge, MA: Harvard University Press, p. 123.

23 Robert Pope (2001), 'Battling for God in a Secular World: Politics and Fundamentalisms', in *Fundamentalisms*, ed. Christopher Partridge, Carlisle: Paternoster Press, p. 183.

24 Abdul Aziz Said and Nathan Funk (2003), 'Peace in Islam: An Ecology of the Spirit', in *Islam and Ecology*, ed. R. Foltz, F. Denny and A. Baharuddin, Cambridge, MA: Harvard University Press, pp. 167–74.

25 George Hourani (1985), *Reason and Tradition in Islamic Ethics*, Cambridge, UK: Cambridge University Press, p. 86.

26 Haqq (2003), p. 125.

27 Yasin Dutton (2003), 'The Environmental Crisis of Our Time: A Muslim Response', in *Islam and Ecology*, ed. R. Foltz, F. Denny and A. Baharuddin, Cambridge, MA: Harvard University Press, p. 323.

28 P. 325.

29 Daniel Pipes (2002), 'What is Jihad', *New York Post*, 31 December.

30 Muhammad Sirozi (2004), 'Perspectives on Radical Islamic Education in Contemporary Indonesia: Major Themes and Characteristics of Abu Bakar Ba'asyir's Teachings', *Islam and the West Post 9/11*, ed. R. Geaves, T. Gabriel, *et al.*, Aldershot: Ashgate.

31 John Esposito (1999), *The Islamic Threat: Myth or Reality*, Oxford: Oxford University Press, p. 30.

32 Mohammed Abdul Malek (2001), 'The Islamic Doctrine of Jihad Does Not Advocate Violence', in *Islam Opposing Viewpoints*, ed. Jennifer Hurley, San Diego: Greenhaven Press, p. 121.

33 Qur'an 3:110.

34 Qur'an 4:76.

35 Mir Mustansir (1987), *Dictionary of Qur'anic Terms and Concepts*, New York and London: Garland Publishing, p. 112.

36 Sirozi, p. 174.

37 Imam Khomeini (1985), *Islam and Revolution*, trans. Hamid Algar, London: KPI, p. 132.
38 Ibid.
39 P. 149.
40 Ibid.
41 P. 132.
42 P. 149.
43 D. Behrend (2003), *Reading Past the Myth: Public Teachings of Abu Bakar Ba'asyir*, http://www.arts.auckland.ac.nz/asia/tbehrend/radical-islam.htm, p. 8.

Chapter 6

1 Shaikh Abdullah Quilliam, in *Islamic World*, July 1896, Vol. 4, p. 74.
2 Pew Research Center's Forum on Religion and Public Life, 2009, reported in *The Guardian*, Friday 9 October.
3 According to the census returns, there are 3.7 million people of 'possible Muslim faith' in France (6.3 per cent of the total population of Metropolitan France in 1999) but the numbers are highly disputed by right-wing organizations (see 'Les vrais chiffres' by Gilbert Charles and Besma Lahouri, *L'Express*, 12 April 2003; see also Michèle Tribalat, 'Counting France's Numbers – Deflating the Numbers Inflation', *The Social Contract Journal*, 14 (2), Winter 2003–4).
4 Http://www.dw-world.de/dw/article/0,,4419533,00.html, accessed 16 October 2009.
5 Http://www.state.gov/r/pa/ei/bgn/3997.htm, accessed 16 October 2009.
6 Only a minority of the Muslims residing in Germany are members of religious associations. The ones with the highest numerical strength are: Diyanet İşleri Türk İslam Birliği (DİTİB), German branch of the Turkish Presidency for Religious Affairs, Cologne; Islamische Gemeinschaft Milli Görüş, close to the Islamist Saadet Partisi in Turkey, Kerpen near Cologne; Islamische Gemeinschaft Jamaat un-Nur, German branch of the Risale-i Nur Society (Said Nursi); Verband der islamischen Kulturzentren: German branch of the conservative Süleymanci sect in Turkey, Cologne; Islamische Gemeinschaft in Deutschland organization of Arab Muslims close to the Muslim Brotherhood, Frankfurt; Verband der Islamischen

Gemeinden der Bosniaken, Bosnian Muslims, Kamp-Lintfort near Duisburg. There are two central umbrella organizations: Zentralrat der Muslime in Deutschland, dominated by the 'Islamische Gemeinschaft in Deutschland'; and the 'Islamisches Zentrum Aachen', Islamrat in Deutschland, dominated by Islamische Gemeinschaft Milli Görüş and its suborganizations. In addition, there are numerous local associations including Sufi movements without affiliation to any of these organizations.

7   Estimates of the number of Muslims in France vary widely. In accordance with a law dating from 1872, the French Republic does not ask about religion in its census. Nor does it ask for ethnic origin. In 2006 the United States Department of State placed it at roughly 10 per cent, while two 2007 polls placed it at 3 per cent of the national population. The CIA World Factbook places it at 5–10 per cent. In 2000, the French Ministry of the Interior estimated the total number of people born into Islam as 4.1 million and converts as about 40,000. Estimates of numbers of Muslims, and the alleged dangers in the housing projects of the suburbs by the Renseignements Généraux, the intelligence agency, have often been criticized. Critics in particular are the *Monde diplomatique* and the *Canard Enchaîné*. A study conducted by Michèle Tribalat based on 1999 French census returns showed that claims of 5 to 6 million Muslims in France were overestimated.

8   An Interior ministry source in *l'Islam dans la République*, Haut Conseil à l'intégration, November 2000, p. 26.

9   From the same source. Statistics for illegal immigrants are based upon those awaiting regularization and for obvious reasons there are no reliable estimates for others who have not made themselves known to the authorities.

10 *L'Islam en France et les reactions aux attentats du 11 septembre 2001, Résultats détaillés*, of the Institut Français de l'Opinion Publique (IFOP) (HV/LDV No. 1–33–1, 28 September 2001.

11 The history of *laïcité* dates to the French Revolution. In the Revolution of 1789 the French people sought to overthrow not only the monarchy and its supporters, but also the whole social and political system, including the Roman Catholic Church. Although the Church survived the Revolution, according to the ideology of the new republic it could no longer remain a separate estate with its own possessions. The state also attempted a huge restructuring of the Church hierarchy and demanded that the

clergy swear allegiance to the French Government ahead of the Church. This dispute was only resolved in 1801, when Napoleon Bonaparte signed a Concordat with the Pope, which officially brought the Catholic religion under state control. However, the document stated that so long as the Church confined its authority to religious affairs and kept within the rule of the law it would be allowed to run itself. France had begun to view faith as a matter for each individual citizen rather than for the nation as a whole. Despite this, it was not until 1905 that the principle of secularism in France was fully developed and set down as a law. This was mainly due to increased conflict between atheist government ministers and members of the Catholic Church, who had been allowed to work in schools and hospitals. In 1880, Jules Ferry (an ancestor of the education minister who oversaw the 2004 law) sought to completely eliminate religious personnel from state-run schools as part of his education reforms. This was taken a step further by Emile Combes, who, in 1902, closed the majority of religious schools and as Prime Minister was behind the movement in favour of a law guaranteeing the independence of the state from religion. The main terms of the law of 1905 were enshrined in a number of already-applied principles in law, but it also officially ended Napoleon's Concordat and imposed a number of new measures. The main terms of the law were: (1) no religion could be supported by the state, either by financial aid or political support; (2) everyone had the right to follow a religion, but no one had an obligation to do so; and (3) religious education at school was strictly forbidden.

12 This information comes from the Renseignements Généraux, the intelligence service of the French police, but its reports on security issues have often been criticized, for example by *Le Monde Diplomatique*, a current affairs magazine, and *Le Canard Enchaîné*, a satirical monthly publication.

13 R. A. Geaves (2005), 'Negotiating British Citizenship and Muslim Identity', *Muslim Britain*, ed. Tahir Abbas, London: Zed Books pp. 66–77.

14 Pnina Werbner (2002), *Imagined Diasporas among Manchester Muslims*, Oxford: James Currey, p. 49.

15 The labels of 'participationist' and 'rejectionist' were coined by Anthony McRoy (2006), *From Rushdie to 7/7: The Radicalisation of Islam in Britain*, London: The Social Affairs Unit.

16 Tariq Ramadan (2004), *Western Muslims and the Future of Islam*,

Oxford: Oxford University Press, p. 83.

17 Tariq Ramadan (2000), 'Who Speaks for European Muslims?', *La Monde Diplomatique*, June.
18 N. Le Quesne (2000), 'Trying to Bridge a Great Divide', in *Time Magazine*, 11 December.
19 Cited from Magda El-Ghitany (2005), 'Enemy Within', Al-Ahram Weekly On-Line, 14–20 July, No. 751.
20 Ibid.
21 Renata Goldirova (2007), 'Brussels Questions EU Capitals over Approach to Islam', in the *EUobserver*, 6 July.
22 Andrew Rippin (2005), 3rd edn, *Muslims: Their Religious Beliefs and Practices*, London: Routledge, pp. 181–8.
23 Hefner (2005), Eickelman and Piscatori (1996), Esposito (1991) and (1987), Esposito and Voll (1996), and Makris (2007).
24 John Esposito and John Voll (1996), *Islam and Democracy*, New York: Oxford University Press, p. 3.
25 The medieval Islamic scholar Ibn Taymiyya, in his *al-Wasaiyyah as-Sughraa* in *Majmoo al-Fataawa*, was probably the first to use the term to describe backsliding in contemporary Muslim society as opposed to pre-Islamic Arab society. It was picked up again by Maulana Mawdudi and Sayyid Qutb, who used the term to describe contemporary Muslim societies that were not applying *shari'a* law in totality. It can sometimes be used to describe non-Muslim societies.
26 Samuel Huntingdon (2002), *The Clash of Civilisations and the Remaking of World Order*, London: Free Press. Amongst other academics that implicitly promote such a view of Islam and Muslim cultures are Daniel Pipes and Bernard Lewis.
27 J. Clarke (1997), *Oriental Enlightenment: The Encounter between Asian and Western Thought*, London: Routledge, p. 225.
28 F. Heeren (1976), *Women in Islam*, Leicester: The Islamic Foundation.
29 Edward Said (1978), *Orientalism*, London: Routledge and Kegan Paul.
30 Bruce Lawrence (1998), *Shattering the Myth: Islam Beyond Violence*, Princeton, NJ: Princeton University Press, p. 5.
31 Norman Daniel (1993), 2nd edn, *Islam and the West: The Making of an Image*, Oxford: Oneworld, p. 17.
32 Ibid., p. 24.
33 Franklin Graham, quoted in Giles Fraser (10 November 2003), 'The Evangelicals Who Like to Giftwrap Islamophobia', *The*

172   Notes

Guardian.

34 William Boykin, quoted in Giles Fraser, ibid.

35 John Wansbrough (1977), *Qur'anic Studies: Sources and Methods of Scriptural Interpretation,* Oxford: Oxford University Press, quoted in Malise Ruthwen (2004), *Fundamentalism,* Oxford: Oxford University Press.

36 Dominic Cascioni (29 September 2002), 'Pledge to Wipe Out Islamophobia', BBC News Online Bulletin.

37 Mark Wark (1994), *Virtual Geography: Living with Global Media Events,* Bloomington: Indiana University Press, p. 23.

38 Quoted in Cascioni (2002).

39 Gordon Conway (1997), 'Islamophobia', *Bulletin – the University of Sussex Newsletter,* No. 7, November.

40 Said (1978), p. 1.

41 Montgomery Watt (1988), *Islamic Fundamentalism and Modernity,* London: Routledge.

42 Yvonne Haddad (2004), 'The Shaping of a Moderate North American Islam: Between "Mufti" Bush and "Ayatollah" Ashcroft', in *Islam and the West Post 9/11,* ed. R. Geaves, T. Gabriel, *et al.*, Aldershot: Ashgate, p. 99.

43 Haddad (2004).

44 Ibn Warraq (2007), *Defending the West: A Critique of Edward Said's Orientalism,* New York: Prometheus Books, p. 44.

45 P. 38. Goldziher, a Hungarian scholar of Islam, describes the moment 'I became inwardly convinced that I was a Muslim ... Never in my life was I more devout, more truly devout, than on that exalted Friday'; see Raphael Patai (1987), *Ignaz Goldziher and his Oriental Diary,* Detroit: Wayne State University, p. 28.

46 Gritt Klinkhammer (2009), 'The Emergence of Transethnic Sufism in Germany: From Mysticism to Authenticity', in *Sufis in Western Society: Global Networking and Locality,* ed. Markus Dressler, Ron Geaves and Gritt Klinkhammer, London: Routledge Sufi Series.

47 P. 131.

48 L. Seidentop (2000), *Democracy in Europe: Europe, Christianity and Islam,* Harmondsworth: Penguin, p. 209.

49 The *fatwa (fetva)* is as follows:

In the name of Allah, the most merciful and compassionate! Peace to all True Believers to whom this shall come!

Know ye, O Muslims, that the British government has

decided to commence military and warlike operations against the Muslims of the Soudan, who have taken up arms to defend their country and their faith. And it is in contemplation to employ Muslim soldiers to fight against these Muslims of the Soudan.

For any true believer to take up arms and fight against another Muslim who is not in revolt against the Khalif is contrary to the Shariat, and against the law of God and His Holy Prophet.

I warn every true believer that if he gives the slightest assistance in this projected expedition against the Muslims of the Soudan, even to the extent of carrying a parcel, or giving a bite of bread or a drink of water to any person taking part in this expedition against these Muslims, that he thereby helps the Giaour against the Muslim, and his name will be unworthy to be continued on the roll of the faithful.

Signed in the Mosque of Liverpool, England, the 10th Day of Shawal 1313.

W. H Abdullah Quilliam Sheikh al-Islam of the British Isles.

(*The Islamic World*, Vol. IV, No. 37, May 1896, pp. 86–7)

50 P. 89.
51 *The Crescent*, 1 March 320, 1899, the weekly newspaper published by Abdullah Quilliam from 1883 to 1908.
52 The *Islamic World*, Vol. IV, No. 37, May 1896, p. 90.
53 Rippin (2005), p. 195.
54 Rahman (1979), p. 633.

The Future

1 See Maleiha Malik (2008), 'In Broken Images': Faith in the Public Sphere', and Michael Nazir Ali 'Christian Faith and National Belonging', in *Building a Better Bridge: Muslims, Christians and the Common Good*, ed. Michael Ipgrave, Washington, DC: Georgetown University Press.
2 *Nostra Aetate*, caption 3.
3 The 2000 declaration of the Congregation for the Propagation of the Faith, *Dominus Iesus*, promulgated under the Prefecture of Joseph Ratzinger, then Cardinal, now Pope Benedictus XVI,

invites theologians of the Church 'to explore if and in what ways the historical and positive elements of other religions may fall within the divine plan of salvation'. Article 841 of the Catholic Catechism states that God's plan of salvation includes Muslims who 'acknowledge the Creator'.

4   A sentiment expressed in the concluding page of *Building a Better Bridge: Muslims, Christians and the Common Good*, ed. Michael Ipgrave, Washington, DC: Georgetown University Press, p. 177, and developed by the editor in Michael Ipgrave (2005), *Bearing the Word*, London: Church House, pp. 124–40.

5   Qur'an 10:99.

6   Paul Heck (2009), *Common Ground: Islam, Christianity and Religious Pluralism*, Washington, DC: Georgetown University Press, p. 221.

7   Malcolm Evans (2009), 'Human Rights and the Freedom of Religion', in *Justice and Rights, Christian and Muslim Perspectives*, ed. Michael Ipgrave, Washington, DC: Georgetown University Press, p. 109.

8   P. 110.

9   Ibid.

10 Mary Jelen, Ted G. Cochran and Clarke E. Segers (1998), *A Wall of Separation? Debating the Public Role of Religion* (Enduring Questions in American Political Life Series), Lanham, MD: Rowman & Littlefield, p. 5.

11 John Rawls (2005), *A Theory of Justice*, Boston: Belknap Press of Harvard University Press.

12 P. 137.

13 John Rawls and Samuel Freeman (ed.) (2001), *Collected Papers*, Cambridge, MA: Harvard University Press, p. 427.

14 Jelen, Cochran and Segers, p. 53.

15 Nicholas Wolterstorff and Robert Audi (1997), *Religion in the Public Square: The Place of Religious Convictions in Political Debate*, Lanham, MD: Rowman & Littlefield.

16 P. 105.

17 Hasan Hanafi (1995), *Islam in the Modern World*, Cairo: Anglo-Egyptian Bookshop.

18 P. 15.

19 P. 29.

20 P. 32.

21 Bassam Tibi (2008), *Political Islam, World Politics and Europe*, London: Routledge, p. 3.

22 P. 4.
23 Pp. 15, 17.
24 P. 19.
25 Taha Jabir Al-Alwani (2006), *Islamic Thought: An Approach to Reform*, London: The International Institute of Islamic Thought, p. 7.
26 Francis Fukuyama (1992), *The End of History and the Last Man*, New York: Avon Books.
27 Tibi, pp. 18–19.
28 Michael Sandel (2009), *Justice: What's the Right Thing to Do?* London: Allen Lane.
29 Interview with Michael Sandel by Oliver Burkeman, 31 October 2009, *Guardian Review*.

Bibliography

Aboul-Enein, H. Yousuf and Zuhur, Sherifa, *Islamic Rulings on Warfare*, p. 22, Strategic Studies Institute, US Army War College, Diane Publishing Co.

Abu-Lughod, Lila (1998), *Remaking Woman: Feminism and Modernity in the Middle-East*, Princeton, NJ: Princeton University Press.

Adams, Charles (1983), 'Mawdudi and the Islamic State', in *Voices of Resurgent Islam*, ed. John Esposito, New York: Oxford University Press.

Ahmad, Fauzia (2003), '"Still in Progress?" – Methodological Dilemmas, Tensions and Contradictions in Theorizing South Asian Muslim Women', in *South Asian Women in the Diaspora*, ed. Nirmal Purwar and Parvati Raghuram, Oxford: Berg.

Ahmad, K. and Ansari, Z. I. (eds) (1979), *Islamic Perspectives: Studies in Honour of Sayyid Abul A'la Mawdudi*, , Leicester: Islamic Foundation.

Ahmed, Ishtiaq (1987), *The Concept of an Islamic State – An Analysis of the Ideological Controversy in Pakistan*, London: Francis Pinter.

Ahmed, Leila (1992), *Women and Gender in Islam*, Newhaven: Yale University Press.

Al-Alwani, Taha Jabir (2006), *Islamic Thought: An Approach to Reform*, London: The International Institute of Islamic Thought.

Appleby, R. Scott (1995), *Fundamentalisms Comprehended*, Chicago: Chicago University Press.

Arberry, A. J. (1956), *Sufism*, London: George Allen & Unwin.

Badawi, Jamal A. (1971), 'The Status of Women in Islam', *Al-Ittihad Journal of Islamic Studies*, 8 (2), September.

Bauman, Z. (1993), 'Modernity', in *The Oxford Companion to the Politics of the World*, ed. Joel Kriegar, Oxford: Oxford University Press.

Behrend, D. (2003), 'Reading Past the Myth: Public Teachings of Abu Bakar Ba'asyir', http://www.arts.auckland.ac.nz/asia/tbehrend/radical-islam.htm.

Betts, Robert Brenton (1988), *The Druze*, New Haven: Yale University Press.

Bontekoe, Ronald and Stepaniants, Mariëtta Tigranovna (1997), *Justice and Democracy*, University of Hawaii Press.

Brown, Daniel (2004), *A New Introduction to Islam*, Oxford: Blackwell.

Caplan, Lionel (1987), *Studies in Religious Fundamentalism*, London: Macmillan.

Cascioni, Dominic (29 September 2001), 'Pledge to Wipe Out Islamophobia', BBC News Online Bulletin.

Choueiri, Youssef (1997), *Islamic Fundamentalism*, London: Pinter.

Clarke, J. (1997), *Oriental Enlightenment: The Encounter between Asian and Western Thought*, London: Routledge.

Conway, Gordon (November 1997), 'Islamophobia', *Bulletin – the University of Sussex Newsletter*, No. 7.

Cragg, Kenneth (1987), *Islam and the Muslim*, Milton Keynes: Open University Press.

Daniel, Norman (1993), *Islam and the West: The Making of an Image*, 2nd edn, Oxford: Oneworld.

Donohue, John and Esposito, John (eds) (1982), *Islam in Transmission*, Oxford: Oxford University Press.

Dutton, Yasin (2003), 'The Environmental Crisis of Our Time: A Muslim Response' in *Islam and Ecology*, ed. R. Foltz, F. Denny and A. Baharuddin, Cambridge, MA: Harvard University Press, p. 323.

Dutton, Yasin (2007), *Original Islam*, London: Routledge.

El-Ghitany, Magda (2005), 'Enemy Within', Al-Ahram Weekly On-Line, 14–20 July, No. 751.

Esposito, John (1988), *Islam – The Straight Path*, Oxford: Oxford University Press.

Esposito, John (1999), *The Islamic Threat: Myth or Reality*, Oxford: Oxford University Press.

Esposito, John (2002a), *Unholy War: Terror in the Name of Islam*, Oxford: Oxford University Press.

Esposito, John (2002b), 'Islam and Secularism in the Twenty-first Century', in *Islam and Secularism in the Middle-East*, ed. John Esposito and Azzam Tamimi, London: Hurst & Co.

Esposito, John (2005), *Islam*, Oxford: Oxford University Press.

Esposito, John and Voll, John O. (1996), *Islam and Democracy*, New York: Oxford University Press.

Evans, Malcolm (2009), 'Human Rights and the Freedom of Religion', in *Justice and Rights: Christian and Muslim Perspectives*, ed. Michael Ipgrave, Washington, DC: Georgetown University Press.

Feldman, Noah (2008), 'Why Shariah?', *New York Times*, 16 March.

Foltz, Richard, Denny, Frederick and Baharuddin, Azizan (eds) (2003), *Islam and Ecology* (Religions of the World Ecology Series), Cambridge, MA: Harvard University Press.

Fraser, Giles (2003), 'The Evangelicals Who Like to Giftwrap Islamophobia', *The Guardian*, 10 November.

Fukuyama, Francis (1992), *The End of History and the Last Man*, New York: Avon Books.

Gardner, Frank (2001), 'Saudi Women Defy Business Curbs', BBC News Middle-East World, 21 January.

Gari, L. (2002), 'Arabic Treatises on Environmental Pollution Up to the End of the Thirteenth Century', *Environment and History*, 8 (4), pp. 475–88.

Geaves, Ron (1996), *Sectarian Influences within Islam in Britain* (Community Religions Project Monograph Series), Leeds: University of Leeds.

Geaves, Ron (1999), 'Islam and Conscience', in *Conscience in the World Religions*, ed. R. Hannaford, Canterbury: Gracewing.

Geaves, Ron (2000), *The Sufis of Britain*, Cardiff: Cardiff Academic Press.

Geaves, R. A. (2005), *Aspects of Islam*, London: Darton, Longman and Todd and Washington, DC: Georgetown University Press.

Geaves, R. A. (2005), 'Negotiating British Citizenship and Muslim Identity', in *Muslim Britain*, ed. Tahir Abbas, London: Zed Books, pp. 66–77.

Gibb, Hamilton (1963), 'The Community in Islamic History', *The American Philosophical Society Proceedings*, 107 (2), April.

Goldirova, Renata (2007), 'Brussels Questions EU Capitals Over Approach to Islam', in *the EUobserver*, 6 July.

Goldziher, I. (1966), *Muslim Studies*, trans. C. R. Barber and S. M. Stern, London: George Allen & Unwin, Vol. I.

Haddad, Yvonne (2004), 'The Shaping of a Moderate North American Islam: Between "Mufti" Bush and "Ayatollah" Ashcroft', in *Islam and the West Post 9/11*, ed. R. Geaves, T. Gabriel, *et al.*, Aldershot: Ashgate.

Hadden, Jeffrey, K. and Schupe, Anson (1989), *Secularisation and Fundamentalism Reconsidered*, New York: New Era Books.

Halm, Heinz (1991), *Shiism*, trans. Janet Watson, Edinburgh: Edinburgh University Press.

Hanafi, Hasan (1995), *Islam in the Modern World*, Cairo: Anglo-Egyptian Bookshop.

Haqq, S. Nomanul (2001), 'Islam', in *A Companion to Environmental Philosophy*, ed. Dale Jamieson, pp. 111–29, Oxford: Blackwell Publishing.

Haqq, S. Nomanul (2003), 'Islam and Ecology: Towards Retrieval and Reconstruction', in *Islam and Ecology*, ed. R. Foltz, F. Denny and A. Baharuddin, Cambridge, MA: Harvard University Press.

Hardy, Roger (2003), 'Saudi Women Join Reform Call', BBC News Middle-East World, 30 September.

Hawley, Caroline (1999), 'Egyptian Women's Rights: A Century On', BBC News Middle-East World, 23 October.

Hawley, Caroline (2000), 'First Egyptian Woman Files for Divorce', BBC News Middle-East World, 29 January.

Hawley, Caroline (2000), '"New Era" for Egyptian Women', BBC News Middle-East World, 12 March.

Hawley, Caroline (2000), 'Arab Women Demand Equal Opportunities', BBC News Middle-East World, 20 November.

Heck, Paul (2009), *Common Ground: Islam, Christianity and Religious Pluralism*, Washington, DC: Georgetown University Press.

Heeren, F. (1976), *Women in Islam*, Leicester: The Islamic Foundation.

Hiro, Dilip (1989), *Holy Wars: The Rise of Islamic Fundamentalism*, New York: Routledge.

Hirst, David (1999), 'Educated for Indolence', *The Guardian*, 3 August.

Hobsbawm, Eric (1992), *The Invention of Tradition*, Cambridge, UK: Cambridge University Press.

Holy Qur'an, The (1405AH revised Abdullah Yusef Ali English translation), The Presidency of Islamic Researches, Mushaf Al-Madinah An-Nabawiyah: King Fahd Holy Qur'an Printing Complex.

Hourani, George (1985), *Reason and Tradition in Islamic Ethics*, Cambridge, UK: Cambridge University Press.

Huband, Mark (1995), *Warriors of the Prophet*, Boulder, CO: Westview Press.

Huntingdon, Samuel (2002), *The Clash of Civilisations and the Remaking of World Order*, London: Free Press.

Ibn Warraq (2007), *Defending the West: A Critique of Edward Said's Orientalism*, New York: Prometheus Books.

Ipgrave, Michael (2005), *Bearing the Word*, London: Church House.

Irving, Stephanie (2000), 'Morocco Women Win Rights', BBC News Middle-East World, 20 November.

Jelen, Mary, Cochran, Ted and Segers, Clarke E. (1998), *A Wall of Separation? Debating the Public Role of Religion* (Enduring Questions in American Political Life Series), Lanham, MD: Rowman & Littlefield.

Kamalkhani, Zahra (1998), *Women's Islam*, London: Kegan Paul International.

Kepel, Gilles (2002), *Jihad: The Trail of Political Islam*, Cambridge, MA: Harvard University Press.

Khalid, Fazlun (2003), 'Islam, Ecology, and Modernity: An Islamic Critique of the Root Causes of Environmental Degradation', in *Islam and Ecology*, ed. R. Foltz, F. Denny and A. Baharuddin, Cambridge, MA: Harvard University Press.

Khomeini, Imam (1985), *Islam and Revolution*, trans. Hamid Algar, London: KPI.

Khuri, Fuad (1990), *Imams and Emirs*, London: Al-Saqi Books.

Klinkhammer, Gritt (2009), 'The Emergence of Transethnic Sufism in Germany: From Mysticism to Authenticity', in *Sufis in Western Society: Global Networking and Locality*, ed. Markus Dressler, Ron Geaves and Gritt Klinkhammer, London: Routledge Sufi Series.

Lawrence, Bruce (1998), *Shattering the Myth: Islam beyond Violence*, Princeton, NJ:

Princeton University Press.

Lazreg, Marnia (1988), 'Feminism and Difference: The Perils of Writing as a Woman on Women in Algeria', *Feminist Studies*, 14, Spring, pp. 81–107.

Lemsine, Aicha (2001), 'The Suffering of Algeria's Women at the Hands of Islamists', *Middle East Times*, 16 March, Cairo.

Le Quesne, N. (2000), 'Trying to Bridge a Great Divide', in *Time Magazine*, 11 December.

Lewis, Bernard (1994), *Islam and the West*, Oxford: Oxford University Press.

Ling, Martin (1983), *Muhammad: His Life Based on the Earliest Sources*, Cambridge, UK: The Islamic Texts Society.

Llewellyn, Othman (2003), 'The Basis for a Discipline of Islamic Environmental Law', in *Islam and Ecology*, ed. R. Foltz, F. Denny and A. Baharuddin, Cambridge, MA: Harvard University Press.

Malek, Mohammed Abdul (2001), 'The Islamic Doctrine of Jihad Does Not Advocate Violence', in *Islam Opposing Viewpoints*, ed. Jennifer Hurley, San Diego: Greenhaven Press.

Malik, Maleiha (2008), 'In Broken Images': Faith in the Public Sphere', in *Building a Better Bridge: Muslims, Christians and the Common Good*, ed. Michael Ipgrave, Washington, DC: Georgetown University Press.

Marty, Martin E. and Appleby, R. Scott (eds) (1994), *Accounting For Fundamentalisms*, Chicago: Chicago University Press.

McRoy, Anthony (2006), *From Rushdie to 7/7: The Radicalisation of Islam in Britain*, London: The Social Affairs Unit.

Mernissi, Fatima (1991), *Women and Islam*, Oxford: Blackwell.

Mir-Hosseini, Ziba (1999), *Islam and Gender*, Princeton, NJ: Princeton University Press.

Mir, Mustansir (1987), *Dictionary of Qur'anic Terms and Concepts*, New York and London: Garland Publishing.

Momen, Moojan (1985), *An Introduction to Shi'i Islam*, New Haven: Yale University Press.

Naseef, Fatima (1999), *Women in Islam*, London: Institute of Muslim Minority Affairs.

Nazir Ali, Michael (2008), 'Christian Faith and National Belonging', in *Building a Better Bridge: Muslims, Christians and the Common Good*, ed. Michael Ipgrave, Washington, DC: Georgetown University Press.

Nicholson, R. A. (1966), *The Literary History of the Arabs*, Cambridge, UK: Cambridge University Press.

Nicholson, R. (1989), *The Mystics of Islam*, 4th edn, Harmondsworth: Arkana.

Paladin, A. Vanzan (1998), 'Ethics and Neurology in the Islamic World: Continuity and Change', *Italian Journal of Neurological Science*, 19, pp. 255–8 [257], Springer-Verlag.

Partridge, Christopher (ed.) (2001), *Fundamentalisms*, Carlisle: Paternoster Press.

Patai, Raphael (1987), *Ignaz Goldhizer and his Oriental Diary*, Detroit: Wayne State University.

Pipes, Daniel (2002), 'What is Jihad?', *New York Post*, 31 December.

Pope, Robert (2001), 'Battling for God in a Secular World: Politics and Fundamentalisms', in *Fundamentalisms*, ed. Christopher Partridge, Carlisle: Paternoster Press.

Rahman, Fazlur (1979), *Islam*, 2nd edn, Chicago: Chicago University Press.

Ramadan, Tariq (2000), 'Who Speaks for European Muslims?', *La Monde Diplomatique*, June.

Ramadan, Tariq (2004), *Western Muslims and the Future of Islam*, Oxford: Oxford University Press.

Rawls, John (2005), *A Theory of Justice*, Boston: Belknap Press of Harvard University Press.

Rawls, John and Freeman, Samuel (eds) (2001), *Collected Papers*, Cambridge, MA: Harvard University Press.

Rippin, Andrew (2005), *Muslims: Their Religious Beliefs and Practices*, 3rd edn, London: Routledge.

Roald, Anne Sofie (2001), *Women in Islam: The Western Experience*, London: Routledge.

Rogerson, Barnaby (2003), *The Prophet Muhammad*, London: Little, Brown.

Rosmini, Antonio (1867), *Principles of Ethics*, trans. Terence Watson and Dennis Cleary (2nd edn 1989), Durham: Rosmini House.

Ruthwen, Malise (2004), *Fundamentalism*, Oxford: Oxford University Press.

Saeed, Abdullah and Saeed Hassan (2004), *Freedom of Religion: Apostasy and Islam*, Aldershot: Ashgate.

Said, Abdul Aziz and Funk, Nathan (2003), 'Peace in Islam: An Ecology of the Spirit', in *Islam and Ecology*, ed. R. Foltz, F. Denny and A. Baharuddin, Cambridge, MA: Harvard University Press.

Said, Abdul Aziz and Sharify-Funk, Meena (eds) (2003), *Cultural Diversity and Islam*, Lanham, MD: University Press of America.

Said, Edward (1978), *Orientalism*, London: Routledge and Kegan Paul.

Sandel, Michael (2009), *Justice: What's the Right Thing to Do?*, Harmondsworth: Allen Lane.

Schacht, J. (1952), *The Origins of Muhammadan Jurisprudence*, Oxford: Oxford University Press.

Schacht, J. (1964), *Introduction to Islamic Law*, Oxford: Oxford University Press.

Seidentop, L. (2000), *Democracy in Europe: Europe, Christianity and Islam*, Harmondsworth: Penguin.

Shepherd, John (2004), 'Self-critical Children of Abraham? Roots of Violence and Extremism in Judaism, Christianity and Islam', *Islam and the West Post 9/11*, R. Geaves, T. Gabriel, *et al.*, Aldershot: Ashgate, pp. 27–50.

Sirozi, Muhammad (2004), 'Perspectives on Radical Islamic Education in Contemporary Indonesia: Major Themes and Characteristics of Abu Bakar Ba'asyir's Teachings', in *Islam and the West Post 9/11*, R. Geaves, T. Gabriel, *et al.*, Aldershot: Ashgate.

Sivan, Emmanuel (1985), *Radical Islam: Medieval Theology and Modern Politics*, Newhaven: Yale University Press.

Stowasser, Barbara (1994), *Women in the Qur'an: Traditions, and Interpretation*, Oxford: Oxford University Press.

Thompson, J. (trans.) (1984), *The Ethics of Aristotle*, Harmondsworth, Penguin.

Tibi, Bassam (2008), *Political Islam, World Politics and Europe*, London: Routledge.

Vahiduddin, S. (1979), *Studies in Islam*, XVI (2), Indian Institute of Islamic Studies.

Visram, Rozina (2002), *Asians in Britain: 400 Years of History*, London: Pluto Press.

Wallis, Roy (1979), *Salvation and Protest: Studies of Social and Religious Movements*, New York: St Martin's Press.

Wolterstorff, Nicholas and Audi, Robert (1997), *Religion in the Public Square: The Place of Religious Convictions in Political Debate*, Lanham, MD: Rowman & Littlefield.

Wark, Mark (1994), *Virtual Geography: Living with Global Media Events*, Bloomington: Indiana University Press.

Watt, Montgomery (1961), *Islam and the Integration of Society*, London: Routledge and Kegan Paul.

Watt, Montgomery (1988), *Islamic Fundamentalism and Modernity*, London: Routledge.

Webb, Gisela (ed.) (2000), *Windows of Faith*, New York: Syracuse University Press.

Weeramantry, Christopher G. (1997), *Justice Without Frontiers*, Leiden: Brill Publishers.

Werbner, Pnina (2002), *Imagined Diasporas among Manchester Muslims*, Oxford: James Currey.

Yamani, Mai (ed.) (1996), *Feminism and Islam*, Reading: Ithaca.

Zuhur, Sherifa (1992), *Revealing Reveiling*, Albany: State University of New York.

Index